Praise for Cu

MW00913315

"Hear ye, hear ye! This little gem of a book is filled with delightful tidbits about Provincetown, spread out in bite-sized chapters for an easy read. I am now incorporating many of these interesting facts into my daily spiel!"

—Provincetown Town Crier, Daniel Gómez Llata

"Take one 295-year old village, over-brimming with history and mystery, sprinkle in knowledge of several generations of natives and locals, stir well by a writer with a living presence in the village and a voracious appetite for every taste it has to offer—then spread these pages across your table and happily consume this book!"

—Char Priolo, Provincetown Chamber of Commerce concierge of 19 years, Trolley Tour Guide 6 years

"My family [Atkins] has lived here for generations, but I learned a lot from reading the stories in this book—all told with charming wit and humor!"

—Barbara Atkins Grandell

"Having grown up in Provincetown, I was delighted to read this book written with affection and respect for my hometown."

—Janet Whelan, MD

"As a full time resident of Provincetown for over 50 years, I thought I knew a lot about the town until I read this book. Throughout, Odale drops little previously unknown factoids about the town like spices that bring a dish to its fullest flavor."

—Priscilla Jackett

"This fascinating book reveals a world of colorful historical and contemporary people and places in town, while exploring its picturesque streets lined with wonderful places to stop and eat!"

—Kristy Meyer, out-of-town visitor

"I've never been to Provincetown, but reading this book inspired me to make reservations to visit. I can't wait to see the historic sites where these stories took place!"

—Vivien Kirchner, future visitor to Provincetown

"These well-researched stories left impressions of art and history that attuned us to many sights in Provincetown, making them more relevant and memorable."

—Tim and Kelly Burt, visitors from upstate New York

"This entertaining book will take you on a culinary tour that is as much fun to read as good food is to eat!"

—Pat Medina, 30 years as Trolley Tour Guide
and Tour Operator in Provincetown

Cuisine is a Dialect

A Leisurely Stroll Through the
Edible History of Provincetown

Odale Cress

Dialect Press
Provincetown, Massachusetts

Cuisine is a Dialect:
A Leisurely Stroll Through the Edible History of Provincetown

Revised Aug 2022

Dialect Press, LLC
Provincetown, Massachusetts

Copyright © 2022 Odale Cress

It is with deep gratitude I thank the following for permission to include pieces of their work in this volume:

Peter Donnelly's lyrics, "Road with No End"; Zoë Lewis's lyrics, "Bicycle" and "Squid Song"; Bill Fitt's drawing, *Monster*, Mark Adams's portrait of the author; John Wiley Nelson's lyrics, "Red Cranberries" and "Provincetown Rag"; Daniel Trotter's contribution of sketch of *Lady Fin*; Nick Flynn's poem, "Daughter," from *I Will Destroy You*; Michael Cunningham's excerpt from *Land's End: A Walk through Provincetown*; Debra Lawless's excerpts from *Provincetown: A History of Artists and Renegades in a Fishing Village* and *Provincetown Since World War II*; Lenny Alberts for excerpt of poem by David Matias, "Eyes to the Sun"; Chef Greg Atkinson's excerpt from his *Seattle Times* article "Treasures of the Tide Flats: On a beach or at a bash, oysters are worthy of celebration" and the Peary–MacMillan Arctic Museum for Rear Admiral MacMillan's journal entry.

ISBN 978-1-7376125-0-6

"If more of us valued food and cheer and song above hoarded gold, it would be a merrier world."

— *The Hobbit*, J.R.R. Tolkien

For Milo. Thank you for coming into my life; it's been a privilege to be your mother and an unparalleled hoot to travel this wild, wondrous world with you.

This book is also for my relatives and chosen family, in Provincetown and around the world, who make me feel at home, wherever I am.

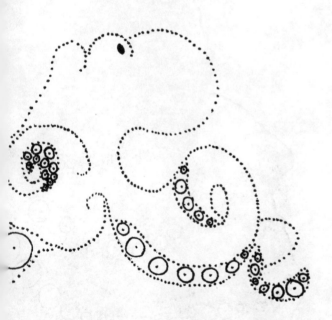

INTRODUCTION

FOOD IS A LANGUAGE; CUISINE IS A DIALECT

"The History of every major Galactic Civilization tends to pass through three distinct and recognizable phases, those of Survival, Inquiry, and Sophistication, otherwise known as the How, Why, and Where phases. For instance, the first phase is characterized by the question 'How can we eat?' *the second by the question* 'Why do we eat?' *and the third by the question* 'Where shall we have lunch?'"

— Douglas Adams, from *The Hitchhiker's Guide to the Galaxy*

These stories, anecdotes and musings, with a bit of poetry, artwork and song lyrics tossed in, tell of the cultural history of Provincetown as seen through culinary traditions, foodways and cuisines of people who have lived at the very tip of Cape Cod.

Food, which has no inherent messaging or meaning, is saturated in social connotations and symbolism bestowed on it by the people who eat it or—equally telling—decline to. Cultures are differentiated, defined and judged, in large part, as much by what they eat as by what they refuse to. Humans eat only the tiniest fraction of the available types of edible plants and animals on the planet. Which kinds of plants and animals are eaten is not entirely, but predominantly, culturally dictated. At times, people have starved rather than eat food that, in spite of being nutritious and abundant, is repellent to them. Culinary distinctions help make up the cultural identity of a community living in a particular place and time.

Food traditions and foodways, as well as which foods are eaten and how, reveal the social, political and economic structure of a society. Who cultivates, harvests or hunts the food, as well as who prepares, serves and consumes it, defines and illuminates stratifications within the community. Social messaging is embedded in every aspect of food consumption, too, from who sits where at the table (if eating at a table), which plates and utensils are used—not only the sort of plates and utensils—but also whether it's the "everyday" set or the "good" set being used. In some cultures and households it is customary to leave a couple of bites of food on the plate, indicating that diners are so full they couldn't possibly eat another bite, whereas in other cultures, this gesture may be interpreted to mean the food was not tasty. In some cultures belching loudly is the ultimate compliment to the host. It is intended to convey that the meal was superb; in other cultures or settings, a diner who unleashes a thunderous belch at the end of a meal is likely not to be invited back. The order in which courses are eaten; who is served first, last or the choicest piece; which portions are discarded (if these bits are edible, whether they are eaten and by whom); how the food is prepared and presented and by whom, all contain social and cultural connotation and significance—sometimes even moral implications. In specific contexts, foods may be imbued with sacred or mythical qualities.

Cuisine brings place to the plate. Food is merely an edible ingredient; cuisine is the culturally relevant dish made with it. The cuisine of a region is prepared by people or groups of people of the area, using the natural or cultivated bounties indigenous to that geographic region. As Linda Civitello points out in her book *Cuisine & Culture: A History of Food and People*, cuisine is an intentional preparation of food, not accidental, and is not just a style of cooking, but an awareness of how and when it is prepared and eaten, and by whom. Patterns created by food acquisition, preparation and consumption help to both create and define culture.

Meals are the metronome of our lives. The organization and repeated patterns of meals measure the passage of time. Meals are universally experienced—the details of them are decidedly not. We eat certain foods at certain times of the day, on particular days of the week, for specific days and times of the year and to mark important milestones in our lives. Special foods are prepared for birthdays, weddings, funerals and commemorative events during the year. Some types of foods are eaten only during specific times of the year. In general, the time of day and the passage of time are measured by the rhythm at which foods are prepared and eaten, a rhythm that is primarily culturally dependent.

In addition to eating certain foods at given times, we shun foods we deem inappropriate to consume at particular times. In the United States, for example, among those who consume alcohol, it's socially acceptable to drink at breakfast, but only certain kinds of booze are considered appropriate first thing in the morning. Ordering a Bloody Mary, or mimosa or adding a splash of Bailey's to your morning coffee won't raise too many eyebrows, whereas ordering an old fashioned, a pinot noir or a frothy mug of beer with your eggs Benedict likely will. Followers of certain religious mandates eat fish rather than red meat on Fridays or prepare specific foods for holy days and religious occasions. Some are restricted to eating only specific food or no food at all during times of fasting. Norms are neither inherent nor universal, but rather, culturally dictated and defined. No one food is consumed by everyone.

The stories in this book, in their varying forms, are offered up like tapas laid across a table: As each entry is a stand-alone piece, pages can be sampled in any order without losing an overarching thread. If you choose to start at the front of the book and read forward, the stories invite you on a figure-eight tour through the picturesque streets of Provincetown, uncovering its unique culinary and cultural history along the way.

— Od.

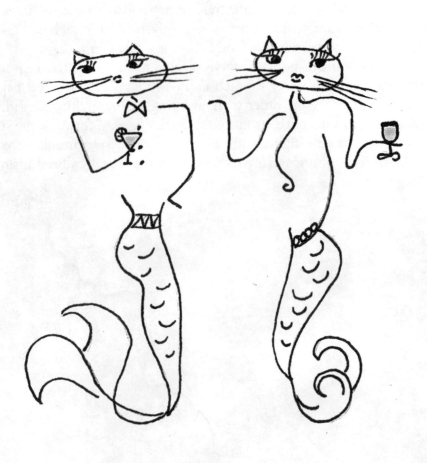

PREFACE

It's often said that the four major food groups of Cape Cod are breakfast, seafood, ice cream and booze. Now that sounds like my kind of walking tour! The layout of the routes for these two walks through the East and West End are designed with the intention that those reading the book, rather than strolling around town, may get a sense of the town and its character, while those walking the suggested route, in addition to touring the town, will have ample opportunity to sample the eclectic eateries on offer in Provincetown.

This is not a restaurant guide offering recommendations as to where to eat or not to eat in Provincetown. For one thing, restaurants come and go and change addresses with head-spinning frequency here, so it would be a nearly impossible feat with a very short shelf life. However, a few restaurants from the past and a handful that are in business now are described in the book, with the goal of illustrating some of the ways in which restaurants promote and facilitate cross-cultural understanding, as well as how they help define the cultural aspects of communities within Provincetown and of the town itself. Whether mentioned here or not, each of the restaurants, past and present, has contributed, socially and culturally, to the ever-expanding, ever-shifting foodscape here.

Creating a culinary tour based on "breakfast, seafood, ice cream and booze" immediately brings to light the diverse cuisines of Provincetown—and presents us with a most pleasurable dilemma: shall we have Mexican chilaquiles, or Portuguese flippers and linguiça, or maybe New York bagels with smoked salmon and lox, or some Greek yogurt with nuts and honey? We could have Canadian poutine, or an invigorating Asian miso soup or a few scrambled eggs with hash browns and toast … so many options. The range of choices for seafood in town stretches from Italian to Greek, to French, Portuguese, Asian, Yankee, Latin American, Caribbean options and beyond. (You can even find seafood-based cocktails!) Regarding ice cream and its close cousins, there are countless shops which sell gelatos and sorbets in addition to ice cream. As for the final course, booze, many bars serve signature cocktails, often inspired by the house cuisine. Most feature local Cape-crafted spirits, wine and beer. Individually, these foodways and cuisines are edible expressions of cultures, past and present, that have influenced the history of this place. Collectively, they illustrate the singular nature and character of Provincetown itself.

Most everything we see around us as we meander through town, revolves in some way around the cultivation, harvesting, preparation or consumption of food. Many of the local writers and artists depict the stories and lives of the people engaged in the foodways of Provincetown. Some of the better-known scenes portray people catching fish, tilling fields, gathering beach plums, clamming, preparing stews, hawking pastries and waiting tables. Several artists in town are known for incorporating squid ink, wine, tea and other food into their artwork. (Even slabs of fish or chunks of vegetables may be inked then pressed onto paper, revealing the pattern of its scales or other designs.) Walking these streets we see food images carved on wooden archways, stone gateways, fences, doorways, printed on kitchen curtains, atop festive hats and embedded in clothing patterns. Provincetown's foodways and traditions, in endless forms, are all around us, and help tell the stories of this special place.

Who's up for some breakfast?

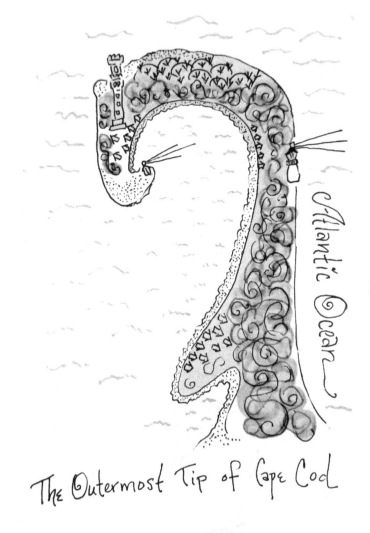

The Outermost Tip of Cape Cod

At Land's End, the tip of Cape Cod, hangs a sandy question mark, sculpted by the alternating battering and caressing of water and wind. Cupped in its curve floats the sheltering bay and harbor of Provincetown. Along its shores the waves unfold and retreat, like a curled hand opening onto the sand, dropping shells and other sea treasures, then sliding back into the depths, pulling shoreline stones and sand with it. The town and its people are fed and nurtured, literally and figuratively, by the bounty and beauty of the surrounding sea and sand.

It's along the narrow, winding streets laced through this eccentric, provocative and tenacious little town that our walk takes us, as we stroll through the culinary and cultural history of Provincetown.

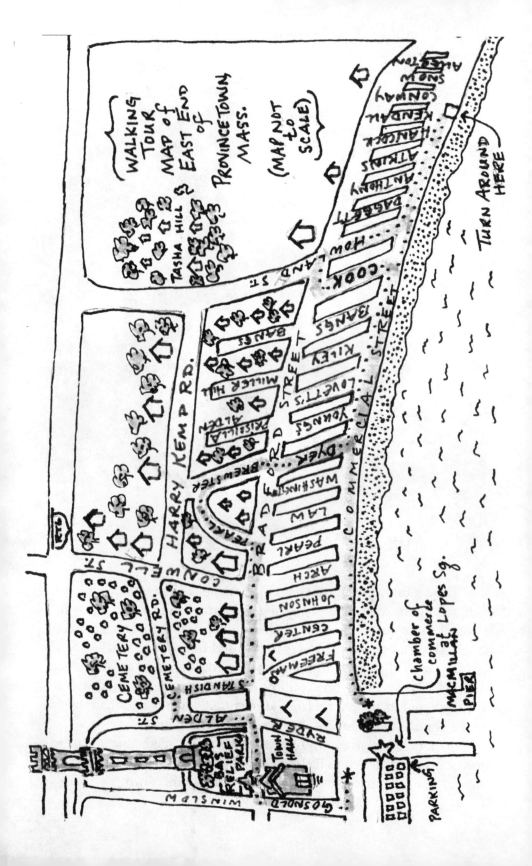

WELCOME TO PROVINCETOWN:
A FEAST FOR THE SENSES

It's a lovely day in the prettiest town on the Cape.

This stands true through all seasons, in any weather. Sunshine, fog, rain and snow each embroiders its own variegated hues into the land and seascape that is Provincetown enhancing an elusory beauty that has bewitched and beguiled artists and writers and local inhabitants for centuries.

But to notice only its postcard qualities is to miss the essence of this place. "Provincetown lives by skill and daring, by luck and by chance," wrote town chronicler Mary Heaton Vorse. Provincetown (known to many as Ptown) has long been home to stalwarts and sojourners— courageous fishing families, folks whose folk have lived here for generations, wash-ashores who've found a home among their kith, if not kin, expatriates and fugitives from a conformist outside world, as well as bold creatives seeking new directions and ideas. It's a place steeped in tradition and culture, while forever shaping history and shifting cultural boundaries.

Over the centuries leading to this moment in time, the feet of countless before us have trodden this nook-shotten shoreline: Native Americans, seafarers, farmers, shopkeepers, bootleggers, bohemians, artists, poets, politicians, immigrants, outcasts, scoundrels and heroes. All have left their mark on the sandy nib.

Let's follow their trail of crumbs and see where it leads us, shall we?

We'll begin our stroll in the heart of the historic district of Provincetown. Grab a coffee and a bite at one of the nearby eateries, if you like, and meet me in front of Town Hall. We'll start our walk there.

TOWN HALL

The current town hall, built in 1885, was the second to be built in Provincetown. The first, called Town House, straddled Pole Hill where the Pilgrim Monument now stands sentry. When the Town House burned down, the fire took most of the town's historical records with it.

The Ryder family moved their own house from this location to around the corner on Winslow Street to make way for the construction of the new Town Hall. Philanthropy seems to have run in the family. A preceding generation of Ryders was among principal donors of the land on which the first Town House was built. In appreciation, the town named the street to the east of Town Hall in the Ryder family's honor.

One candied-cherry topping short of resembling an oversized petit four, Town Hall stands proudly at the corner of Commercial and Ryder Streets. The outside is coated in scrumptious colors that may look as if they're inspired by the pistachio and cream taffies sold in the candy store next door, but which are, in fact, the original colors of the building.

Town Hall serves as both a municipal and cultural hub. Its auditorium has seen theatrical performances, concerts, costume balls and even women's wrestling competitions in its tenure. It's here that residents assemble every April for Town Meeting to decide on local issues in that quintessentially New England democratic manner: each voice to be heard, each hand to be counted. These lively meetings have been known to carry on for days and occasionally capture headlines in distant newspapers.

The weekly Town Hall dances, which Mary Heaton Vorse describes in her book, *Time and the Town*, were attended by everyone across town, "Portuguese, New Englanders and summer people." Tourists as well as townsfolk of all ages and stations—sea captains, dairy farmers, storekeepers, family, friends and neighbors—came together to get acquainted, dance and socialize. At that time, refreshments were served "under the Town Hall," a "euphemistic term for the town jail," Vorse notes. The guard on duty would call out periodically to revelers, reminding them "not to offer the prisoner ice cream or cigarettes."

After being closed to the public in 2020 due to the coronavirus, the Town Hall was reopened to the public in 2021. Thrilled to be able to gather together once again, throngs of community members and visitors flocked to events like the Tennessee Williams Festival, music performances and Provincetown's inaugural Food & Wine Festival.

Before we start walking, it might be worth mentioning that there are public bathrooms in Town Hall. If you head into the building and suddenly find yourself sidetracked, wandering the halls captivated by the array of artwork, you would be neither the first nor the last to do so. The interior of Town Hall features the rich caramel and dark chocolate complexities of oak and mahogany. Its hallways are studded with some 100 murals, paintings and sculptures by legions of local artists, many of whom became nationally and internationally known. The art depicts the cultural life of Provincetown—illustrations of fishing and farming families, clammers and oystermen, the Blessing of the Fleet and scenes from the rowdy annual Carnival. The exhibit reflects a smörgåsbord of foodways and traditions of the people here and the eras in which they lived.

It's an extensive collection well worth taking time to explore. At your leisure, please be our guest.

A SPOONFUL OF FRIENDLY ADVICE

Provincetown has a seemingly unlimited capacity for the unexpected. One immediately noticeable idiosyncrasy of Provincetown is the irregular flow of traffic on Commercial Street. Trucks, cars and trolleys may only travel in one direction, while bicycles and bike taxis may travel in any direction, and often do so at insane speeds. Traffic on two-lane Bradford Street travels both ways, usually moving closer to the posted speed limit.

If you arrive in Provincetown by car, it is universally recommended to park your car as soon as you can and leave it parked for the duration of your stay if possible. If you are lodging in or day-tripping to nearby Truro, it's easy to get a bus or taxi between the towns during summer months. There's usually no need for a car: bike taxis, cabs and buses are handy for getting a lift wherever you need to go, including to nearby beaches. Entertaining, informative sightseeing tours are available from walking tour guides, as well as from trolley and dune tour companies.

The town is but two streets wide and a bit over a mile long, so exploring it by foot is perhaps the best way to take in its wisteria-arcaded back streets, distinctive Cape architecture, voluptuous gardens, bay views—and the endlessly entertaining parade of people: people-watching is a round-the-clock pastime in Provincetown.

PORTUGUESE SQUARE

On the grounds surrounding Town Hall are historical markers saluting battles of various eras. In the front corner of Portuguese Square stands the *Doughboy* statue commemorating World War I. This statue was created by an internationally acclaimed woman artist, Theo Alice Ruggles Kitson, whose war memorials stand in nearly every state in the country. In 1893, at the noteworthy age of 22, she became the first woman inducted into the National Sculptors Society.

Although the World War I quota for Provincetown's approximately 3,800 residents was set at 38 men, more than 300 locals answered the call to duty, at least six of them women. These volunteers' names are listed on Ruggles's *Doughboy* sculpture. On the east side of Town Hall, near Bradford Street, sits the Veterans Park Honor Roll memorial, which lists the names of Provincetown women and men who served in World War II and more recent conflicts.

Nearby, the thought provoking AIDS Memorial, a gleaming slice of granite, with smoothed sides and uncalm waters rippling across the top, memorializes a different battle, and one that is still being fought. When HIV/AIDS hit town, platoons of locals pulled together to prepare and deliver homemade food to people afflicted and to help with shopping, housekeeping and dog walking. Squadrons of others drove carloads of people several hours away to Boston for medical appointments. Medical workers and volunteers have worked tirelessly for decades to fight this epidemic that had killed one-in-ten of the total year-round population within a few years of its arrival. A far greater percentage had become infected with the virus. Everyone in town was impacted in some way as coworkers, neighbors, friends, relatives, lovers and partners fell ill. At the height of the epidemic, Provincetown had the nation's second highest per capita population of people living with AIDS. Although the overall picture regarding HIV/AIDS in Provincetown is much improved, a cadre of locals continues to provide homemade dishes and other support to help neighbors overcome challenges of this ongoing health issue.

Next, the very large boulder on the lawn in front of Town Hall celebrates the Lipton Cup Race triumph in 1907 by Provincetown schooner, *Rose Dorothea*. Today, a large replica of the winning ship and the silver trophy are on display at the town Library.

Looking to our left, as we face the front of Town Hall, the first building we see up-along Commercial Street was, once-upon-a-time, Café Poyant, one of the first sidewalk cafés in Provincetown.

CAFÉ POYANT

This locale has long been prized as a prime people-watching perch throughout its many iterations, selling everything from European pastries to Caribbean dishes, tropical cocktails to Vermont ice cream, and specialties running the gamut of global cuisine. In the 1960s, Café Poyant, then a French-style bakery with pretty little tables scattered beneath red-and-white striped awnings, opened as a sidewalk café and quickly became a favorite of locals, summer drift-ins and tourists. It was a hot spot for famous, soon-to-be-famous and wannabe creatives who gathered to trade gossip, debate artistic styles and political views and to keep an eye peeled for their next subject to paint or write about. Well-known local artist Harvey Dodd often set up his easel at a table here to paint portraits of tourists by commission.

Though its tenants will continue to morph over time, I imagine this lively spot in the center of town will remain a popular place for locals and visitors alike to pull up a seat and stay a while, observing and amusing one another.

TOWN CRIER

Gene Poyant, proprietor of Café Poyant and a colorful customer himself, vehemently disapproved of the increasing numbers of hippies, beatniks and gay people coming to town and, to his mind, cluttering the streets and his café. He'd loudly denounce them to anyone who would listen, urgently warning of the imminent demise of the character of the town if the tide of this unsavory influence was not turned, and soon, by golly!

In the 1980s, he took up the seasonal, ceremonial post of town crier. Dressed as a caricature of a Pilgrim, complete with a black buckled hat and buckled boots, Poyant rang his bell, posed for photos with tourists, and regaled listeners with tales of fishing adventures. He made national news when *The New York Times* ran the story of his abrupt removal from the post of town crier after he'd unfurled a tirade upon a group of tourists, lambasting the gay and lesbian community and ranting that the Unitarian Universalist church had been co-opted by the devil.

Poyant's departure from the post brought a temporary halt to the long line of lively town criers to walk the streets in Pilgrim garb, but the custom has since been revived. Folks can once again ask directions of, get restaurant suggestions from, and have their picture taken with the current colorful, but decidedly less inflammatory, costumed town crier.

JAMAICAN INFLUENCE

In earlier times, most young men coming up from Jamaica arrived on whalers, seeking adventures on the seas and fortunes in whale oil. In recent decades, Jamaican women and men have come to town for seasonal work, primarily in the construction and tourism industries. Increasingly, they are deciding to stay on, open their own businesses and raise families here.

A Jamaican friend of mine, John, told me of foods he remembers from the island of his birth, many of which he's happy to be able to find on menus here now, but he misses meals prepared in the way his family makes them. In particular, he misses his sister's salt fish. Salt fish is considered by many to be the national dish of Jamaica. Enslaved Jamaicans, using their characteristic culinary panache, transformed this normally lackluster food into a dish that is now revered as a delicacy.

Another food John misses is ackee fruit. He says that, out of all the Caribbean countries, only Jamaicans eat ackee. He explains that this pear-shaped fruit "resembles a warm Jamaican sunset until it leaves behind its bright red coloring for a happy yellow-orange that sings out that it is ripe and ready to eat." John notes that on other Caribbean islands, ackee is dismissed as merely something pretty to look at. "But oh, they are missing out!" he says, shaking his long graying braids and chuckling.

A few decades ago, when John first arrived, it was nearly impossible to find Jamaican foods in stores or restaurants on the Cape. It's much more common these days to find, not only salt fish and ackee, but other traditional Jamaican dishes as well, like curry goat, oxtail, Jamaican patty (a spicy mix tucked into a flaky pastry shell), stewed cows' feet, conch soup, fried fish with pickled vegetables, callaloo, dumplings and the distinctive coco bread.

Then there's jerk chicken which, like salt fish, is regarded as a national dish. John told me he learned that jerk chicken was first cooked up by enslaved people who broke free and lived in the woods. To flavor meats roasted over a wood fire, they developed a distinctive blend of spices from plants they found growing wild. This became the special seasoning now used for jerk chicken.

These days it's increasingly common to see menus at restaurants all over town offering dishes made "with a Jamaican twist." This usually means the chef has incorporated jerk seasoning or added a blend of hot peppers into the recipe, lifting flavors of the meat or seafood and adding layers of character to the dish. Jamaican cuisine has become a staple in Cape Cod's school lunch cafeterias and local grocery stores now stock Jamaican ingredients and brands.

On Shankpainter Road is Iria Eats, a Jamaican store and deli run by two Jamaican women. At lunchtime a line streams out the door, made up of customers craving hot jerk sandwiches and cold fruit juices. The women's loyal following is happy to wait as long it takes to get their fix of flavor.

In Provincetown and throughout the Cape, in addition to Jamaican foods, you can find a variety of styles of Jamaican music and singers, and Provincetown's community radio station, WOMR, airs a Jamaican music program. You can also catch Jamaican produced films at Provincetown's Jamaican Film Festival.

From here, let's take a right onto Gosnold Street.

GOSNOLD STREET

For reasons that are not immediately apparent, this narrow, nearly treeless way was called Forest Street back in the day. At some point the road was rechristened in honor of Bartholomew Gosnold, whose name for this long strip of land, Cape Cod, wound up having more staying power than all of the others tacked to it over the years.

Native Americans named it first, then several explorers who came both before and after Gosnold called the land by other names. But Gosnold's choice stuck and today, Cape Cod is the name that appears on maps, t-shirts, bumper stickers, coffee mugs and the occasional tattoo. Gosnold, like others, was struck by the "great stoare of codfysshes" which his crew caught here. While bearing in mind that oft-repeated stories lend themselves to exaggeration in the retelling, it remains clear that there were an awful lot of cod in these waters. So abundant were they, that visitors insisted that one could fairly skip across the top of the water on the backs of the massive schools of fish. Although for his part, Gosnold didn't give as much as a fig about the land he called Cape Cod, he was utterly smitten by the lush, vine-covered island not far from here, which he named Martha's Vineyard in honor of his daughter, the apple of his eye.

THE *ADVOCATE* BUILDING AND NEWSPAPER

Where Gosnold Street meets Bradford Street, we can see a pretty red brick house on the corner. In 1975, the local *Advocate* newspaper moved into this building which had, in bygone days, been the home of the New England Telephone and Telegraph Company, bringing news to town by wire.

Launched in 1869, the *Advocate* offered up the latest news as well as commentaries on restaurants, arts, and culture in Provincetown and the Outer Cape. From this corner, the *Advocate* operation moved to a spot tucked behind the Post Card Shop on Commercial Street, which, as it happens, was also owned by the proprietor of the *Advocate*. Debra Lawless writes in her book on the history of Provincetown that in 1911, it's estimated that an astounding 10,000 one-cent postcard stamps were sold in town daily. These stamps were stuck onto the cool half million postcards sold town-wide, 150,000 of them from the *Advocate*-owned Post Card Shop.

The *Advocate* newspaper ran for 131 years before being bought by the *Provincetown Banner* in 2000. Not long after that, Provincetown came to have two newspapers reporting cultural events, restaurant reviews and local news: the *Provincetown Banner* and the *Independent*. There are also a couple of widely circulated culture-focused magazines: the *Ptownie* and the *Provincetown Arts Magazine*.

We'll cross Bradford here at the crosswalk. On our left we come upon the Bas Relief Park. The little park with the big stone at the center is also known as the Town Green. It rests at the base of High Pole Hill, beneath the omnipresent Pilgrim Monument keeping an eye on things from on high.

The Town Green sits more or less at the center of Provincetown. Bradford Street was originally called Back Street (Commercial Street was Front Street). This roadway is named for Governor William Bradford, the second elected and the longest-serving Governor of Plimoth Colony. (The name of the colony has undergone several spelling changes over time, and now goes by one of its historical spellings: Plimouth Colony.) Bradford Street was the first proper road to be built in town. Up until then, squiggling sandy paths knitted the smattering of houses and shops along the shoreline.

THE "SWEET SHIP" THEY CALLED THE *MAYFLOWER*

Prior to her transatlantic voyage, the *Mayflower* had never carried passengers. She'd ferried English woolens, French wines, Spanish salt, hops and vinegar across the English Channel. She'd hauled wine in her hold, the contents of which frequently sloshed out, saturating the wooden flooring. The *Mayflower* and other wine-ferrying ships were known as "sweet ships" owing to the booze-soaked boards from which emanated a powerful (and cooped-up passengers might say cloying), plummy aroma. It was in this whiffy hold that over 100 passengers lived during their voyage across the Atlantic.

In addition to being a bit musty-on-the-nose, the passengers' quarters were cramped. Initially, two ships, the *Mayflower* and the *Speedwell*, rendezvoused in Southampton, England, and set out to make the Atlantic crossing in tandem. The pair got off to a stuttered start, however, as the *Speedwell* repeatedly sprang leaks, requiring the ships to return for repairs at Dartmouth, then again at Plymouth. Finally, it was decided that all onward passengers would travel together aboard the *Mayflower*, leaving behind the beleaguered *Speedwell* and several of her passengers who had, not surprisingly, grown skeptical of the venture.

For over two months the passengers ate, slept—and became very well acquainted, I'd imagine—in the "tween decks." The 102 adults and children were sandwiched into a space less than 60 feet long, no more than five-and-a-half feet high, and at its widest point, only 24 feet across. Passengers were permitted above deck, but most of their time was spent in the *Mayflower's* mephitic belly.

Once the *Mayflower* anchored at Plimoth/Patuxet, male passengers lived ashore building homes for the budding colony, while women and children, as well as anyone who fell ill, continued to live aboard the ship. As a result, the *Mayflower's* dank and dirty hold was home for months on end for the women and children who'd climbed aboard at the ship's initial departure in London in July of 1620, remaining right through the early spring of 1621, when the *Mayflower* returned to England.

LAND HO!

After 66 trying days at sea, the band of Pilgrims arrived at the bay which appeared on their English map as Milford Haven, and is now called Provincetown Harbor. The 102 *Mayflower* passengers and approximately 30 crew (and, according to the Provincetown Dog Park Association, one mastiff and a springer spaniel) anchored in the calm waters tucked into the top of the question mark–shaped scribble of land punctuating the tip of Cape Cod.

The voyage had been an eventful one. In addition to being waylaid by their troubles with the *Speedwell*, they were thrown off course by storms, a passenger was nearly lost when he went overboard, a crew member and a young passenger perished and a baby boy was born along the way.

The bounty of fresh summer vegetables and fruits the passengers enjoyed at the beginning of the voyage had long since been depleted. For as long as the supply lasted, lemons were squeezed into beer, but the lemons, too, were gone and beer was running low. By the time they arrived at the Cape, their meals were made up of dwindling rations of rice, root vegetables, hard cheese, dried peas, hardtack, fish, salted pork, dried beef and cow tongue, pickled foods and oatmeal. In addition to cider, children and adults were each allowed a quart to a gallon of beer per day, until allotments of food and drink were reduced to stretch supplies.

Given such a long stint at sea, any view of land must have seemed a relief. However, the subtle, nuanced beauty of the Cape in mid-November may well have been lost on the passengers who were hoping to find a land of milk and honey. The colors here at that time of year are reduced to variations on the theme of gray. Beyond a few dark green conifer trees, those aboard the *Mayflower* would have been looking out upon a scene of darkish-gray, leafless trees protruding from whitish-gray snow, ice and sand, giving onto a steel-gray bay beneath bleached gray skies. Far from looking like the land of plenty, this outermost stretch of darkly-bristled woods and shrub-stubbled sand must have seemed to the travel-weary arrivals to be as unpromising as a pauper's tin plate.

To top it off, although Captain Gosnold named Cape Cod for the abundance of cod in the surrounding sea, the fish were more or less inaccessible to those on the *Mayflower*, as they lacked adequate fishing tools and had no experienced fishermen among them. The ship carrying wool carders, shoe makers, milliners, printers, preachers, weavers, carpenters and the like, watched from the ship's deck as schools of cod swirled past in the water far below them.

In an added twist of tragic irony, while the *Mayflower* passengers and crew suffered from hunger and undernourishment throughout their first winter, just 50 miles off shore, fleets of fishing vessels were bouncing merrily among the waves, hauling in untold tons of codfish and returning to Britain and the European continent, their holds brimming with so-called "British gold."

Though all the passengers were Pilgrims in search of a new life, they fell into two camps: Saints and Strangers. In a nutshell, the Saints were seeking a land in which they could practice their religious beliefs freely, whereas the majority—two-thirds, in fact—of the passengers were Strangers who'd been hired to help build and found the colony.

Of the 102 passengers who traveled on the *Mayflower*, only 17 children, five women and 35 adult male passengers survived the first winter at the Plimoth Colony. All told, half the passengers and nearly half the crew had perished before the first green bean sprouted and first apple tree blossomed in the spring. In April, 1621, the surviving *Mayflower* crew members set sail back home to England, leaving the Pilgrims and one crew member, cooper John Alden, behind in their new home.

THE TOWN GREEN

BAS RELIEF: *SIGNING OF THE COMPACT*

The center of the Town Green is dominated by the Bas Relief, a large copper depiction, framed in granite, titled *The Signing of the Compact*. Smaller historical markers stand off to either side, together telling the passengers' story of the arrival of the *Mayflower*.

When the Mayflower Compact was signed in 1620, the 41 male signatories may have sealed the deal with shots of aqua-vitae they'd brought on board. It could be that a belt of this strong liquor might have proved fruitful in smoothing the ruffled feathers of some of the disgruntled Strangers. A few of them had let it be known that they had a beef with sticking to their contract to help build the colony, since the ship had landed outside the jurisdiction of their contract (today's Manhattan). Alarmed by a simmering mutiny, leaders of the Saint contingent drew up a binding agreement, known thereafter as the Mayflower Compact.

In many ways they were as apples and oranges, these Saints and Strangers who had crossed an ocean to build a colony together. The agreement they reached was a covenant which bound the entire party on ostensibly equal terms, as a "civil body politic." It defined the community as one that was self-governing and democratic to a large degree. Somewhat less democratically from several angles, until the document was signed by all adult male passengers, no one was allowed to disembark. Finally, on November 11, the Compact was signed, and the shipmates went ashore, their feet touching land for the first time in nearly 10 weeks. The Mayflower Compact remained active until 1691 when Plimouth Colony became part of Massachusetts Bay Colony.

The dedication ceremony in 1920 of the Bas Relief Monument marked the 300-year anniversary of the signing of the Mayflower Compact. The ceremony included a reenactment of the signing of the Compact, with members of the Mayflower Society playing the roles of the signatories and their families. In a striking detour from historical record, smiling Native Americans (played by non-Native American actors) looked on, though Native Americans are not known to have been on board the *Mayflower* for the signing, smiling or otherwise. Straying even further off script, there were several actors portraying pirates, whose presence are not mentioned anywhere in the available historical record. (Regarding the somewhat random addition of pirates, it may have been a case of having more people wanting to play roles than there were historical roles to fill, so perhaps pirates were added to accommodate a demand for roles—similar to what happens every Christmas when it comes time to put on the nativity play. Several kids inevitably wind up in the final manger scene dressed as historically unsubstantiated lobsters or elephants, or as wives, cousins and butlers of the three wise men.)

When the Bas Relief was dedicated in 1920, merrymakers may have donned their fancy gowns and the ol' soup-and-fish (men's formal wear) for the Grand Ball held that evening at Town Hall, but as the unveiling took place during Prohibition, it is unlikely that champagne glasses were raised, in public view anyway. Private parties were a different kettle of fish. Even before the advent of Prohibition, Provincetown was a dry town and, according to accounts from the time, private parties during Prohibition—at least as much or more than before—were awash with champagne, rum, whiskey, beer and most any other liquor that revelers desired.

AS AMERICAN AS APPLE PIE

As is often noted, the two groups of voyaging passengers were as different as apples and oranges. From the wide gap in their motivations for venturing across an ocean, to the divergence in their personal and religious beliefs, there was a measurable distance between the two groups. Yet, they say, variety is the spice of life. In the case of the Pilgrims, the Mayflower Compact bound them, their common efforts united them, and together, with help from their Native American neighbors, the disparate group successfully built and grew their new colony.

By fortuitous coincidence, a delightful dish awaits the cook who adds a squirt of orange (or lemon) juice to their favorite apple pie recipe. This melding of apple and orange gives a bright, exciting lift to America's favorite dessert.

THE OTHER TOWN GREEN MARKERS

In 1873, while laying out Bradford road, workers unearthed a small cemetery. The graves were presumed to have been those of the young *Mayflower* passenger who died en route and others who died while the ship still sheltered in the harbor. In 1921, the Historic Memorial Plaque was placed to the left of the Bas Relief Monument by the Massachusetts Society of Mayflower Descendants in tribute to the five departed passengers: William Butten, who died just before the *Mayflower* landed, Edward Thompson, Jasper More, Dorothy Bradford and James Chilton, who all died while the ship lay anchored in the harbor. The crew member who died en route to the Cape was buried at sea and is not named on the plaque.

The marker to the right of the Bas Relief details the wording of the Mayflower Compact, the date it was signed and lists the names of its signatories. (Note: November 11, 1620, was the date of the signing according to the Julian calendar used by *Mayflower* passengers, whereas November 21, 1620, is the date we ascribe to the event today, in accordance with the Gregorian Calendar in use now.) Once they left the Cape, the remainder of the freshly covenanted community of Pilgrims worked together to build their settlement, Plimoth Colony.

DOROTHY BRADFORD

Having left the women and children on the *Mayflower,* safely anchored in the harbor, William Bradford was ashore with a scouting team when young Dorothy, his wife and "dearest consort," went overboard and drowned, prompting the uncomfortable question as to whether Dorothy had accidentally fallen overboard or had thrown herself into the bay.

Although theories have been advanced which suggest or concoct various configurations of love triangles that might have led Dorothy to take her own life, these theories have generally been discredited by historians. Still, setting real or imagined romantic troubles aside, Dorothy had ample reason to feel deeply sad and possibly despondent: she and her shipmates had recently experienced a spate of deaths in quick succession—a crew member immediately followed by three passengers—the most recent being little seven-year-old Jasper More, who had died only the day before. Another passenger, James Chilton, was extremely ill. (He succumbed the day after Dorothy died.) William and Dorothy had left their own three-year-old son behind, intending for him to join them at the colony later. Bradford wrote in his journals of the deep sense of despair many passengers felt upon landing hundreds of miles north of their intended destination with winter coming on, a deadly illness on the rise and food stores running low.

A debate still runs among historians as to whether this combination of painful circumstances would lead Dorothy to leap from the ship, as both her faith and her community would have strongly discouraged and condemned that course of action. In the absence of a reliable account regarding Dorothy's own state of mind at the time, speculation continues.

THE *DOROTHY BRADFORD* FERRY

For years, Provincetown's summer season was deemed underway when the *Dorothy Bradford* ferry sailed into the Provincetown Harbor each May; when her trips stopped after Labor Day, it marked summer's unofficial end. The *Dorothy Bradford*, operated by the Cape Cod Steamship Co., sailed between Boston's Long Wharf and the Provincetown Harbor for nearly three decades.

A colorful 1889 poster advertised the round-trip fare between Boston and Provincetown as $1. A later poster, this time for a 1920 "Annual

Outing" of a Boston Masonic Lodge, offered round trip tickets, including "continuous lunch on boat" for $5. An ad in a 1939 pamphlet for the Provincetown Art Association accentuates the *S.S. Dorothy Bradford's* modern amenities: state rooms, refreshments, orchestra and dancing. By then, the one-way fare had gone up to $1.75; round trip within the same day was $2, and a round trip with an overnight stopover, $3. The trip took approximately four hours each way in 1939.

By comparison, there are now a couple of ferry companies making several trips per day in the summertime. Today's ferries still depart from Long Wharf (and the Seaport World Trade Center) in Boston and land in downtown Provincetown. The "slow" ferry takes about three hours and the Fast Ferry makes the journey in half that time. Today's fares? In 2022, the slower ferry costs $30 one way, $60 round trip. The faster one is approximately $60–70 one way, $80–100 round trip. There are no staterooms or orchestras on these boats, but there is a small bar on some runs where you can get a bag of chips and a soda for just under ten bucks.

NATIVE AMERICAN INFLUENCE ON US CONSTITUTION

The Mayflower Compact is largely credited with laying the groundwork for both the United States Constitution and the Declaration of Independence. For inspiration, however, the framers of the Constitution looked also to democratic structures already employed by Native Americans. At the time of the *Mayflower's* landing, various concepts of democratic governance were already in use by some Native Americans, including Wampanoag tribes in the Cape Cod region.

Architects of the US Constitution borrowed from democratic frameworks established by the Iroquois Confederacy government in particular. The Iroquois, who call themselves the Haudenosaunee, are made up of several distinct, independent tribes. Theirs is credited as being one of the oldest surviving participatory democracies in the world. By the time of the Declaration of Independence and the writing of the Constitution, the Iroquois government had already evolved into a multi-state system, permitting each state governance over affairs of its own region. In 1776, the Great Council members of the Iroquois were invited to address the Continental Congress on the topic.

Notably, the architects of our Constitution deviated from the Iroquois example with regard to reliance on hereditary leadership roles by instituting, instead, leadership by elected officials, and in adding its abiding cornerstone principle: The power of the government comes from the "consent of the governed" and from the Constitution itself.

CONGRESSIONAL RESOLUTION

In 1988, Congress passed a resolution formally recognizing that "[The] confederation of the original 13 Colonies into one republic was influenced by the political system developed by the Iroquois Confederacy as were many of the democratic principles which were incorporated into the Constitution itself." The resolution also acknowledged "[The] continuing government-to-government relationship between Indian tribes and the United States" as established by the US Constitution, as well as recognizing the sovereignty and legitimacy of Native Nations and their respective governments.

WAMPANOAG MEMORIAL

As this book goes to print, a Wampanoag Memorial project is currently in the works designed to tell the story of the people of the Wampanoag Nation, who inhabited the Cape at the time of the *Mayflower's* landing. The Wampanoag tribes had been living on the Cape since around 3000–2000 BCE and still live here today. The Memorial will honor local Wampanoag history and commemorate the Native American presence here on the Cape at the time of the *Mayflower's* arrival on Native lands, up through the present.

THE PLIMOTH PATUXET MUSEUMS

In 2020, the museums at Plimoth Plantation (at Plymouth, Massachusetts) were updated and modified to more accurately recognize and give a fuller account of the lives of Native American tribes who have lived in this area for thousands of years, long before and since the arrival of the *Mayflower* passengers up through the present day. The site and museums were renamed as the Plimoth Patuxet Museums.

From here, we will follow the zebra crossing to the opposite side of the street. We'll hang a left, taking us eastward.

IF THESE WALLS COULD TALK, THEY'D SING

If we were to listen closely to the echoes in the walls at 119 Bradford, we might hear the lilting hum of oaths and rituals of the King Hiram's Lodge of Ancient Free and Accepted Masons, by which the house was constructed in 1797. Provincetown's King Hiram Lodge was first established in 1795 by Paul Revere himself, America's most well-known noctivagant horseman.

We'd hear jaunty jingles taught to local girls and boys who were educated (in separate classrooms) here as part of the Lodge's initial charter. The Lodge also pledged to help provide for members' families whose breadwinners died at sea and in other unfortunate happenstances. Lodge logs tell of turkey dinners being delivered to bereaved families at holidays, as well as other assistance given to its members' widows and orphans.

As we listen, we'd hear the walls ring with the canticles and incantations of Catholic masses amid a quiet thrum of confessions shared here in the mid-1800s. This was the spiritual home of the local Catholic church, until the growth in numbers of parishioners outpaced the space and a new church, St. Peter the Apostle, was built.

We'd hear, ricocheting down the hallways, the warbling strains of children learning to play the recorder, the flute or maybe the saxophone. We'd hear the laughter, play and clamor of large, happy families who've flourished here in the decades since.

If these walls could talk, the cacophony of their voices would rise to weave a chorus—equal parts hymn, serenade, fado and lullaby, singing the as-yet-unfinished ballad of Provincetown.

COD'S OUT-SIZED INFLUENCE ON HISTORY

Looking across the street at the Clarendon House you may notice a large golden cod mounted above the door frame. It's one of a school of codfish images floating around town.

When not gilded, though, the cod is nothing remarkable to look at compared to fish with flashier colors, or swords jutting from the front of their heads or glow-tipped protrusions dangling lantern-like in front of rows of glinting teeth. But the unassuming codfish has had an outsized impact on the culture, politics and history of Cape Cod and, indeed, the United States and beyond.

The abundance of this fish, the ability to easily preserve it through drying and salting, and its adaptability to cuisines around the world helped cod become one of the most sought-after catches of the northern Atlantic waters. It also became a lucrative leg in the Triangular Trade between the Colonies, Europe, Africa and the Caribbean, particularly the unsavory entanglement of cod, rum and enslavement. The colonists' use of codfish, quite literally, as a trading currency, made the exchanges challenging for the Brits to control and even harder to tax. The trade in cod also brought many Massachusetts colonists staggering sums of wealth.

In fact, so important was the codfish to the growth, influence and prosperity of Massachusetts that, to this day, a nearly five-foot long "Sacred Cod" carved of wood hangs in the chamber of the House of Representatives in Boston. It swims in one direction when the Democrats are in power and in the opposite when Republicans hold the reins.

COD IN CUISINES AROUND THE WORLD

Cod: it's boiled, baked, dried, deep fried, smoked, salted, stewed, sautéed, marinated, stuffed with things, stuffed into things, made into fish fingers or a Provincetown specialty, skully-jo, a sort-of salt-drenched, wind-dried fish jerky—an acquired taste, say some. Infinite variations on the preparation of cod proliferate throughout the world.

In Italy, salt cod appears on menus as baccala, in Brazil and Portugal as baccalau and in Mexico as bacalao. The French make a delightful cod dish called brandade, a puree of salt cod, olive oil, and milk or cream. Sometimes potatoes, garlic or truffles are added, then crowned with croûtons. Salt cod is a national dish of Jamaica and is highly prized elsewhere in the Caribbean and in parts of Africa. Cod sperm is considered a delicacy in Japan. Choice bits and manavelins alike are incorporated into dumplings in China, and into soups, stews and chowders in a multitude of countries.

All parts of the fish can be eaten or otherwise put to use: the head, including the throat, (usually called the tongue) as well as the cheeks, roe, milt, stomach, tripe, liver and sperm. Up until the 20th century, the Icelanders ate cod bones softened in sour milk. Extracted from the liver, cod liver oil has long been believed to offer health benefits, though some of the benefits are more well-documented than others. The early colonists used the unpalatable parts of the fish to fertilize crops.

Those who settled on the Cape in the past few centuries have brought their cod cooking traditions with them, continuously shifting and redefining cod-based dishes you find in kitchens up and down the Cape today.

From here, let's cross back over Bradford and head up narrow little Alden Street.

THE ALDENS

Young John Alden, being single, adventurous and skilled in woodworking, joined the *Mayflower* crew in Southampton as the ship's cooper. His job was to build, repair and maintain the wooden barrels filled with food and drink. *Mayflower* historian Caleb Johnson describes the kinds of foods that were kept in these barrels as hard tack, butter, salt, vinegar, oatmeal and grains, dried cow tongue, salt pork and various additional salted or dried meats. Pickled foods like herring, various vegetables and eggs went into barrels of brine to keep them from spoiling. There were barrels of wine, cider and beer to tide the voyagers over while at sea where no fresh water was available.

John Alden's marriage to Priscilla Mullins, who had been orphaned during the course of the first winter, inspired a whimsical poem about a love triangle—probably fanciful—between John Alden, Priscilla Mullins, and Captain Miles Standish. John Alden was repeatedly elected to serve as Assistant-to-the-Governor at Plimoth Colony. Later, along with Standish and several others, John and Priscilla helped found Duxbury, Massachusetts. In 1687, John died at age 89; he was the last surviving signer of the Mayflower Compact.

In restaurants and snack bars around Provincetown throughout New England, you can find menu items named for John and Priscilla Alden. Usually, these are turkey in some form, slathered in a sauce historically reminiscent of Plimoth Colony, such as cranberry sauce or brown gravy. There's a street nearby named for Priscilla Alden, which intersects with Bradford Street, just a few blocks east of Alden Street.

ALDEN STREET

There is a surprising array of fruit and nut-bearing trees lining the streets and in the yards in Provincetown. Apple, crabapple, pear, plum, peach, cherry, chestnut, walnut, beech, maple, bayberry, hickory, hazelnut and even grape vines grow here. Orchards scattered around town have waxed and waned under different caretakers and weather patterns over the years. Here, between Alden and Standish, there is believed to have been an apple and pear orchard at one time.

One of the pear trees in town offers pears for the taking.

CIRCULAR CELLARS

Built sometime in the mid to late 1880s, the house at 12 Alden is said to have originally had two circular cellars. The rounded walls were designed to withstand the strain of constantly shifting sands better than conventional rectangular cellars. Several houses in town boast at least one round cellar, sometimes two. Historian Nancy Paine wrote that in houses with two circular cellars, one was generally used to capture rainwater, while the other served as a frost-proof storage area.

Several local cellars were specially outfitted to receive and store contraband liquor, especially during Prohibition. The handmade contraptions rigged up for this purpose are still found "down cellar" in some homes.

In households without cellars, illicit bottles were sometimes hidden, buried in a back garden. Peas might be planted above the gin, for example, carrots above the whiskey, lettuce above the rum and so forth, so the bottles could be easily relocated later.

THIS OLD HOUSE

Though now a building of residences, the Town Asylum was here at number 26 before it became Cape End Manor, a nursing home whose mission was to house, feed and care for elder and indigent residents. (The nursing home was later moved and expanded to include assisted and non-assisted elder housing. Interestingly, it's located just across the street from the largest of the town cemeteries.)

After its run as the Cape End Manor, the building was renamed in honor of the esteemed Grace Gouveia, who in 1915, at age six, skipped happily off the boat from Portugal and grew up to become revered as a local legend. She was a school teacher, a poet and an activist for elder rights. The Council on Aging, which she founded, operated here and for many years served free luncheons every Wednesday. The cookbooks the Council sells to raise funds feature a wide range of recipes spanning the endless variety of cuisines prepared by and shared among the people of Provincetown. (NOTE: This is now private residences. Copies of the cookbooks may be bought from the Friends of the Council on Aging, at the Senior Center, 2 Mayflower Street, near the Monument.)

THE WARM WELCOME ROOMING HOUSE

At one point this quaint home at number 29 was a rooming house offering a warm meal and a clean bed to newly-come Portuguese fishermen. Young men who'd just arrived in town could get room and board here without paying upfront. Instead, they paid their keep from wages earned on their first fishing voyage. Many newcomers came from the Azores, and at this welcoming boarding house they were able to meet others from the same or nearby islands, swap stories, get advice and share news from home gathered around a table filled with comfortingly familiar dishes from home.

THE TOWN CEMETERIES

We arrive now at the largest of the town's cemeteries, sown with head-stones, markers and mausoleums of remarkable people who've lived and died in Provincetown. As is the case up and down the Cape, a heart-breaking number of graves here are empty, the headstones having been placed on land to commemorate people whose bodies were never recovered from the sea.

Excepting the Winthrop Cemetery, all of the town's cemeteries are here, stitched together quilt-like. Edge to edge, they drape across this stretch of knurled and tussocked knolls between Alden and Conwell Streets, in tribute to the lives of infants, children and adults, creatives, curmudgeons, rascals and heroes; people of all ages, races, and genders, who've lived, loved and died here over the past four centuries.

WHALING, WHALERS AND THOSE LEFT BEHIND

In 1897, a ship with a crew of 18 men and one boy went down, leaving behind 16 widows and 37 children without a father. A storm in 1900, took a crew of 29 men and a boy, creating 15 more widows and ren-dering another 54 children fatherless. Within a span of less than two years, two more shipwrecks resulted in 91 additional fatherless children in Provincetown.

From the mid-1700s until the great whaling bust in the late 1800s (when alternative sources of oil suddenly became available), whaling was the third largest industry in Massachusetts, fifth largest in the country and certainly one of most dangerous occupations one could have. In some parts of the world whales were (and are) harvested for food, but in the US, whaling was not directly part of the food industry, rather part of the lucrative oil industry.

Wages for whalers were not guaranteed and sometimes, after weeks or months at sea in grueling conditions, sailors returned to port empty-handed. So brutal were the conditions and so uncertain the outcome, that 90 percent of sailors went on only one whaling voyage. Still, large paydays happened often enough to make the gamble appealing to men looking for fortune and adventure.

Historian Skip Finley writes that many men of color who went to sea found that they faced less discrimination on board than on land. On board the ship, a crew member's abilities as a sailor were more important than the color of his skin. Before, during and after the American Civil War, whaling was one of the few occupations that offered equal pay and equal treatment for men of color, at least while on board the ship. For many, this liberty, together with opportunities for promotion and financial success, outshone the risks inherent in chasing whales for a living.

In the later years, somewhere between 20 to 40 percent of the whalers were men of color and at least 64 of them achieved the rank of captain. With seven of them based out of Provincetown, this port had more Black whaling captains than any other in the country. As time went on, although some crews were entirely men of color, most were made up of men of various races and ethnicities. The last Provincetown-owned and -registered whaler was the *Charles W. Morgan*, which returned from her final trip in 1921. Her master, Captain John T. Gonsalves, and his crew were all men of color from Cape Verde. All seven of Provincetown's Black captains ranked among the top 15 most successful New England whalers in terms of numbers of whales killed. Among them, they brought in a cache of oil worth an estimated value of over $100 million dollars in today's currency. The lives and achievements of several captains of color are honored in museums, including the New Bedford Whaling Museum and the Whaling Museum on Nantucket.

Sailing the seas on whaling and fishing vessels and merchant ships was a treacherous business, and not all survivors fully recovered from the impacts of shipwrecks, piracy, privation and other traumatic events. The experience of near-starvation at sea induced some sailors to stash away food in hidey-holes around their homes for the remainder of their days. Scraps of food have been found hidden in rafters, under floorboards and behind the chimneys in the homes of some of older fishermen after they died.

Commercial fishing remains one of the more dangerous occupations around. In spite of this, Provincetown women and men proudly and courageously carry on the tradition.

CAPTAIN COLLIN STEVENSON (STEPHENSON)

Regrettably, although he is listed in Provincetown's Historic Cemeteries booklet, Captain Collin Stevenson, one of Provincetown's most successful Black whaling captains, has no headstone bearing his famous name. Stevenson sailed on a remarkable 16 voyages in 15 years and was one of few Black men at that time to become a member of the local Masons. The quantity of whale oil he is believed to have harvested would be valued in today's money at a whopping 3.1 million dollars.

Born in the West Indies in 1847, Collin Stevenson arrived in Provincetown at age 18. He worked hard and rapidly rose to captain. He was appointed master of the *Carrie D. Knowles*, a whaling ship owned by a fellow King Hiram Lodge member. In January 1904, Stevenson and his crew of 12 men, along with the ship he captained, disappeared inexplicably while on a trip that was supposed to have been a quick, 20-day "plum pudding" voyage—a fishermen's term for a trip that is short, rich and sweet.

Five years later his widow, Hannah, believing Stevenson to be dead, became engaged to marry another man. About that time, *The New York Times* published an article citing a report that the missing ship's crew was being held prisoner in Venezuela. Hannah called off her wedding. No further evidence ever surfaced to support the story of the incarceration of the crew of the *Carrie D. Knowles* or her captain. Hannah never remarried.

We will leave the cemetery and head back toward Bradford along Standish Street.

As we walk, I will tell you of the harrowing, modern day whale adventure of local lobsterman, Michael Packard. In tribute, his friend and rescuer Josiah Mayo, a local fisherman himself and the award-winning chocolate magician of Chequessett Chocolates, created a chocolate bar called "Everything Whale be Alright!"

DISPATCHED FROM THE MOUTH OF A WHALE

One day in June of 2021, a local fisherman was swimming with the fishes—not euphemistically—he was scuba diving among schools of little sandeel fish in search of lobster. As fate would have it, sandeel are a favorite snack of the humpback whale. Suddenly, a whale slurped him up, but it couldn't slosh him down. In spite of how enormous a humpback whale is (around 66,000 lbs.), and how much food it eats every day (around 3,000 lbs.), a baleen whale cannot swallow anything much larger than a watermelon, let alone a grown man floundering madly about in full scuba gear. Still, it's a miracle that the lobsterman was not seriously injured or killed. Instead, the whale swished him around in its mouth a bit before spewing him back into the sea. His friend Josiah quickly fished him out of the bay and plunked him back into the boat. (For their troubles, the two men appeared on late night television, enthralling the nation and stealing global headlines for days.)

I wrote this little limerick for Michael Packard and Josiah Mayo, who well deserve to dine out on their story for the rest of their days.

> A fisherman of wide renown
> Went lobster diving in Ptown;
> On that same day
> In that same bay,
> A whale was chasing sandeel down.
>
> Down it plunged, its jaws agape,
> Landing Michael in a scrape;
> Sucked into the maw,
> He stuck in its craw,
> So it spat him straight back to the Cape!
>
> —Od.

STANDISH STREET

Being a captain in Her Majesty's military, and the only man aboard the ship to hold that rank, Captain Miles Standish is sometimes mistaken for having been the captain of the *Mayflower,* but the man who captained the *Mayflower* on her historic voyage was Master Christopher

Jones. Captain Standish, on the other hand, was hired by the Pilgrims for his military prowess, though later they denounced and rejected his unconscionable brutality and cruelty toward his enemies.

Standish is also known for inland forays he led with William Bradford while the *Mayflower* was docked at Cape Cod. During these exploratory trips to the area where Truro is now, they found a freshwater source (now Pilgrim's Pond) in addition to a stash of corn belonging to local Native Americans. The *Mayflower* scouts took the corn, along with artifacts from Native graves they'd uncovered.

Captain Standish may be best known, however, as a jilted suitor, the likely fictitious image of him created by Henry Wadsworth Longfellow and baked into the minds of American middle schoolers made to memorize the poem, "The Courtship of Miles Standish." The poem purports a love entanglement between Miles Standish, John Alden and pretty Priscilla Mullins. In the poem, Standish, who prides himself for his agility with a sword but less so for his skill with words, engages his silver-tongued sidekick, Alden, to convey messages of love on his behalf to young Priscilla Mullins. Alden, in spite of being in love with Priscilla himself, takes on this duty to his elder in the name of loyalty and friendship. Priscilla, miffed that Standish has sent a proxy instead of courting her himself, ends up falling for young Alden. A furious Standish compares this perceived betrayal by Alden to that of Caesar by Brutus. Eventually, Standish forgives the lovers and blesses their marriage, saying, "I should have remembered the adage, 'If you would be well served, you must serve yourself; and moreover, no man can gather cherries in Kent at the season of Christmas!'"

Priscilla and John raised 10 children and are often credited with having more descendants than any of the *Mayflower* voyagers, among both passengers and crew. Turns out, Longfellow, too, was one of Priscilla's descendants. His family connection to her might have had some bearing on his fanciful retelling of her story. However, historians note that Longfellow frequently applied artistic license in lieu of historic facts when penning this and other poems, including his even more famous (and equally inaccurate) accounts of "Paul Revere's Ride" and his poem "The Song of Hiawatha."

The intersection of Standish and Bradford is known as McQuillan Square. At 21 years of age, Everette McQuillan, Seaman First Class in the US Naval Reserve, succumbed to the 1918 flu. He was the first of eight Provincetown service members to die serving in the Great War. The first of these commemorative markers were put up just as WWII loomed on the horizon. Not every Provincetown service member who died while serving has been honored with a marker. In the Vietnam War alone, 96 people from Provincetown gave their lives.

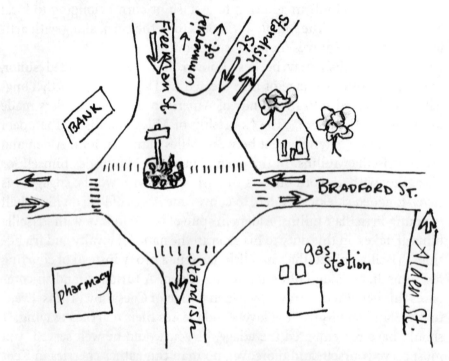

Ding, ding, ding!

We will soon be arriving at the intersection of Standish and Bradford, near where the Old Colony Railroad Depot once stood.

FI-LI-MI-OO-RE-OO-RE-AY!

Most of the men who built the Cape Cod line of the Old Colony Railroad were Irishmen, although some in the ranks were local fishermen who'd fallen on hard times. In other parts of the country it was the Irish, as well as immigrants from around the globe, together with Americans of a wide range of racial and ethnic extractions, who worked to build the vast railway system which knits the rest of the lower 48 states together. It took the men 17 months to build the Cape's Old Colony line. On the Cape, Irish "gandy dancers," as railroad builders called themselves, usually slept in tents, shacks or boardinghouses alongside the rails, surviving on brown bread, boiled beef, boiled potatoes, black coffee and booze. A half pint of whiskey per day was considered a standard component of a worker's wage. It was not uncommon for Cape rail worker's letters home to Ireland to arrive months on, edged with smudges of dirt-blackened fingers, and the lingering stench and stains of smoked fish and spilt whiskey.

Gandy dancers invented songs like "Poor Paddy on the Railway" to help synchronize the swinging of their sledge hammers and the hoisting of the iron rails, easing their workload by joining their strength in rhythm. Singing while working also helped to pass the time and entertain one another. The music of country singers such as Jimmie Rodgers were influenced by the songs of African American gandy dancers in the South, especially.

In addition to helping the gandy dancers keep time in their work, lyrics of songs such as "Poor Paddy on the Railway" tell the sad story of the difficult life of an Irish lad who leaves his home in Ireland in search of work in the States. Paddy meets and marries "sweet Biddy McGee" and takes up work as a gandy dancer working on the railway. It's hard work; he's poorly paid and poorly treated. In the labor riots of 1840s, he's attacked with "sticks and stones" in anti-immigrant violence against foreign-born workers. Paddy's wife dies, leaving him with several children to feed. The song ends with Paddy drowning his sorrows in whiskey: "In eighteen hundred and forty eight/ I learned to take me whiskey straight/ 'Tis an elegant drink and can't be bate/ For working on the railway/ Fili-mi-oo-re-oo-re-ay!"

OLD COLONY RAILROAD DEPOT

By July of 1873, the gandy dancers had finished their jig; the railway was complete and the air was filled with merry train whistles announcing the arrival of four trains per day carrying city passengers and off-Cape products into Provincetown from Boston. The trains then turned around and carried seafood and sunburned tourists back again. The three dozen or more stops en route stretched the 120-mile trip into a four-and-a-half hour crawl between Boston and the tip of the Cape. In celebration of the new railway, President Grant traveled the length of the Cape by train, from Hyannis to Provincetown the following year.

Before long, the age of train travel to the Cape was overtaken by the automobile. The completion of a paved road the length of the Cape enticed increasing numbers of tourists to travel by bus and car, not only from Boston, but also from New York City and beyond. In his book, *Building Provincetown*, David Dunlap writes:

> The last scheduled passenger train left the Bradford Street depot on 17 July 1938 — 65 years, almost to the day, after service began. The station was mournfully draped in crepe and a dirge was played as the train pulled out.

Railroad service, followed by the arrival of automobiles, both had a profound impact on the food industry here on the Outer Cape, as it enabled frozen and nearly fresh seafoods to expand into new markets far inland, and a wider variety of foods from across the country could reach even the tippity-tip of Cape Cod.

The Provincetown train depot adapted to the demise of the train by reinventing itself as a bus depot. In the 1940s, the It's Hubert's restaurant was added to meet the burgeoning demand of hungry travelers. In response to the notoriously unpredictable nature of early automobiles, entrepreneurial mechanics opened an auto repair shop at the busy intersection. Today's self-service filling station selling overpriced packaged snacks seems a predictable, if less exciting, progression from this intersection's grander days as the Old Colony Railroad Depot.

THE GLORY DAYS OF RAILROAD CAR DINING

Early travel by rail didn't include food service or a dining car. On the Cape, at brief but frequent stops, throngs of passengers would swarm off the train to tussle for a coffee or a bite to inhale before racing back onto the train before its departure moments later. Wiser passengers packed a lunch basket. Before long, enterprising young men, known as News Butchers, began to board trains to peddle their apples, sweets, books and, of course, newspapers. After a few stops, they'd disembark and board a train headed back, selling their goods in the opposite direction until they got back to their original station.

According to James D. Porterfield, who wrote *Dining by Rail*, a comprehensive book on the topic and includes over 300 recipes from railroad menus, beginning in the 1860s, meals were served on select train lines in designated train cars. Oftentimes, a dining car was added to a train for just long enough to serve a meal, then removed from that train to be attached to another. Beer and wine in elegant glassware accompanied multiple-course meals served in timed seatings. These luxurious meals were presented on logo-embossed china plates, with silver plated flatware, atop crisp white tablecloths and served by waiters in white. Fresh flowers graced each table.

Dining car meals were an extravagance in which only well-heeled passengers could indulge. Rail companies vied fiercely for high-end passengers by hiring innovative chefs who created signature dishes and specialties from top-quality meats, dairy and fruits. Rail lines competed to serve dishes unique to that line, highlighting culinary elements specific to the region of the country it rolled through. Even the wine labels, brands of beer and specialty cocktails were specific to individual train lines.

These golden days of luxury railroad car dining were financially unsustainable for the rail lines. Today, on some rail lines, passengers may still find a food car. Most of these offer hot and cold snacks, a can of beer or a glass of wine. Very few lines now offer a sit-down dinner served on ivory linen by white-suited waitstaff reminiscent of the past.

There is no longer a train line running out to Provincetown, but on weekends from Memorial Day through Labor Day, the CapeFLYER caters to the Boston crowd, making a daily jaunt from South Station in Boston to Hyannis and back. Both first class and general seating are available. First class passengers can enjoy the two-hour, twenty-minute journey in large "comfy leather seats" with food and drinks served on tray tables. The Café Car is open to all passengers and its light menu lists snacks of bagels and cream cheese, pastries, a fruit cup, sandwiches, chips and salsa. They have a selection of beers, wines, coffee and sodas to accompany meals.

Just across Standish Street you can see a large building with the Eye of Horus keeping watch over the intersection below. Once a shamble of sheds, shacks and garages, the rambling building became the inimitable Napi's Restaurant.

NAPI'S RESTAURANT

This is a storied restaurant with a personality of its own, revealing a sense of humor and adventure as original as that of its first proprietor, Napi Van Derek. The current building grew from a disjointed row of garages that served as a trash-and-treasure shop. It was constructed by creative local craftsmen, fueled by unfettered imagination and unhindered by convention—or building regulations. Many of its materials were souvenired and scavenged from old ships and disused structures from hither and yon. Antiques collected back in the day adorn the walls; the Eye of Horus offers a glance back at Napi's travels in Egypt in his youth. Artistic puns pop up all around the place, including one in the form of a polar expedition scene painted on a cold air duct. (Is that our Arctic explorer Admiral MacMillan, perhaps?) The requisite wooden codfish swims above the front door, and a clowder of cats—both the alive sort and artistic sort—roam the grounds and snooze in corners. Napi's restaurant boasts one of the earliest sculpted brick creations by artist Conrad Malicoat and a museum-sized (and museum-worthy) collection of notable works by local artists, past and present.

In Napi's day, the menu featured classic dishes and fusions of flavors from around the globe, reflecting the spectrum of tastes and traditions of people who live in and visit Provincetown. Offerings range from traditional Yankee-style New England seafood to spicy Jamaican jerk, from Portuguese staples and Italian pastas to Indian curries, Asian dishes, Mexican favorites and Greek specialties. Napi's menu read like an explorer's map of the world.

We'll head up the gentle hill now as we carry on along Bradford. Right away, we see a sun-yellow fence decorated with delightful pineapple cut-out panels.

THE "KING OF FRUIT"

Around the globe, pineapples are emblematic of friendship, warm welcome, hospitality and sometimes of fertility and abundance. Images of pineapples decorate kitchen curtains, the tops of banisters, even bedposts. Owning the fruit was once indicative of extreme wealth, as a single pineapple could cost thousands of dollars. The "King of Fruit" was displayed as an ornamental table centerpiece in the homes of affluent hosts to flaunt their wealth. For hosts who could not afford to purchase a pineapple to brandish at a dinner party, pineapples could be rented, discretely, overnight.

The pineapple is also a curiosity for both mathematicians and artists. Its outer shell is a botanical example of a naturally formed Fibonacci sequence (a series of numbers in which each consecutive number is arrived at by adding the two previous numbers together). Fibonacci sequences found in flowers, fruits and vegetables, for example, tend to be appealing to the human eye. Just one more reason the pineapple deserves its place at the center of a well-appointed table!

PINEAPPLES IN THE AZORES

Provincetown wives who sailed with their sea captain husbands to the Azores regarded pineapples as a special treasure. Pineapples are not native to the Azorean islands but have been grown there in large quantities since at least the 17th century. They've become a major source of revenue and deeply integrated into the Azorean cultural identity, especially on São Miguel, which holds fiercely competitive pineapple cooking contests every year. The pineapples of São Miguel are considered by pineapple connoisseurs to be amongst the best in the world. Azoreans who left home to come here brought their love of pineapple with them, and it's common to find the fruit in both sweet and savory Portuguese dishes here.

As we meander up Bradford Street we will pass the Provincetown Brewing Company that, conveniently, affords me an opportunity to talk a bit about a beverage with a long and fascinating history in Massachusetts: beer.

BEER

"In wine there is wisdom, in beer there is strength, in water there is bacteria."

—David Auerbach

BEER AND THE *MAYFLOWER*

American beer lore, probably teetering somewhere between hard fact and compelling storytelling, has it that passengers of the *Mayflower* wound up settling at Plimoth/Patuxet, rather than soldiering on to their original destination, because they were running low on beer.

The theory stems from the fact that storms, mishaps and other factors had delayed their journey, bringing the *Mayflower* passengers to the shores of the "new world" much later in the year than anticipated. By that point, all the ship's food stores were running low, including beer. As water did not keep well in wooden barrels, tending toward slime and grime in fairly short order, beer was the most dependable way to stay hydrated on board. Beer rations had already been decreased to make the supply last longer, but the ship's crew had, not only to get through the winter with nothing but the food and drink already on board, but also had to get all the way back to England before running out.

Once the passengers decided that the Cape did not offer the resources and fertile ground they'd need to start a colony, they debated whether to continue on to their original destination, a couple hundred miles to the south, or to find a closer location in which to settle. In the end, given the precarious winter weather and short rations, it was decided to settle their colony nearby where the *Mayflower* could moor over the winter and return to England in the spring.

Once arriving at Plimoth/Patuxet, all healthy adult male passengers, according to William Bradford's writings, were "hastened ashore and made to drink water, that the seamen might have the more beer." Bradford wrote that Master Jones staunchly refused to share the ship's precious store of beer with any man, whether well or ailing, even were it his own father. Apparently, Jones's stance was softened (albeit briefly) by the Christmas spirit; on that day, passengers and crew reportedly shared a meal and a round of beer aboard the *Mayflower*.

BEER IN THE BAY STATE

Brewed initially as a safe, reliable way to stay hydrated, and later for both pleasure and profit, beer has long been an important part of New England's culinary, economic and political history. At Plimoth Colony, women brewed beer in their homes from ingredients on hand, such as corn, barley, oats—even carrots. Ten years later, the Puritans came over, bringing fortifications of 10,000 gallons of beer, 120 casks of malt for brewing, 12 gallons of Dutch gin and bags of seeds to grow wheat, rye and barley. This got them off to a good start in their new home in Boston. In 1634, the first licensed tavern opened in Boston, followed three years later by the creation of the first commercial brewery.

By 1689, in Boston there was one pub for every 20 adult men; beer was even brewed on the Harvard campus. Harvard lore has it that their beer was brewed from a recipe taught to the founder of Harvard College by his friend, William Shakespeare. Niggling questions regarding the accuracy of that tidbit aside, beer was taken very seriously at Harvard which, at one point in the 1700s, boasted three breweries on its campus. After graduating from Harvard with the Class of 1743, Samuel Adams began making malt for beer brewers. Over a century later, the Boston Beer Company began brewing Samuel Adams lager, named in honor of the Founding Father and maltster. More recently, New England-brewed Harpoon beer was founded by a handful of enterprising Harvard graduates from the Class of 1982.

While most commercial brewers in New England were men, women brewed small batches of beer at home, as women have done in various parts of the world for nearly 4,000 years. While most early commercial beer brewers in New England were men, women brewed small batches of beer at home, as women have done in various parts of the world for nearly 4,000 years. Today in the US, women still make up only a small fraction of commercial brewers, though their numbers are rapidly on the rise and, increasingly, their brews are taking home top prizes nationally and internationally.

THE PROVINCETOWN BREWING COMPANY

The punned names of menu items at the Provincetown Brewing Company salute both Provincetown and American culture and history. Their Crandaddy Sour features the local "must" ingredient: cranberries. The Double Rainbow IPA, Asphalt Glitter Stout and Love Conquers Ale all nod to the LGBTQ+ community. Spilt Tea and Provincetown 400th Commemorative brews clearly salute history-making events impacting broader New England and American history.

The next point of interest as we walk up the block, is tucked into the basement of what once was a funeral home.

RUTHIE'S BOUTIQUE

Ruthie's is a long-standing, much-cherished thrift shop in Province-town where boas and bargains abound! The wild, ever-changing assortment of clothing and household items donated to Ruthie's are sold at bargain prices, and the proceeds are distributed to local organizations which feed, house and assist community members in need.

Provincetown is an increasingly difficult place for many to afford to live. Basic groceries are expensive, rental housing options are slim pickings and the rates are stratospheric and rising. Nowadays, Provincetown is trending sybaritic. There are ever more Mazaratis around than Mazdas, more BMWs than VWs, more Teslas than Toyotas. At an increasing number of restaurants, for the price of a single entrée, one could purchase enough ingredients to feed a small family for a couple of days. Most jobs at the tip of the Cape are seasonal and, all too often, pay meager wages. For decades, contributions from the sales at Ruthie's Boutique have helped local folks weather rough times.

Directly across the street from Ruthie's, meet Provincetown with a Southern accent. This is the John Randall guesthouse, offering an ambiance of Southern elegance and hospitality.

THE JOHN RANDALL HOUSE

Aptly billed as "Provincetown's Inn for art-lovers," this guesthouse is a tapestry woven of art, history, food and culture, run by a congenial wash-ashore from North Carolina. For breakfast, guests are treated to fresh pastries made locally, in an atmosphere of tastefully blended Southern hospitality and New England charm. The walls and halls are lined with artwork drawn from a rich African American heritage, together with local art reflective of Provincetown's eclectic culture and history. Though Don, proprietor of the John Randall House, is not Provincetown's first African American guesthouse owner, he's one of very few to date. The first was Helen Caddie-Larcenia, née Brown, who ran a popular women's guesthouse called Aspasia, on Pearl Street in the 1980s.

While relaxing in your deck chair in the John Randall garden, taking in your surroundings over an afternoon cocktail, you may notice the inn straddling the crest of the hill and find yourself thinking, "Hmmm, where have I seen that house before?" The guesthouse in question, now the Sunset Inn, was the subject of a painting done by Edward Hopper in 1945 titled *Rooms for Tourists*. On the canvas, the inviting, ember-orange glow in the upper window feels to me as if a friend has just poured a nightcap in anticipation of my arrival. I want to call up to the open window in the painting, "I'll be right up!"

Among Hopper's other paintings of Provincetown is the building that now houses the Provincetown Library.

FAR LAND PROVISIONS

Though not located at the precise geographic center of town, the corner of Conwell and Bradford has arguably been the social center of town for nearly a century, as a prevailing string of civic-minded proprietors have offered up hearty provisions and warm hospitality to the community.

A veritable Provincetown institution since the day its doors opened in 2004, Far Land Provisions is a year-round gift to the community. Inspired by the owners' mothers, who loved to bring friends and strangers together over a good meal, Far Land is where people come to meet old friends and make new ones; it's a place to come celebrate joyful occasions or to gather and find solace in hard times.

In winter, it's an everyone-knows-your-name kinda place. In summer, it is thrumming with the excitement and energy of visitors and locals mingling, popping in to pick up a pastry and coffee, or a few picnic fixings and a bottle of wine. Or just to share a hello and a hug. During the height of summer there's a Far Land outpost open at Herring Cove Beach.

With an appreciation for the environmental and economic benefits to the community of sourcing locally, the ingredients at Far Land are generally Cape-sourced and made from scratch. Many are named after popular locations, recalling local history. The "Marconi" sandwich leans Italian, in honor of the renowned inventor whose radio tower stood up-Cape from here; the "Pilgrim Lake" features turkey, cheddar and cranberry chutney.

In pride-of-place are framed photos of Jim and Tom's mothers, alongside a photo of John Perrone, a Far Land cashier, and a DJ for WOMR (the community radio station), who tragically died of COVID-19 in April 2020, at the onset of the pandemic. John was the first person in Provincetown known to have died of the coronavirus.

Before we continue along Bradford Street to Pearl, let's pause briefly and talk about doings on Conwell Street.

CONWELL STREET

A bit up the street from here, where the Conwell Lumber and Hardware store is now, was a railroad hub from the 1870s to the 1950s, when foods and goods were brought into Provincetown by rail from up-Cape and off-Cape. The location has served as a lumber and hardware store since 1945, continuing to thrive long after the railroad was shut down. In addition to lumber, patrons these days can find construction materials, a few household appliances, a basic selection of artists' supplies as well as candies—including bags of Australian-style licorice. (An Australian candy company named Darrell Lea claims to have inadvertently invented the world's first soft licorice recipe, a style of sweets they now sell the world over, including here.)

Provincetown's first supermarket set up shop in 1958, just down the street from the hardware store. The market was owned by the Great Atlantic & Pacific Tea Company, more widely-known as the A&P. In the 1980s, A&P closed its Conwell location and upped-stakes for Shankpainter Road, across town. Later, an affordable housing development was built on Conwell and christened Old Ann Page, in tribute to the popular A&P house brand of that name. As many still recall, the Ann Page label appeared on bottles of salad dressing, ketchup, tapioca, cans of beans and more.

Continuing along Bradford Street, we come next to Pearl Street. Turning left, almost straight away, we come to the world-renowned Fine Arts Work Center at number 24 Pearl.

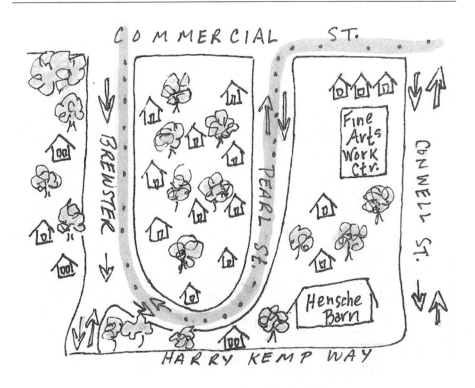

FINE ARTS WORK CENTER

Frank Days, a forward-thinking, Azorean-born immigrant to Provincetown, built a row of rustic art studios here on Pearl Street in

1914 and began renting them out at affordable rates to artists of Provincetown's swelling art colony. These inexpensive, seasonal accommodations were instrumental in enabling the stability and growth of the arts and writing community. The commune flourished. Today, Provincetown proudly upholds its title as the oldest continuous art colony in the country, and many of the nation's top writers have been fellows and teachers here.

The Fine Arts Work Center (FAWC), founded in 1968, has been a driving force behind the success of the colony. Several artists and patrons, including Hudson and Ione Walker, Phillip Malicoat, Josephine and Salvatore Del Deo, Stanley Kunitz, Robert Motherwell, Myron Stout, Jack Tworkov and others got the FAWC off the ground. Their work and that of others helped to lay the foundation for the success that FAWC and the art colony still enjoy.

Not only does the FAWC offer fellowships to emerging and established artists and writers, but anyone can sign up to take summer classes taught by well-known artists and writers like Jo Hay, Mark Adams, Pete Hocking, Jessica Jacobs, Vicky Tomayko, Porsha Olayiwola, Rowan Ricardo Phillips and many others.

But artists and writers don't just need a place to sleep and paint—they also need to eat. In its early years, artists at the FAWC beat a path to the door of Nellie Barnes, who ran a boardinghouse and restaurant up the street at 33 Pearl. She fed artists, as well as fishermen, boatmen and anyone else who showed up—whether they could pay or not. Charles Hawthorne was one of her patrons in those days. In appreciation for her kindness, he painted her portrait. Later in his life, Hawthorne's portraits could fetch north of $4, 000 and now, of course, far more.

PEARL STREET

Whether or not this street is named for the pearls of oysters is unclear, but it is common on maps of other oyster-harvesting towns and cities around the world, to see a Pearl Street running through them. While all oysters (and other mollusks) have the ability to produce pearls, most types of oysters are less likely to do so, including those most commonly found hereabouts. The chance of finding a pearl in a wild oyster is estimated to be 1 in 10,000.

ON OYSTERS

'Twas "a bold man who first ate an oyster," mused Jonathan Swift.

Indeed. Though many have taken a shine to the squishy critters since. I, admittedly, am among them. In fact, the first time I was taught to slurp oysters, the exhilaration was akin to a religious experience.

If you woke up one morning to find you were of a mind to eat nothing but oysters all day, you would be looking at consuming 250 of them in order to meet your recommended daily intake of calories. However, very few people could afford to do that these days. At today's going price, 250 oysters will set you back around 725 clams!

THAT AGE-OLD DILEMMA:
WHAT TO DRINK WITH OYSTERS?

As oysters are influenced by their meroir–the soils, waters and temperatures surrounding them—it's often suggested that wines coming from near where the oysters are sourced, having a similar terroir, will pair best.

Others in the know say that, regardless of the wine's region, leaning toward a dry, uncomplicated wine, usually a mild-mannered white that will not interfere with the briny flavors of the oyster, is preferred. To this end, Chablis and muscadet are frequently recommended, *mais bien sûr*, with oysters, one cannot go amiss with a good champagne!

Some oyster-philes swear by a smooth, high-end vodka, served up, a little bit dirty, with a big fat olive. Some opt for a simple gin martini, or even a margarita if it's not too sweet. Certain friends of mine delight in the downright hedonistic practice of slipping the oyster into a shot of lemon vodka mixed with spicy pepper vodka, splashed gently with a good tart mignonette.

A bit of that shared among friends, and all is right with the world.

FORMERLY ASPASIA GUESTHOUSE, AT 31 PEARL

Prior to becoming the first African American guesthouse owner in Provincetown, Helen Caddie-Larcenia had been the first woman and the first African American to become a full-time police officer in the city of Danbury, Connecticut.

From the mid-1980s, through the end of the decade, Helen and her then-partner, ran Aspasia. It was a hospitable women's guesthouse, a haven for women of all races, ethnicities and backgrounds from around the globe, to meet and share stories over a breakfast of yogurt and fruit, warm muffins, and strong coffee. Hours of leisurely conversation in the sun room led to new friendships and a sense of belonging that the women seldom found elsewhere.

THE HENSCHE BARN AT THE TOP OF PEARL STREET

When Charles Hawthorne came to town, he started his art school atop Miller Hill in the Hawthorne Barn (now run by the art organization Twenty Summers) and set up his work studio here in the barn at the end of Pearl Street. This studio location is now called the Hensche Barn, in honor of one of Hawthorne's students who taught art classes here. Hawthorne's school is credited with being the first to teach outdoor figure painting. Although it was the best known of Provincetown's early art schools, his school was not the first on the scene. A woman named Dewing Woodward had been running her school for art in town for three years by the time Hawthorne arrived.

Charles Hawthorne lived and taught in Provincetown, exhibited nationwide, died in Baltimore, was given a funeral in New York City then buried here in Provincetown.

NORMAN ROCKWELL AND NOTIONS OF THANKSGIVING

One of Hawthorne's students was "America's most popular illustrator," Norman Rockwell. Rockwell created slice-of-life scenes which offer insights into his own perspective of American life. Although his paintings are often described as portraying "typical" American lives, in many aspects they are typical only of a portion of the American population. Foodways are at the heart of much of our cultural expression, and Rockwell's use of food scenes, in particular, helps illustrate the version of America he knew best. Perhaps Rockwell's most famous illustration and, as it turns out, one of his more controversial is *Freedom from Want*, which depicts a 1940s, white, middle-class American family having just sat down to enjoy a "quintessential" Thanksgiving dinner. On the table the viewer can see celery, pickles, a bowl of fruit, cranberry sauce and a covered casserole dish. The glasses for both adults and children are filled with plain water. The centerpiece is a steaming roasted turkey. The scene is frequently described as Puritan-esque for its lack of frills regarding the types of food served, its simple presentation and the muted tones in the clothing of the diners.

Food scenes in writing, films, artwork and other forms of storytelling are used as shorthand to convey underlying messages and story elements. Rockwell was particularly adept at incorporating food into his paintings to help flesh out a picture's multi-layered stories. The cultural messaging in *Freedom from Want* is so powerful that, from the time it was first published in the early 1940s to this day, the painting has continued to evoke strong responses among viewers. As its title suggests, this painting depicts people whose lives are filled with plenty—plenty of family, friends and food. When the painting became public in 1943, it caused an uproar in Europe, where it was felt Rockwell was flaunting the abundance enjoyed in America while Europeans were suffering the pain and deprivations of war.

In America, many found the picture to be profoundly heartwarming and reflective of their own life and family. Other Americans felt it represents a narrow fraction of American families, rather than recognizing America's varied family structures, its multitude of races and cultures, as well as the plethora of Thanksgiving foods this diversity brings to the table.

The various premises portrayed in the painting have been challenged by artists for decades in countless parodies. The iconic scene has been re-envisioned to depict families of color, mixed raced families, non-nuclear families, families which include LGBTQ+ members and families of different religious faiths and traditions. Some spin-off paintings celebrate cuisines besides the turkey an' fixins of Rockwell's scene. Parodies and remakes of the painting highlight differences—and perhaps more importantly—the fundamental similarities between the loving, laughing family portrayed in the painting and the loving, laughing array of families that make up America.

Essayists and journalists have used the painting to address the legend of the First Thanksgiving and to bring attention to the history of the harvest meal shared with Native Americans, as documented by colonists, as well as to explore a broader account and context of the historic feast. Many within the Native American Nations gather to commemorate the day as one of reflection and mourning, rather than one of celebration.

In his time, George Washington called for a day of celebration, prayer and giving thanks; however, the feast was not celebrated on a yearly basis until Lincoln declared Thanksgiving an official annual holiday in 1863. As such, the holiday itself is a relatively recent annual tradition, though creating Rockwell-like turkey dinners derived from popular notions about the First Thanksgiving stretches back centuries.

Today, in households in Provincetown and around the country, Thanksgiving is observed, if not celebrated, each in its own meaningful way. Regardless which foods grace the table, the occasion marks a time for family, friends and neighbors to gather to share a meal and a sense of community and to express gratitude for having good food and one another's company.

THE HARVEST CELEBRATION 1621, PLIMOTH COLONY

Of the 18 women who boarded the *Mayflower*, only five of them survived beyond the first winter. When Governor John Carver died of heatstroke, followed shortly after by his wife Katherine, apparently of a broken heart, only four adult women remained. By time the legendary harvest celebration rolled around, it was up to these four women to put on days of feasting for 150 or so people (while looking after 25 children and teens). At the gathering, the 50 colonists were joined by more than 90 Native Americans for the three-day harvest celebration, diplomatic bridge-building and a few joint military exercises.

What we know of the foods served at the first harvest meal shared between the colonists and Native Americans comes primarily from the writings of William Bradford and Edward Winslow. Although most of the dishes served at this celebration would not have looked like those featured in Norman Rockwell's famous painting, many of the same ingredients were on hand. The Wampanoag guests contributed five deer and other foods. There was probably wild turkey on the table, though likely not as a centerpiece. The tables were loaded with waterfowl, cod, bass, shellfish, and, possibly, lobster. There were no potatoes, but plenty of nuts, vegetables and fruits. Garlic, along with wild and cultivated herbs added flavor to various dishes made with chestnuts, walnuts, corn, onions, beans, carrots, pumpkins, parsnips, leeks, sunchokes and cabbage. There would have been melons, berries and grapes.

And, of course, cranberries.

BREWSTER STREET

Although "brewster" is the term for a woman who brews beer, this street is named for William Brewster, the *Mayflower* passenger who was a church leader in Leiden, where he and others found refuge when they fled England seeking to practice their religion more freely and openly. When members of the Leiden congregation left to establish a colony on the European Continent, the Leiden pastor opted not to travel with the first wave of Pilgrims. The next highest-ranking member, Elder Brewster, was tapped to fill the role.

William Brewster's wife, Mary, was one of the four women who survived to see the three-day fall harvest meal often called the First Thanksgiving. In researching Mary's life, I learned that she named her children: Jonathan, Patience, Fear, Love and Wrestling.

In that order. An intriguing progression.

Let's cross over Bradford Street here and start down picturesque Dyer Street. Both tangible and intangible aspects of Provincetown often defy description, but that doesn't keep people from trying. Putting pen to paper, paintbrush to canvas, hands to clay, generations of creatives have striven to capture the essence of the landscape, the flora and fauna, architecture and people here and to impart the feelings that being here stirs within.

HOW DOES YOUR GARDEN GROW?

Some of the houses you see in town are trim and stately, adorned with staid blue-ribbon gardens showcasing a cortège of roses in bold, rich, perfectly harmonized hues. Tall, debonair lupines patrol the picket fence in lock-step with a retinue of royal purple iris and navy-blue delphiniums. Delicate white sprays of lobelia and sprightly blue bachelor's but-

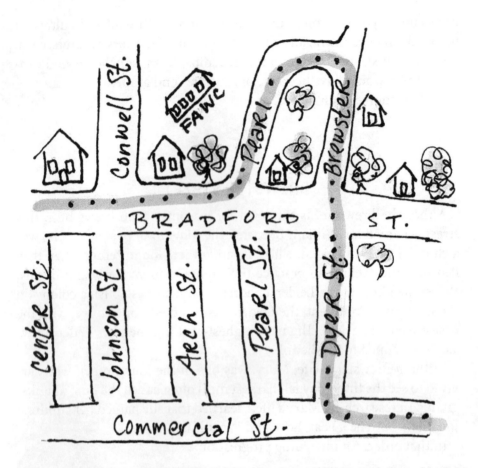

tons dance a strictly choreographed waltz in red pots that march up the staircase in parallel rows: little red-white-and-blue floats in a patriotic parade. In two stout, ceramic planters, posted on either side of the wide stone portico, robust Martha Washington geraniums survey the garden below with a calm, knowing eye.

The inhabitants in the garden next door may be less well-behaved. Skirting the fence line, coquettish peonies flounce their voluptuous heads above the pickets to flirt at passersby. Portulaca swirl in a carousel of colors far below huge laughing yellow faces of sunflowers dancing on tall bendy stalks. A lively mix of candy-colored impatiens spill from several window boxes, spoiling for a place at the party. Wispy honeysuckle vines wander away from their trellises to spiral up the porch posts, stretching ever higher to dangle out over the garden and feel the breeze through their leaves. From up there, they can see sailboats playing tag in the harbor as the summer moon, a shimmering slice of crystallized ginger, rises over the bay above the Truro hills.

The plump rosehips left behind by the dusky blossoms of the Rosa rugosa can get as big as fat-cheeked crab apples. Not only are the rose hips dried and brewed to make a vitamin C-rich winter tea, but they can also be a substitute or supplement for tomatoes in stews and sauces and such.

DYER STREET

Sometimes you're the diner, sometimes you're the dinner. Earlier in the tour we had the story of the lobsterman who recently survived his meeting with a humpback whale. Here on Dyer Street lived a whaling captain who had a more unfortunate encounter with a shark—though, he too, lived to tell the tale. On a whaling voyage to the West Indies in the mid 1800s, Captain John Thomas Dunham took a tumble overboard and lost a leg to a shark waiting for him below. When Dunham got back to Provincetown he left sailing behind and took up the dry land post of Keeper of Long Point Light for the remainder of his days.

As we follow Dyer down onto Commercial Street, we'll turn left in front of number 409 Commercial, which for decades was a popular ice cream and candy store.

FORMERLY JO'S SODA SHOP

Penny candy, candy cigarettes, bubble gum cigars, wax lips, candy necklaces, lollipop rings, Squirrel Nut Zippers, Atomic Fireballs, Turkish Taffy, Dad's Root Beer Barrels, Zero Bars, Sugar Babies, Sugar Mamas, and Boston Baked Bean candies.

Many of these sweets are no longer on store shelves today, but way back when, these were coveted treasures, even serving as a bartering currency by children. One woman told me that as a girl she bought a live peeper frog off her friend in exchange for two bubble gum cigars and a packet of Sugar Babies. Each girl came away feeling she'd got the better end of the deal.

This location was a soda fountain, ice cream and candy store, beginning as far back as 1918. It was a daily destination for neighborhood children for decades. Old timers say that they especially enjoyed strewing multicolored sprinkles over the top of their ice cream. Here in New England the sprinkles are called "jimmies," but in Britain, Australia and New Zealand, they go by the delightfully optimistic name "hundreds and thousands."

Turning left onto Commercial now, we will come next to a tall building, tall for Provincetown anyway, at 411 Commercial.

DINNERS, CHEZ DOWD

one pot of spaghetti
three friends
two forks
a summer of nights chasing stars with a butterfly net

An art gallery occupies the first floor, while on an upper floor facing the water sits one of several, ever-so-teeny-tiny studio apartments that, decades ago, was the home of landscape artist, John Dowd.

I remember he had a piano wedged into his apartment, leaving little room for his cot, a small sink and a stove. The hammock strung up on the deck was a lovely place to dangle above the harbor with a book of Olga Broumas poems on a sunny afternoon.

Friends of John's—poets, playwrights, novelists, musicians, actors, comedians and the occasional world traveler—wandered in at all hours of day and night. Many's the summer night a handful of us would end up back at his place for a bite to eat after a night out dancing.

We danced most every night. When we weren't dancing in the clubs, we'd take John's Victrola and vinyl records and pile like jackstraws into his baby blue Ford Falcon convertible. We'd drive out to Long Nook beach where we'd swing-dance on the sandy cliff top, bejeweled star clusters twinkling just above our outstretched fingertips. Later, we'd wander down to the beach and wade into cool, black velvet waves, suddenly aflame with glowing green ribbons entwining our legs as each step, each swoop of our hands through the water ignited the phosphorescence beneath the surface. When cupped, the glowing sea water slipped like starlight between our fingertips. Exhausted, we'd climb the cliff back to the car, a galaxy of fireflies chasing one another through the grass at our feet.

It was the early 90s and AIDS was ravaging the town around us with a relentless fury. In this town of about 3,000 residents, another person was dying every few days. Dancing was our flight into an interim reality where Death could not reach us or our friends. All over Provincetown, in restaurants and bars, churches, art organizations, gyms; chess, book, travel or dog-walking clubs and AA meetings, people were seeking ways to cope with the unfathomable loss of coworkers, neighbors, friends, lovers. My friends and I, we danced, ate spaghetti and consorted with constellations.

PROVINCETOWN STREETS

As we walk through town, you might notice that, unlike many American towns, Provincetown is not crisscrossed with generically labeled 1st and 2nd Streets, Elm Avenues, Pine Lanes and Cottonwood Courts.

Instead, Provincetown street names archive the people and events that sculpted the town's history: Mayflower Street, Capt. Bertie's Way and Hensche Lane, for example. Streets given names such as Baker, Dyer, Johnson, Conant, Atkins, Holway, Atwood, Small, Ryder, Nickerson, Conwell, Freeman and Snow salute the influential roles—past and present—of these families, many of whom serve(d) as members of Provincetown's King Hiram Masonic Lodge, local politicians and business owners. Of course, a few streets are named after founding American fathers Washington, Franklin, Hancock, and the rest go to local writers, artists and ship captains. The street map of Provincetown serves as a historical catalog through which we can catch glimpses of the town's long, complicated story.

A PROVINCETOWN DRIVE ... IN SALINAS, CALIFORNIA?

I stumbled on a surprise recently on a map of Salinas, California. In addition to street names I expected to find on a California map—Mariposa, Los Gatos, Natividad, Pescadero, for example, running alongside the more-or-less obligatory Independence and Constitution streets—the map also had streets with names I was not expecting to find in a town 3,286 miles away from here: Provincetown Drive and Nantucket Boulevard, for starters. But there are also New Salem, Lexington, Burlington, Canterbury, Snug Harbor, Beacon Hill, Berkshire, Harrington,

Hancock, Georgetown, Wellington streets, too. And the tribute to New England doesn't stop there. They have a Boston Way, a Massachusetts Drive, as well as Longfellow, Hartford, London, Londonderry, Manchester, Newport, Rockport and Cabot streets. And then come streets named for Hemingway, Melville, Falkner and Fitzgerald.

Perhaps the person in charge of doling out street names in Salinas was a New Englander with an affinity for classic American literature and a severe bout of homesickness?

BLUE PLAQUES

You may notice that on the front of the house at 422 Commercial hangs a distinctive plaque with alabaster-white strokes on a background of bottomless inky-blue. While in his 90s, Claude Jensen and his son Hank began making the blue plaques you see on buildings around town. The plaques indicate that the building has historical significance. It may have once been the home of someone well known, or the location of an important happening or, if the plaque depicts the image of a house gliding merrily over the waves atop a barge, it means that the house is believed to have been floated to town across the bay from the former Long Point colony. After Jensen's death, the torch, along with the requisite kiln and supplies, was passed to the McKown family who have carried on making the now-iconic blue enameled plaques and historical markers ever since.

WE'LL ALWAYS HAVE THE MEWS

The ornately carved mahogany panels look like they belong in a wealthy ship captain's stateroom. Instead, they adorn the well-appointed bar at the Mews Restaurant & Café, owned by Rockin' Ron Robin.

For several decades prior to acquiring the award-winning restaurant, Ron was a popular Boston DJ. He owned "The Dunes" radio station here on the Cape for several years. Ron's legacy and continued contribution to the music scene is featured at the Music Museum of New England, an organization created "to preserve, honor and showcase New England's musical heritage."

Ron Robin has spent a good deal of his life entertaining people, not only by playing his favorite tunes on the radio and serving award-winning meals at his restaurant. For the Carnival Parade in 1984, he brought Ruth the Elephant to the party. People are still talking about it decades later, over oysters and martinis at the Mews.

Beyond being a fine dining restaurant, Ron's is a place locals and visitors gravitate toward to mark life's milestones, whether it's celebrating accomplishments, birthdays, weddings, or gathering in sorrow to mourn a loss. The humor, kindness and generosity with which he leads his team has made this into one of those special places with an essence deeper, broader, larger than the walls that shelter it.

Ron teamed up with Peter Donnelly, songsmith and show producer, to entertain townies on cold winter nights. For over three decades they've run the "Coffeehouse at the Mews" open mic night, in which anyone can participate, and for which there is a special performer featured each week as the centerpiece. An hour of the show is broadcast live on the local radio station. Wintering residents trudge through wind and snow every week to join their neighbors in the crowded warmth of the Mews to eat and drink, to entertain and be entertained. While seasonal visitors may long for Provincetown's summer beach days, many year-rounders can't wait for the bonhomie of winter coffee house nights.

One of my very favorite songs of Peter Donnelly's is this happy tune which takes me straight to memorable "days long with sun," those friend-filled, sun-splashed, halcyon afternoons on the beach.

ROAD WITH NO END

I've got nothin' to do
No one to see
Nowhere to go
No, no, nowhere to be
I've got nothin' to lose
No reason to hide
On this road with no end
Oh, with time on my side
I'm just trippin' along
With nothin' to fear
Movin' and groovin' year after year
I don't know where it all began
Or if it's gonna end
I don't care, I don't care,
Just leave me to be
I've got some time
To spend here with you
Take me as I am
Oh, no don' don' dontcha make me —
I've got some time to spend here with you-ooh-ooh
Don' don' dontcha make me blue

Love that sweet ocean air
With birds in the sky
With free-running dogs
Where the people are high
On the lives that they lead
And days long with sun
And nights where the sky turns
And thun- thun- thunder shakes the ground
I've got some time to spend here with you
Take me as I am
Oh, no don' don' dontcha make me —
I've got some time to spend here with you-ooh-ooh
Don' don' dontcha make me blue

I've got nothin' to do
No one to see
Nowhere to go
No, no, nowhere to be
I've got nothin' to lose

No reason to hide
On this road with no end
Oh, with time on my side
Remember me in your heart
And think of me when
You see snow fallin'
Flowers bloomin'
Summer's soulful end
I don't know where it all began
Or if it's gonna end
I'm movin' and groovin'
On a road with no end
Na, na, nana, na, na,
nana, na, nana, na
I've got some time to spend here with you-ooh-ooh
Take me as I am
Oh, no, don' don' dontcha make me —
I've got some time to spend here with you-ooh-ooh
Don' don' dontcha make me blue
Dontcha make me blue!

POOR RICHARD'S LANDING

In the early 2000s when Harvey Dodd had his art studio here, he'd perch on his stool, munch on a sandwich and paint, with these wide French doors thrown open, as he chatted with passersby and friends who dropped in at the studio.

Back in the day, this was the Avellar's Wharf and home of the prominent Portuguese fishing family of the same name. Having met as teens in the late 1800s aboard the ship that carried them to America from their home island of Flores, the young Avellars soon married and raised their family of 10 children in this charming, crooked old building. Their neighbor Mary Heaton Vorse wrote of countless meals shared here among neighbors, friends, extended family and visitors stopping by. For the generous Mother Avellar, "extended family" included many of the local young fishermen, writers and artists, several of whom took to calling her "mother." Vorse recalls fondly that there was always a pot of something enticing simmering away on Mrs. Avellar's stove, ready to feed any hungry visitor who chanced by.

CIRO & SAL'S ON KILEY COURT/HUNT'S LANE

World-renowned foodie, the late Anthony Bourdain said, "Food is everything we are. It's an extension of nationalist feeling, ethnic feeling, your personal history, your province, your region, your tribe, your grandma. It's inseparable from those from the get-go." Bourdain worked in the kitchen at Ciro & Sal's during his early days in Provincetown, but that's far from this restaurant's only claim to fame. Most everyone who's anyone who's come to Provincetown has eaten at this restaurant at the end of the long alleyway. Ciro and Sal were artists on canvas and in the kitchen, though neither had any prior cooking experience. A love of good food propelled and guided them, and before long, the casual hangout of fishermen and artists became the "in" spot in town for hearty Italian food, wine and storytelling.

Throughout the decades, locals and visitors, the famous and infamous, fishermen, musicians, actors, writers, artists and gourmands have found themselves in this sepia-lit cellar. Beneath the spent Chianti bottles dangling in clusters from the ceiling, and lampshades made of cheese graters shooting jagged patterns across the pitted brick and stone walls, the initials of names of locals and people passing through, lovers, artists, writers, as well as a few past staff members, are carved into the wooden tables between the knife gouges and cigarette burns.

HUNT'S LANE

Before the name of this shell-stippled alleyway where Ciro and Sal opened their restaurant was changed to Kiley Court, it was named for local folk artist and cookbook author Peter Hunt whose bright and cheerfully painted furniture became sought-after nationwide. One great admirer of his work was Helena Rubinstein, who owned a house in the West End of Provincetown in those days.

Hunt's refinished furniture and woodworks were feverishly coveted by collectors. Many of his works featured distelfink-like birds and other images reminiscent of stylized works in the Pennsylvania Dutch tradition. The distelfink is that chipper-looking finch design you often see on kitchen curtains, cabinets and crockery. The bird's cheerful presence is said to bring happiness and good fortune to the kitchen, the very heart of a home.

ILONA

I would be remiss if I did not mention Ilona. Across the street from Ciro & Sal's resided—one might say reigned—a cultural icon who lived for over a century, much of it in Provincetown, though she also spent a good deal of her time in New York City and abroad.

Ilona Royce Smithkin's obituary in *The New York Times* in 2021 noted that she always served coffee or vodka to her guests, as she claimed these were the only things she knew how to make. They might be the only things she knew how to make in the kitchen, but outside the kitchen Ilona was an extraordinarily creative woman. To her own mind, she felt that she truly began to blossom once she hit 80 years old. Ilona was known for painting portraits, for singing hits by Edith Piaf and Marlene Dietrich, and for her in-demand performances alongside musician Zoë Lewis. In her '80s and '90s, Ilona was a fashion model, admired for her sense of style, punctuated by her signature eyelashes, as long and thick as a shag carpet, which she made herself. She became well-known for ending her cabaret performances in a dramatic swirl of skirts and a drop into full splits, as lithe and limber as a cat even into her late 80s.

In honor of her 100th birthday, in the spring of 2020, Ilona sang for a crowd of properly, socially-distanced friends, neighbors and admirers toasting her health from the sandy beach below her balcony.

We're now coming up on Bangs Street.

REMEMBERING BANGS & SMALL

Members of the Bangs family first arrived at Plimoth Colony in 1623, a couple of years after the *Mayflower*, on the good ship *Anne*. Generations of Bangs have populated the Cape and New England for centuries since. There have been several notable Bangs along the way, not the least of which was Provincetown businesswoman Rosilla Bangs. Her death is the only fatality connected to the construction of the Pilgrim Monument. Rosilla had the unfortunate luck to be walking along the road below the Monument, which was under construction at the time. Apparently, lightning hit a rail car full of stone that was parked at the top of the hill, propelling the rail car headlong down the hill, where it struck and killed Rosilla.

A second death associated with the Monument happened many years later, running up to the 300-year anniversary celebration of the landing of the *Mayflower*. Several structures near the prospective park site were demolished to make way for the Bas Relief Park, including the home of Joshua Small. He took his life rather than see his home taken from him.

THE HULK

On the water, where Bangs Street meets Commercial, an unassuming wooden building squats with its back turned to the busy street as it ponders the bay. The "Hulk," as it's called, is the home of the fabled fraternity of male artists known as the Beachcombers. The Hulk is attached to what used to be the Flagship Restaurant. For a time, meals for Beachcomber meetings were prepared by the Flagship. The Flagship is also where Anthony Bourdain worked his first kitchen gig in town. Bourdain noted that, "Meals make the society, hold the fabric together in lots of ways that were charming and interesting and intoxicating to me. The perfect meal, or the best meals, occur in a context that frequently has very little to do with the food itself." I've a feeling the Beachcombers would heartily agree.

The Beachcombers' initial meeting was celebrated over a meal at Cesco's Italian restaurant in 1916. The members have continued to meet for dinner and fellowship on Saturdays for well over 100 years. They are known, not only for their fancy balls and (occasionally controversial) theatrical escapades, but also for their charitable deeds. In 1917, when 19 Provincetown mariners lost their lives in a ferocious gale, the Beachcombers rallied together and put on a theater production to raise funds for the fishermen's widows and orphaned children.

THE FLAGSHIP RESTAURANT AND DORY BAR

In addition to the many illustrious artists who have been members of the Beachcombers, the Flagship Restaurant hosted Anais Nin and her various lovers and two First Ladies, Jacqueline Kennedy and Eleanor Roosevelt. While in town, Mrs. Kennedy, together with Gore Vidal, attended a performance of George Bernard Shaw's *Mrs. Warren's Profession* at the then-called Players-on-the-Wharf theater. Word has it that after the performance, Vidal wanted to take her out on the town, but when they arrived at the Ace of Spades Club, the First Lady was turned away as she had not thought to bring along her photo ID.

When Mrs. Roosevelt came to the Flagship, she dined on clam chowder and fried scallops by the fireplace and wrote about it in her column. One of the restaurant's specialties was a baked ham steak topped with sliced pineapples. This was frequently accompanied by another house specialty, Fish House Punch. Instructions for preparing Fish House Punch are entertainingly described in *Peter Hunt's Cape Cod Cookbook*:

> *Dilute every 2 quarts of water with 1 quart Jamaican Rum, 1 quart Bacardi, 1 quart cognac, ¾ pounds sugar, 1 quart lemon juice.*

The recipe is simple, straightforward and strong enough to wake your dead Aunt Nellie. If you happen to overindulge on the punch, Mr. Hunt's cookbook offers a recipe (from his friend Frank Lee), which will surely cure what ails you.

Hunt maintains that "one of the best reasons for anyone to live on Cape Cod, is that they may be near the World's Paramount Hangover Cure at all times, the Prairie Oyster."

Prairie Oyster

With a small glass in your shaking hand, pour into it a teaspoon of good vinegar and knock a shell-less egg into it. Add a sprinkle of Worcestershire Sauce, and add salt and pepper over all.

Upsidaisy.
If one is good, two's better.

Duly noted.

Our ship now righted, on we go. Kitty-cornered across the street. Sculptures of a woman twirling gaily with her child beneath a giant serpent's tail protruding from the lawn, while a woman sleeps peacefully nearby. We have arrived at the renowned Provincetown Arts Association and Museum.

THE PROVINCETOWN ARTS ASSOCIATION AND MUSEUM

The Provincetown Art Association and Museum (PAAM) moved into this location in 1919 and is now listed on the National Register of Historic Places. Various factions within the Provincetown Arts Association have held strong, often opposing views on art since the inception of the organization. The recent expansion of the building brought more opportunity for deliberation and more topics to disagree on, including architectural considerations, financial priorities and other points of contention. In the end, cooperation triumphed, and the Museum opened its remodeled doors in 2006.

One of the wings is named for the Heibert family. During his 53 years of making house calls Dr. Heibert is said to have delivered most of the babies in town, including the son of Eugene O'Neill and his wife. Some of Heibert's medical advice was regarded as unconventional, but as the outcome was more often than not successful, his idiosyncrasies were generally overlooked. When patients were short on cash, he accepted payment in poultry, garden produce, fine jewelry and artwork. Some of the remarkable works from his vast collection are on display at PAAM.

Every year the members and supporters of PAAM put aside their artistic differences and come together to celebrate art and artists of all ilks at its annual gala, an elegant dinner and fancy-dress ball. That's the beauty of sitting down to a meal with people—participants generally rise from the meal on friendlier terms than when they sat down. Breaking bread has been a winning diplomatic strategy since time immemorial. As Oscar Wilde famously said, "After a good dinner, one can forgive anybody, even one's own relatives."

The association celebrated its 100-year birthday in 2014 with an array of events throughout the year and, undoubtedly, a birthday cake large enough to go around.

THE MARY HEATON VORSE HOUSE

She was well past her best-by date when Mr. Fulk fell in love with her.

"She" being the cottage known in her earlier days as the Kibbe House, home of famed whaling captain Kibbe Cook. These days, it's the name of Mary Heaton Vorse that is most closely associated with the house. Vorse was a prize-winning advocate of progressive social and political causes, patron of theater, author, mother, cherished friend and neighbor and perhaps Provincetown's most beloved chronicler.

Vorse loved this house from the moment she saw it. She and her family moved here in 1907, the same year that President Theodore Roosevelt came to Provincetown to lay the cornerstone of the Pilgrim Monument. Widowed twice within five years, Mary Heaton Vorse raised her three children here while writing full time, attending political rallies and labor strikes locally as well as in Boston and New York City. Her invaluable book *Time and the Town* was originally published in 1942. Her account of the town has been treasured by Provincetown-philes and consulted by researchers for well over a half century. Her poignant, humorous, vibrant, narrative of life in Provincetown offers an intimate study of the happenings and characters of Provincetown's past. Much of the town's cultural history would have been lost to us without her writings.

While Vorse lived here, her home was the pulse of the neighborhood, a harbor for artistic fellowship and communal meals during strategy sessions when she and her neighbors gathered to write plays, plan political actions or to cook nurturing food for ailing friends.

When Ken Fulk (the man with the most carefully pronounced name in architectural design) came upon the Vorse House, she was limping along, barely able to stand upright. In 2020, the cottage came back to life when Fulk and his team restored her to the strength and appearance of her Mary Heaton Vorse era. He then opened up the Vorse home to Provincetown's art organizations for an endless variety of cultural events. The Vorse House has once again resumed her place at the heart of Provincetown's thriving cultural scene.

THE BRYANT HOUSE

For a good long while now, the home at number 471 has been known as the Bryant House. (Recently this, too, passed into the loving care of Ken Fulk.) Mary Ann Bryant, who arrived in 1914 as an immigrant from Nova Scotia, ran a restaurant near the busy intersection of Bradford and Standish streets. Her menu offered simple, hardy Nova Scotia–style beef roasts, pork chops, seafoods and steaks. It became wildly popular with both townies and tourists looking for home-cooked, north-of-the-border fare.

Members of the Bryant family ran Bryant's Market next door to their home. It changed hands and later came to be known as Angel Foods. For well over a hundred years, one flourishing market after the next has provided folks in this neighborhood with everything they need, from fresh fish, cold drinks and warm bread, to steamy gossip.

Mary Ann Bryant's grandson was the insatiably curious architectural historian, George Bryant, who archived in his head a library-sized collection of Provincetown history, lore and anecdotes of his family's life and the lives of the people of this town. He was endlessly fascinated by the stories of the people who were born here or made their way here from all over the globe. George and his son delved into the largely invisible and buried history of Black whaling captains of New England. They uncovered a trove of valuable information, and their efforts helped raise public awareness on the subject. For this work, the Mystic Seaport Museum awarded George Bryant the Paul Cuffe Memorial Fellowship for the Studies of Minorities in American Maritime History.

In further pursuit of his interest in architecture and the all-important role that salt-making held in the town's history, George Bryant spent years attempting to replicate a version of the windmill saltworks that used to line the shore of town.

PROVINCETOWN'S WINDMILL SALTWORKS

Looking ever-so like ponderous wooden giants swaggering single file along the shoreline, batting their arms at passing clouds, the columns of windmills sucked saltwater up from the bay, then spewed it into drying vats where, in a few weeks' time, the liquid evaporated, leaving behind mountains of precious salt, glinting in the sunshine. We're talking now about an era belonging to the first half of the 1800s.

Before refrigeration came onto the scene, clean, pure salt was used to preserve fresh fish. According to food historian Mark Kurlansky, 80 pounds of salt required 350 gallons of seawater to produce using these windmill saltworks. Boiling seawater, another common method for salt making, called for burning great amounts of wood and proved even less efficient—400 gallons of seawater yielded a mere 70 pounds of salt. The demand for salt was insatiable, but the supply of wood on the Cape for boiling seawater was limited, and eventually wood had to be shipped in to keep the fires burning.

In the early 1800s, some 700 fishing boats based out of Provincetown where bringing in tons upon tons of fish which had to be preserved immediately, through drying or salting, in order to be transported to shops on and off-Cape. Fish flakes, which are drying racks for fish, occupied most every front yard, backyard and any other space available in town. (I imagine that smelled just lovely!) When salting fish overtook drying as a means of preserving them, making salt became the center of the Provincetown fishing industry—and the town's golden goose. On the Cape there were over 650 saltworks producing 26,000 tons of salt. Provincetown alone churned out some three and a half million pounds annually. The ability to preserve fish and transport it to ever-broadening mainland markets increased the profitability of the fishing industry, as well as adding to the stability of the fish market and steadier wages for fishermen and others in the fish industry.

But Provincetown's salt-making goose was cooked, practically overnight, with the discovery of salt mines in Syracuse, New York, in the 1850s. The opening of the Erie Canal facilitated rapid, extensive distribution of this new source of salt. Shortly after the demise of the salt-works, cold storage facilities popped up in town, enabling fish to be cut into uniform sizes and shapes, then flash frozen. This development re-shaped the fishing industry anew and Provincetown's fishing communi-ty flourished once again.

SALT

The importance of salt worldwide is evidenced, in part, by the variety of roles it plays in cultural traditions. A small pendant containing salt protects from the evil eye in some cultures, while in others, newborns are dipped into a bath of seawater to protect them from harmful spirits. Placing a few grains of salt into the mouth of a baby will ensure a fortu-itous future and protect the baby from evil spirits, according to several traditions. A Welsh custom includes placing a plate of bread and salt upon a coffin for a professional sin-eater to eat the salt, thereby purging the soul of the deceased of its earthly sins. Tossing a pinch of spilt salt over your left shoulder will sting the eyes of the devil seated there, and in doing so protect you from his mischief, say some.

Everyday uses of salt run the gamut: it's used both to remove rust or create rust, depending on the material, as well as to stiffen certain types of cloth, bleach wine stains, put out grease fires, melt ice from roadways, manufacture pharmaceuticals, fertilize fields, make soap, dye textiles, make candles dripless, as well as to treat dyspepsia, sore throats and earaches. A good soaking in Epsom salts dissolved in warm water helps ease the removal of a stubborn splinter or relieve the pain of a sprain.

Use of the word in English idioms is as ubiquitous as it is long-stand-ing: We take information with a grain of salt when we don't give it a lot of credibility, although if we say someone is worth their salt or that they are the salt of the earth, that person has earned our respect and trust. Hurtful words or actions rub salt in the wound of an already difficult situation. In past times, someone sitting below the salt was considered inferior in social standing than those seated above the salt, and therefore not permitted to flavor their food with it. If someone salts their books they may wind up in jail if they're caught. If you appear to be dawdling at work, your supervisor may tell you to get back to the salt mines. To throw salt on someone's game is to attempt to prevent a romantic liaison. Salty language is often not permitted at the dinner table. The examples are unending; they can vary from culture to culture and often change meaning over time.

EATING HUMBLE PIE

According to their neighbor Mary Heaton Vorse, the imposing house at number 468, which was built by one of the Cook captains at the behest of his wife, came about at great expense to its owners, both financially and socially. Its positioning blocked the view of adjacent neighbors, and its ostentatious size left a bad taste in the mouths of the rest of the extensive Cook family. Vorse wrote that when the house was finally completed, the captain turned to his wife and said, "There. Now eat it! Ain't nothin' else to eat."

THE "AMBERGRIS KING"

At number 472, in the graceful white house with a wide front porch unquestionably designed with rocking chairs in mind, lived Provincetown's "Ambergris King," David Stull.

Ambergris is not an appetizing subject. The smelly stuff comes, after all, from the intestines of whales. According to researchers at the Sperm Whale Project, ambergris is formed in the intestines of various squid-eating whales, including the sperm whale, which is, by far, the largest of them. Gray matter forms around the remnants of the tough, indigestible squid beaks, creating globs of glop which may be found floating on the sea, washed ashore, or still within the intestines of a dead whale. These balls can weigh up to 150 pounds, though most are much smaller. Resembling rounded bits of beach glass, they are not immediately noticeable. When fresh, the substance has an atrocious smell. However, when left to be drenched in the sunshine and stroked by a brisk breeze, it firms up and the stench subsides to an aroma resembling violets or lavender.

Though somewhat hard to come by, ambergris was an enormously lucrative product of the whaling industry. It was used in the perfume industry, though it has, for the most part, been replaced by substitutes. It has always been pricey and still commands approximately $40 per ounce. Debra Lawless reports that beach-walkers would drag any ol' stinky lump of goo they found on the beach to Stull, in hopes that it would turn out to be ambergris. However, writes Lawless, "in 40 years Stull only saw two lumps of ambergris that had been found on a beach—and neither was from Cape Cod."

Across the street from the former Stull residence is the MacMillan House which belonged to Rear Admiral Donald MacMillan for whom the big wharf downtown is named.

REAR ADMIRAL MACMILLAN, ARCTIC ADVENTURER

In his lifetime, Rear Admiral Donald MacMillan, who is probably the most famous Provincetown-born resident, made over 30 trips to the Arctic. He was the last survivor of the 1908–09 expedition on which Robert E. Peary believed they had reached the North Pole. Some of the memorabilia of MacMillan's trips is on display at the Provincetown Museum. A larger collection, along with many of his papers and journals, are archived at the Peary-MacMillan Arctic Museum at Bowdoin College, from which both Peary and MacMillan graduated.

MacMillan enjoyed cooking and sampling foods in the far-flung places he explored. He and his crew cooked what they hunted—walrus, seal meat, eider ducks, arctic hare, musk oxen, caribou, even polar bear—supplemented with tinned, dried or salted goods they brought with them. For the Crocker Land Expedition, a trip anticipated to last a couple of years, these items were among the meticulously detailed list of things MacMillan took along:

> There was a teapot, an alarm clock, an 8-day clock, a pudding pan, a bathtub and fixtures (for a house he was building there);
> 500 lbs. butter, 200 lbs. lard and 6 cases of Crisco.
> Dozens of cases of roast beef, mutton, Army bacon, ham, corned beef, salted pork and fish, sausages, clam chowder, salmon, sardines in mustard and 200 lbs. of herring.
> Crates upon crates of tinned pineapple, diced potatoes, turnips,

squash, spinach, onions, baked beans, cranberry beans, corn, peas, rhubarb, cherries, plums, peaches, pears, tomatoes.

Tea, coffee, chocolate, condensed milk, canned plum pudding, molasses, baking powder, corn starch, yellow-eyed beans, yellow split peas, pickles, hominy, flour, corn meal, barley, rolled oats, cream of wheat, rice, brown sugar, syrup, grape juice, lime juice, walnuts, vinegar and salt.

Spices: a case each of allspice, cinnamon, cloves, ginger, mustard, nutmeg, black pepper, paprika and red pepper.

All that and, believe it or not, they still had room for five crates of candy and some Grape Nuts.

MacMillan wasn't a big drinker but he packed a bit of liquor for holidays and for special meals shared with guests. He took more than 20 kinds of cigarettes, including cartons of rolled cigarettes and boxes of loose and plug tobaccos, as well as "assorted pipes." Some of this was for personal use, the rest was for trading or intended as gifts to Native people who worked with his crew. They brought things they felt would be useful to the Inuits such as needles, thread, scissors, thimbles, underclothes, matches, rifles and ammunition, coffee and tea, as well as toy balloons for the children.

One of the more interesting recipes he notes in his journal is for *Eggs Sausage a la Inuit*. The eggs of any number of native bird species available could be used in this recipe: The eggs are broken and poured into the intestines of a bearded seal. This is a very large seal, so the intestines would make a good-sized sausage. MacMillan goes on to describe the piece that he has just eaten. He writes, "would judge it to be excellent food for a cold day as it's percentage of fat is so high." He does not detail how it is preserved, but the director of the museum told me it is likely that it was cached in the early summer to allow it to undergo anaerobic fermentation. This curing process would have given it a ripe, cheesy odor. It would, of course, freeze once the weather cooled. In this way, the sausage could be eaten months after having been made.

MACMILLAN'S THANKSGIVING MISADVENTURE

Although the Rear Admiral was an experienced cook, like all of us, he had his off days. In this entertaining journal entry of 1908, he writes of a Thanksgiving pie gone awry:

Thanksgiving Day and one long to be remembered. I lay in bed and think of the many good dinners I have had and where I have spent some very pleasant Thanksgiving days but this one is unique in many ways: first as to location—the most northern point of land in North America; 2nd the time—at midnight of the great arctic night; 3rd living in a snow house at the base of a 700 foot cliff on the edge of the polar sea with four Eskimos—two men and two women.

I celebrate the day by first having a good wash—some of us wash about once a week and some not at all. Jack and I sing a few old familiar songs—not—familiar to us. We must have something extra for dinner—what—shall it be.

I have one jar of cranberries which might possibly be made into a pie, so here goes. If anyone cares for a good recipe here it is. Grease plates well with butter. Crush up biscuit in your hands into as fine a dust as possible until your hand aches with pain. Mix with medicated musk ox salve from medicine chest—use all of it for crackers are very dry. To be positive of good results, that is to have good flaky crust, put in three large tablespoons of butter in addition to all the salve. Cover plates with thick layer and spread on cranberries. Put on oil stove and bake quickly before the fat has a chance to bubble up through the top. If grease runs out on top of your oil stove creating a dense smoke in your igloo perhaps it would be well to remove the pie and place in open air at a temperature of -40. This is simply another way of hardening the crust if heat fails to do it. Serve cold and eat at once providing each guest with a hammer or a knife according to condition of teeth. The musk ox salve makes an especially appropriate shortening for such a day giving to the crust a peculiar odor as well as taste like that of turkey stuffing, possibly the stuffing made of ground chestnuts of which I have never tasted. If the shortening had been lengthening we would all have been better pleased with results.

P.S. Don't ask the Doctor the recipe for the salve.

After dinner cigars were passed around, a group flashlight picture was taken and then to our musk ox sleeping bags and the day was over.

HOT BUTTERED RUM ON COLD NORTHERN NIGHTS

David Embury (1886–1960), known for his cocktail recipe encyclopedia, said of hot buttered rum, "How anyone can consume it for pleasure is beyond me. I believe the drinking of Hot Buttered Rum should be permitted in the Northwest Passage, and even there, only by highly imaginative and over-enthusiastic novelists."

Legions of us who've withstood winter Nor'easters on Cape Cod with a companionable mug of hot buttered rum in hand might disagree with Mr. Embury. In fact, hot buttered rum is a winter staple at my house. In the interest of those who could use a wintertide pick-me-up, below is a recipe I enjoy, pieced together from several different recipes.

Hot Buttered Rum

Rum, Maple Syrup (or 3 lumps of sugar, Butter, Water.
Cinnamon, Cayenne (optional)

Put a generous tot of rum and a dollop of maple syrup or sugar into a mug, add hot water and stir 'til well blended. Drop in a small knob of butter and sprinkle lightly with cinnamon.
The last step, and to me the most important:
a dusting of Cayenne.

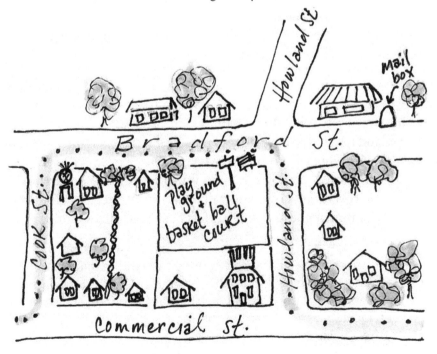

As we turn to walk up Cook Street, making our way toward Bradford, I'll tell you briefly about the Rear Admiral's remarkable wife.

MIRIAM MACMILLAN, EXPLORER

Although it was Miriam who wrote the book titled, *I Married an Explorer*, the rear admiral, too, had married an explorer. Miriam Look MacMillan became a celebrated and decorated adventurer, and in 1981 became one of very few women to be inducted into the esteemed Explorer's Club.

Initially, her husband had refused to let her accompany him on his voyages to the Arctic, as no women had ever ventured to the farther-most reaches of the Arctic. But Miriam was persistent and prevailed. She became a valuable crew member and the first woman to navigate a ship though the heavy ice of Arctic waters, ultimately taking their research ship, the *Bowdoin*, to within 660 miles of the North Pole. She sailed on nine voyages with her husband, recording life in the Arctic and aboard the vessel and charting the waters in which they sailed. She authored a book based on her experiences called *Green Seas and White Ice* and was a sought-after lecturer, becoming an honorary curator of the Peary–MacMillan Arctic Museum at Bowdoin College, from which she received an honorary Doctor of Science degree. She and her husband are buried side-by-side in the Provincetown Cemetery.

We now find ourselves arriving at the Bradford end of Cook Street, where we are greeted by a sign topped with a welcoming golden pineapple. This lemon pie–colored inn, trimmed in sugar-white, has had several past lives and has hosted a number of notable guests in its time, including artists Edward Hopper and Simie Maryles. One winter, writer Michael Cunningham hunkered down here to finish writing his book *Home at the End of the World* in a room now dubbed the "Writer's Room." In the spring and summer, guests can breakfast at shaded tables outdoors.

We'll cross here at the zebra, and continue down the hill toward the intersection at Howland Street. Whereas the sidewalks on Commercial Street are very narrow, along most of Bradford Street they're non-existent, including this stretch of the road, so please be cautious of traffic when walking along here.

BERTA WALKER GALLERY

We pass by the long-established Berta Walker Gallery, where many prominent past and present local artists are represented. On opening nights, visitors may be treated to a sip of wine and some nibbles as they peruse the artwork which is billed as "the history of American art as seen through the eyes of Provincetown." The gallery celebrates Provincetown's long-enduring art colony and its profound impact on the evolution of American art, through the present day.

Artist Nancy Whorf, who lived around the corner on Howland Street, is described by Berta Walker as "the van Gogh of Provincetown." Known for her boldly colored depictions of life in Provincetown, her winter and summer scenes feature the challenges and joys in the lives of fishermen, the vibrancy of local festivals, family picnics, fancy garden parties, women at work and still lifes of food and flowers overflowing from cheerfully decorated crockery.

Directly across the street sits 211 Bradford, which formerly housed the kitchen of the renowned Cesco, "Spaghetti King of Cape Cod."

CESCO, "SPAGHETTI KING OF CAPE COD"

Fred Marvin, who was an art student of Charles Hawthorne (and step-brother to Mary Heaton Vorse), met Francesco "Cesco" Ronga when traveling in Naples, Italy. They returned to Provincetown together and Cesco opened his Italian Restaurant here where the slender wynd, Cesco Lane, pops out of a tangle of beach roses onto Bradford. It soon became a lively spot favored by locals who knew that every night at Cesco's was a party. Guests were assured of copious portions of food and drink and fun.

There are two prominent, official, all-male clubs in town—the King Hiram Masonic Lodge and the Beachcombers. The second is a group of men engaged in the arts which they consider to be painting, etching, engraving, sculpture, architecture, designing, illustrating, writing, music and acting. Men who are patrons of the arts are also welcome as members. The group gathered at Cesco's one July night in 1916 to found their club. Minutes were not taken at the meeting, but it's said the companions dined on great mounds of Cesco's famous spaghetti, washed down with rivers of his homemade red wine. A later member, Ted Robinson, in his book *The Beachcombers*, quoted one of the founding members as saying, "an organization that can masticate and digest the mysteries and miseries of our culinary experts is bound to survive the centuries…" And so it seems. The Beachcombers have been meeting for Saturday dinners and events for over 100 years.

There is a bench at Bradford and Howland which makes for a good resting place as we look around. It sits below a marker declaring this intersection to be the Jesse Arnold Silva Square. This is named for a young staff sergeant who worked at a cold storage facility before becoming a paratrooper, where he died during World War II.

NEIGHBORHOOD MARKETS

There was a time when there were several distinct neighborhoods in town, each with a nearby firehouse, school and shops. Folks did their shopping and much of their socializing near to home. With the exception of attending weekly Town Hall dances, they rarely needed to go to another part of town. Across the intersection from the bench is one of the neighborhood shops sprinkled about town, where you can pick up food and a bottle of wine for dinner or a picnic at the beach, along with some suntan lotion.

Like many of the small markets which have managed to survive over the years, the market at this intersection has changed hands and names multiple times. Even so, it's remained a hub of activity and provides a sense of community within the immediate neighborhood. This particular shop is special for another reason, too: in 1968, Harvey Dodd painted a mural of a birds-eye view of Provincetown on the back wall. It's worth wandering in for a look when you have the time.

EVELYN'S CORSET HOSPITAL

In addition to supplying valuable oils and, in some cases, ambergris, whaling was the backbone, so to speak, of the corset industry. For a while in the 1940s, Provincetown boasted its very own corsetiere. A few houses down from the corner store rose this charmingly named enterprise whose services reportedly included the "washing, repairing, refitting of corsets, girdles, corselettes, brassieres" and, apparently, liberal doses of advice.

Whales such as orcas, sperm, belugas and dolphins have teeth, while blue whales, humpbacks and gray whales have a thick row of baleen in the front of their mouth, which sieves out large particles and allows smaller particles of food to swoop down the gullet into the whale's belly. Baleen, being long, strong, flexible fronds of keratin, proved ideal for making "whalebone" corsets. Before plastics stole the show, baleen was used for making hooped skirts, frames for eyeglasses, spines of folding fans, as well as spokes for umbrellas and parasols. Whalebone necklaces were especially prized.

TASHA HILL

On up the road in the woods behind the little store is the famed Tasha Hill. Over the decades, dozens upon dozens of artists and writers have found inspiration, camaraderie and shelter in the quirky cottages nesting in amongst the trees. Some of my fondest Provincetown memories are from my summer living in one of the shacks.

The Tasha family came over from the Azorean island of São Miguel a couple of generations ago, and they've fostered and cultivated creativity and community here ever since. Several Tasha Hill visitors and tenants have become well-known nationally and internationally. In addition to several accomplished artists within the Tasha family itself, other recognizable names of visitors and residents include "Poet of the Dunes" Harry Kemp, Nick Flynn, Talaya Delaney, David Drake, Mischa Richter, Christopher Bergland, Tawney Heatherton, Taro Yamamoto and countless others.

Down Howland Street we go now, back toward Commercial Street, past one of a couple of outdoor basketball courts in town. More often than basketball players, I see yoga instructors here leading outdoor classes on the court, the participants bending and twisting and looping their bodies into flowy configurations, like ribbons of curling taffy left out in the summer sun.

HOWLAND STREET

Despite the fact that *Mayflower* passenger John Howland went on to sign the Mayflower Compact, assist Plimoth Colony's Governor Carver in creating a keystone treaty with the Wampanoag tribe, become elected deputy to the colony's General Court, marry and raise 10 children, most Americans know John Howland only as the kid who fell into the drink during the *Mayflower's* Atlantic crossing. Fortunately, for his many descendants, young John managed to grab the end of a rope as he flew headlong over the side of the ship, enabling the crew to haul him back on board.

According to the Mayflower Society, of the 102 passengers who arrived in 1620 aboard the *Mayflower*, not all had descendants, but it is estimated that 35 million people or thereabouts are able to trace their roots back to those who came over on the ship. After the fruitful Aldens, it's the Howlands and the Brewsters who are believed to have the most descendants.

THE OLD EASTERN SCHOOLHOUSE

The tall building with the four-pronged belfry at the corner of Howland and Commercial was a schoolhouse for nearly 100 years before taking up a new career as a community center. The center was open to "Portuguese, Yankees, summer and winter folks, Protestants and Catholics," adults and children, who got together to play checkers or dominoes and chew the fat. Later, during WWII, a thousand service members per month found meals, rest and camaraderie here. It did a stint as an American Legion, giving the town's military and veteran population a place to gather and put on special meals and events. Now, as a home to two galleries and the community radio station, this is still a place where locals and visitors come together to enjoy each other's company, exchange ideas and build community.

WOMR

Like a stone soup, WOMR is made up of the contributions of the community it serves. In operation for four decades, the community radio station is an invaluable source of reliable local news and information as well as a cultural hub offering an astounding range of programming. A diverse team of volunteer DJs offers a smattering of nearly every kind of music under the sun—Celtic, bluegrass, Jamaican, opera and classical, reggae, jazz, folk, international blends, dance music, sing-along and cry-along music—as well as forums on arts, food and culture and more. Funding comes largely from listeners' donations. It is truly a combined effort aimed toward benefiting the entire community. One of the DJs, Scott Penn, greets listeners at the beginning of each of his Lush Life jazz programs by saying, "Hello there, Cape Cod, the South Shore and all the ships at sea. Bringing you tunes from the dunes, this is WOMR 92.1 FM in Provincetown and WFMR 91.3 FM in Orleans. We're streaming around the world at WOMR.org." At which point, people from near and far turn up their radio or computer, pour themselves a glass of good wine and settle in to listen.

THE ICE HOUSE

Across the street from the Schoolhouse stands the only industrial ice house building left in Provincetown. Long out of use as an ice house, it's been residential housing for decades. Currently known as the Ice House Condos, back in the early 1900s, this was one of several buildings used to freeze and store fish. For a time it served as a retail ice business. In most cases, ice retailers sold ice coupons to customers ahead of time, to be redeemed upon delivery. The ice was hewn in enormous blocks from frozen freshwater ponds then transported to ice houses where it was insulated with straw. In this way, the ice could usually stay frozen until early summer.

This particular ice house stored cranberries in the 1950s.

THE CRANBERRY

For hundreds of years cranberries have not only been an important ingredient in the local Native American cuisine, but also used medicinally. Cranberry juice is extracted for use in dyeing fabric and decorative threads. A nourishing Native American staple called pemmican is made from dried deer meat and mashed cranberries, mixed together with melted fat.

Domestication and cultivation of the cranberry began up-Cape in Dennis in the early 1800s. Some of the cranberry bushes on the Cape are believed to be over 150 years old. The proliferation of cranberry cultivation has continued unabated since it began, and has spread to parts of the US, into Canada, Chile and beyond. During WWII, one million pounds per year of dried cranberries were packed into the rations of American troops. Today, Americans consume about 400 million pounds of cranberries annually, 80 million of that at Thanksgiving.

According to a WCAI Gastropod radio podcast, the Ocean Spray cranberry company presented romantic cranberry poetry for the 1948 Massachusetts Cranberry Festival. The poems were written on behalf of chickens expressing love for the cranberry. If, at some point, the festival includes songs about cranberries, local musician John Wiley Nelson's little diddy may be just the ticket! It appears on his compilation of Provincetown songs, *Another Day in Paradise.*

RED CRANBERRIES

They've got good coffee at the coffee shop
But I'll tell you now, that's not why I stop
They're baking muffins up until noon
Good enough to make you swoon

Fill 'em with walnuts, yum, yum, yum
Still, that's not why I come
Go tell all the Toms, and the Dicks and the Harrys,
Muffins are full of red cranberries!

Chorus:

Red cranberries, oh so sweet,
Red cranberries, are good to eat
Red cranberries, put 'em in sauce
Put 'em in a salad and give it a toss!

Red cranberries, squeeze 'em down a sluice
Running red with cranberry juice
Red cranberries, put the juice in a jar,
Add a little vodka and there you are!

They got a lotta holidays in the year
Got 'em comin' and goin', got 'em far and near
There's one that separates out from the rest
One among others that I love best!

Now, some say Christmas would suit just fine
Take Thanksgiving every time
Better than Saint Nick and reindeer paws
Thanksgiving turkey with cranberry sauce!

(Repeat chorus)

Where I live, you got cranberries here
Cranberries there, cranberries everywhere
Don't have to truck 'em in under guard,
Got 'em right here in my own back yard!

Walkin' on the water, steppin' on frogs
Sloshing through cranberry bogs
I tell you now, I know there's a God,
Cuz She put red cranberries on Cape Cod!

Red cranberries, oh so sweet,
Red cranberries, are good to eat
Red cranberries, put 'em in sauce
Put 'em in a salad and give it a toss!

Red cranberries, squeeze 'em down a sluice
Running red with cranberry juice
Red cranberries, put the juice in a jar,
Add a little vodka and there you are!

(Repeat chorus)

ST. MARY'S OF THE HARBOR

Both religious and secular gatherings are held at this pretty, shingled church with morning-blue trim, nestled comfortably on the edge of the harbor. Reunions, graduations and baby showers are celebrated here, in addition to weddings and funerals. Many townies and visitors who have never come to a Sunday service here have attended other events and feel at home, too.

Situated on the bay side of the church is a quiet bench and a long, wide wall where you can relax and drink in the view of the harbor and town laid out, *mise-en-scène,* along the sandy arc. We used to sit out here and listen to the now-silenced foghorn calmly intoning its comforting, cadenced G-note from across the bay. The blinking lighthouses you see off in the distance are Long Point Light on the left, flashing green every four seconds, and Wood End Light a bit farther to your right, which flashes red every ten.

FORMERLY TILLIES

Each of the neighborhood markets peppered around town is a Provincetown character unto itself, each known for its distinct personality and for its particular offerings. The shop that used to occupy number 506 Commercial was a neighborhood treasure. Folks brought their chairs here to be re-caned; working men got their bottled beer here; women, their kitchen essentials; and children, their penny candy. It ranked as a town icon during its time. The stories of old-timers at this end of town spill over with fond recollections of the store, especially Tillie and Johnny, its cheerful, quirky, generous-to-a-fault owners.

FROM THE HILLS OF THE AZORES TO THE GARDENS OF PROVINCETOWN

Some places boast skyscrapers or mountains or lakes; Provincetown has humongous hydrangeas.

In spring, the blossoms emerge shyly in tender clusters, the palest whisper of a pre-dawn blue. This hint of blue becomes a promise fulfilled as the petaled globes swell and turn to a blissful azure. By the middle of a crackling summer, the enormous orbs dance on the breeze in joyful cerulean circles among their jade green leaves. These hydrangeas inspire envy in gardeners, wonder in visitors and inflame the creative appetite of artists the summer long. The lacy icing trim on shingled cottages provides a delicious backdrop for this tableau of Cape-Azorean fusion.

It's reckoned that a good number of the hydrangea bushes in Provincetown were brought from the Azores by Portuguese longing to have a blue splash of home blooming in their gardens. The Azorean island of Faial is called the Blue Island for its waves of pretty blue bushes cascading down its hillsides, streaming along its roadways and flooding front lawns across the landscape.

AZOREAN AFTERNOON TEA

The Azores. Nine green islands poking up out of the vast blue Atlantic like the mossy toes of a giant sticking out of a bath—one large one, eight smaller ones (the hidden big toe being a large, mysterious pyramid recently discovered near the islands, just beneath the surface of the water). This lush, green Portuguese outpost is as close geographically to the US as it is to mainland Europe. In addition to a profusion of hydrangeas, the islands' nutrient-rich volcanic soil nurtures crops of sugarcane, tobacco, pineapple and tea.

Since the 1800s, the Azoreans have grown tea, especially on São Miguel. Down from 62 thriving plantations at one point, the Chá Gorreana plantation, planted in 1883, is now Europe's oldest and only tea plantation. Much of the process is still done by hand and many of the harvesting and leaf-processing machines used today are the same ones used in the plantation's early days.

Azorean Afternoon Tea is both a rejuvenating and relaxing affair. A loose-leaf tea is served with Portuguese rolls and fresh butter, glazed cavacas (popovers), suspiros, "meringue kisses," fofas da Povoação, queijadas of various styles, pasteis de nata, filhós or malassadas. Although, those who came here from the Azores initially brought their tea-drinking traditions with them, sadly, this delightful custom did not survive the years after the Atlantic crossing as well as the lovely blue hydrangeas.

As we continue east on Commercial we will pass by Hancock Street.

HANCOCK STREET

This street is named for John Hancock, first signer of the US Constitution, second president of the Continental Congress, a governor of the Commonwealth of Massachusetts, and the man whose autograph was so impressive that the name "John Hancock" became a byword for "signature."

Hancock came into his money when he inherited a mercantile company from a rich uncle, and earned respect among rebel Americans when he was arrested for attempting to avoid paying taxes to the British for a cargo of fine wine.

Bostonians smuggling Madeira wine aboard Hancock's sloop, *Liberty*, locked a British customs official in a cabin for the night while they unloaded the wine cases. Along with fellow agitator and legislator Samuel Adams, Hancock went on to help organize protests and foment revolution, even personally backing the rebellion from his own coffers.

MARY OLIVER

Pulitzer Prize-winning poet Mary Oliver lived in the Waterfront Apartments here at number 535 with her partner, acclaimed photographer Molly Malone Cook. Oliver wrote in *A Poetry Handbook*, "Poetry is a life-cherishing force. For poems are not words, after all, but fires for the cold, ropes let down to the lost, something as necessary as bread in the pockets of the hungry."

FANIZZI'S

In what was once the sail loft in the old Whorf's Wharf, then a thriving fish processing business in a previous incarnation, a succession of popular watering holes have come and gone here for nearly a century. Each has brought its own flair to this spot with its particular cuisine and character. Paul Fanizzi has been feeding Provincetown year-round for a couple of decades, drawing upon local Portuguese and Italian food repertoires for inspiration for his menu.

Suspended over the water as it is, this location always offers a memorable, nearly nautical dining experience—especially at high tide during a Nor'easter, when you can feel the thrill of waves bashing against the underside of the boards beneath your feet. On summer days, the windows surrounding the dining room on three sides allow diners to watch boats sweeping in and out of the harbor and admire the crimson lingonberry-syrup sunsets seeping over the bay and Truro hills in the distance.

THE SUSAN GLASPELL HOUSE

According to Mary Heaton Vorse, a close friend of Susan Glaspell's and a "co-conspirator" in the formation of Provincetown's first theater, life in the Glaspell house was always humming with creative energy. Writers Susan Glaspell and her husband, George Cram "Jig" Cook, along with Vorse and others, gathered regularly at number 564 for marathon writing sessions sustained by potluck meals and fueled by the heady thrill of embarking on something altogether new in the world of theater.

They set out to forge a path that liberated writers from the many confines imposed by commercialism and are credited with spurring unprecedented innovation in American theater. They also worked to include women and little-known writers and actors in their plays. The Provincetown Players performed their first play in 1915 in the Lewis Wharf, a crooked, wooden wharf donated to the theater troupe by Vorse. The play was written by Eugene O'Neill, who lived with his wife behind the big house in a cottage called Happy Home. The collective wrote and performed their award-winning, trend-setting plays in both Provincetown and New York City. In 1931 Susan Glaspell won a Pulitzer Prize for Drama for her play, *Alison's House*.

Around the corner from here on Bradford Street is the Provincetown Theater. Since the demise of the Provincetown Players, there has been a fervent and consistent—though not always concerted—effort to keep theater alive in Provincetown. These efforts have been met with varied successes and numerous, sometimes tragic, setbacks. However, since June 2004, live theater has had a proud and permanent home in Provincetown. To summarize the theater's journey and mission, I give you the theater's own words, "We are proud of our long, turbulent, yet exhilarating history and will continue to pursue art, entertainment, and community on behalf of the singular residents of Outer Cape Cod."

THE CAPE CODDER GUESTHOUSE

For several generations the Mayos, a prominent fishing family, have lived at the home with the stunning garden at number 570 Commercial. Since the 1930s they've have opened their home to Provincetown visitors. Its charm is genuine Old Cape through and through. When guests make their way down to breakfast in the morning, they'll find a continental breakfast featuring seasonal fruits and vegetables and vases brimming with flowers all picked from the house's own abundant gardens. Guests are welcome to spend their days enjoying the Cape Codder's private beach across the street on the bay. The Mayo family has produced a long line of celebrated fishing captains and, more recently, the founder of the Provincetown Center for Coastal Studies.

DEDICATION TO PROVINCETOWN PLAYERS

Thespians, playwrights and theater goers swarm to Provincetown from around the world to stand right here, at the sight of this modest stone marker (beside house number 571 Commercial). Some leave flowers, others proffer scraps of writing anchored with beach rocks. Still others come to read aloud a passage from a play of Eugene O'Neill, Susan Glaspell or another favorite writer.

The stone and its inscription commemorate the location of what once was the Lewis Wharf, converted from a rickety disused fish shed into the still rickety, but dearly cherished, home of the influential Provincetown Player's theater.

The dedication on the stone reads:

> In 1915, on a wharf extending from this site, a fish shed owned by Mary Heaton Vorse was converted to a theater by a group later named the Provincetown Players. On July 28, 1916, the Players staged *Bound East for Cardiff*, the first production of a play by a young and then unknown author, thus launching the career of Eugene O'Neill as a playwright and changing the course of modern drama in America.

In 1963, a model of the historic wharf was made for the Provincetown

Art Museum. In attendance at the unveiling was the inimitable Mary Heaton Vorse herself, sipping her sherry and leaning on her cane.

Poet Nick Flynn graciously offered me this poem to include in this book. It comes from his book titled *I Will Destroy You* published in 2019.

DAUGHTER

So much going on beneath
the waves, that

slo-mo tumbling, the tide
has made you an island. Stare into

the harbor, hold up one hand — this,
love, is all I can offer — *salt,*

the unseen . . . . Others live
inside those windows

that line the shore, held inside
by lightbulbs. Out here

we are the light, out here the salt
holds us. Touch

your tongue to your arm

& taste it. It holds up
this boat

built with these hands, which,

after all, are your hands. Hold yours
up to the sun — see how

it fills you, see how it is you.

The lovely rambling white cottage adjacent to the marker is the former home of John and Katharine Dos Passos.

JOHN AND KATHARINE DOS PASSOS

Here-in lived writers John Dos Passos and his wife, Katharine. John was a post-WWI "lost generation" novelist who once observed, "We work to eat to get the strength to work to eat to get the strength to work."

John wasn't all doom and gloom, though. Once, in a slightly more upbeat mood, he declared, "Life is to be used, not just held in the hand like a box of bonbons that nobody eats."

About three minutes further on you can see, protruding above the roof of number 583, a chimney shaped like the top of the Pilgrim Monument!

Farther east from here, the street is lined with another quarter mile or so of storied homes and bountiful gardens to admire, each with its own fascinating history. If you have the time, it is worth walking to the far east end of town and looking back at the whole of Provincetown splayed out on a crescent of sand. The easternmost end of Commercial Street is one of the best places in town to watch the sun drop behind the skyline at the end of the day.

We will be turning around here, to make our way back into town, pausing at a handful of places we missed on our way down.

THE NORMAN MAILER HOUSE

Here, I feel I must mention another Provincetown Pulitzer Prize winning resident Norman Mailer, who, his neighbors maintain, gained notoriety for his nude cookouts as well as his controversial novels. Mailer liked to describe Provincetown as "the Wild West of the East." He lived at house number 565 with wife number four, Beverly Mailer, and their six children.

One of his many quotable lines comes from his book *Harlot's Ghost*, "Bright was the light of my last martini on my moral horizon."

SOLAR ECLIPSE, 1932

On the afternoon of August 31, 1932, Provincetown lay directly in the path of a total solar eclipse. The Cape and Provincetown were inundated with eclipse watchers who, in spite of the Depression, arrived by the tens of thousands "over land and sea, from far and wide." The harbor was jam-packed with yachts and sailboats squeezed between dories, fishing vessels and commercial ferries. More boats dropped anchor just off the coast. Eclipse vacation packages sold like hotcakes to visitors wanting to come for the celestial show and stay for the beach parties. Everyone joined in on the eclipse naming game. Enthusiastic restaurants temporarily changed their offerings and the names of menu items. A sunny-side up breakfast plate became "an eclipse side up" when a strategically placed slice of tomato obscured the yellow yolk. An "ice cream eclipse" was a scoop of vanilla ice cream hidden under a pool of chocolate.

Spectators crowded the shoreline all along the outermost coast. According to the *Advocate* newspaper, the *Dorothy Bradford* steamboat ferried 800 passengers to Wood End, at the very tip of land's end; four special trains brought 3,500 more viewers into the already-overflowing town. Finally, the police were forced to close the roads and turn back additional tourists at Wellfleet; Provincetown and its beaches were crammed beyond capacity.

The entire solar event—the slow, inescapable adumbration into a bottomless midnight before rebounding, equally inevitably, toward the joyful restoration of daylight—spanned at least a couple of hours, but the sun lay in the clutch of totality for only a couple of minutes.

It was widely reported that, at the moment the sun became fully obscured and the heavens fell dark, there went up a collective gasp. Suddenly, all the bustle halted and there was silence for the duration of the totality. Several planets, normally only visible at night, could be seen flickering in the pitch darkness overhead. When sunlight began to nudge the darkness aside, cheers and laughter rang out.

For days afterward, accounts of strange incidents, liberally attributed to the eclipse, flooded in from locations across New England where the solar phenomenon had occurred. Several newspapers published stories of odd behavior in animals. It was reported that crickets had vigorously belted out their tunes during totality; whereas cicadas had hushed their singing. Curiously, multiple claims popped up regarding the appearance of unusual markings on eggs laid by chickens on the day of and days following the momentous occasion.

LITTLE LIBRARIES

I never know what surprise will turn up in the Little Libraries that have sprouted up around town. The eclectic make up of this community and the people who visit it make it worthwhile to poke my nose into these whenever I pass one on the street. This simple but innovative take-a-book, leave-a-book concept is becoming ever-more commonplace across the country and around the world. I find it exciting. I never know who will pick up a book I've left behind, or what treasure someone will put there for me to find.

THE FIGUREHEAD HOUSE

My imagination is sparked wondering who inspired the face, the hair, the expression of the figurehead mounted on the front of the house at 476 Commercial Street. Was she, perhaps, modeled after a sister, a mother, a wife or lover of the ship's captain? Maybe she was the secret mistress of the person who carved her. What did she look like before the wind and sun and saltwater cracked her wood, scarred her paint, faded her frock? When she was first carved and painted and placed upon the prow of a ship headed to the Indian Ocean, were her eyes lively and bright, excited at the prospect of going to sea, or were they fretful and afraid?

What joys and horrors might she have seen riding high above the waves, before she was found adrift, alone, the ship that bore her there nowhere to be seen? So many unanswered questions.

Speaking of libraries, as we were a moment ago, librarian Abby Putnam, who was the object of Eugene O'Neill's revengeful play, *Desire Beneath the Elms*, lived in the Figurehead House. It bears mentioning that Abby had a rich and fulfilling life of her own beyond the role thrust upon her as punching bag for a young, vindictive playwright. (O'Neill was resentful that she refused to break library policy to lend him books.) She was a voracious learner and perpetually curious. At 64, she resolved to learn to play the trumpet and found an instructor to teach her. At her first concert appearance, Putnam received a standing ovation from the hometown crowd for her solo performance of *Miserere* from *Il Trovatore*.

At 68, Putnam was quoted in a newspaper interview as saying, "Life is just beginning for me."

THE WOMEN INNKEEPERS OF PROVINCETOWN

It all began over a meal, as many great ideas do. The first gathering of what came to be the Women Innkeepers of Provincetown was held at the Ravenwood Guesthouse on Commercial Street. More years ago than most members care to count, a wildly diverse group of women innkeepers came together from more than a dozen guesthouses around town to get acquainted and celebrate the end of the summer season over a potluck supper—a fortuitous gathering that is still fondly remembered by all who were there.

As different as all the women innkeepers were, they realized they faced similar challenges and obstacles in running their houses. They found that, together, they were a happy stew of fascinating women who could get things done when they set their minds to working together. They pooled their time and resources to create an innovative support network that benefited them all, and they had a good time doing it. The fun and formidable Women Innkeepers of Provincetown was born.

Like the Women Innkeepers organization, the end-of-season dinner has become an integral part of Provincetown. The dinner grew into Women's Week, which expanded into introducing a Single Women's Weekend, a Women of Color Weekend and other festive events, which continue to draw women to Ptown from all over the globe. Every fall during Women's Week, the Women Innkeepers put on a huge end-of-season clambake that brings local and visiting women together for great food and a whale of a good time, as they carry on what is now a Provincetown tradition.

WIVES ABOARD

More women traveled with their captain husbands than is commonly understood. In the later years of whaling, it is estimated that one-in-five whaling ships traveled with the captain's wife, and sometimes children, aboard. An even higher percentage of wives sailed aboard trading vessels. When a woman was traveling on board, the ship was sometimes referred to, often disparagingly, as a "hen frigate." The more superstitious among the sailors (and perhaps those resentful that they weren't allowed to bring along their own wives) maintained that having women aboard invited bad luck.

Although a captain's wife, as a rule, did not cook for the crew, she would cook for her husband and usually prepared special meals for guests who were invited onto the ship. These were usually captains and their families whom they met while out at sea. Social meet-ups at sea, called "gams," were exciting occasions as well as an opportunity to don nice clothes, produce a special dinner served on fine china, and open the finest wine and liquor on hand. (Interestingly, a group of whales is also known as a gam.)

Not surprisingly, whaler's meals and bunk accommodations varied according to their rank. Captains ate better food and slept in a stateroom, whereas deckhands were served the most basic meals and slept in bunks or hammocks. Food aboard the ships was prepared by a designated cook and usually consisted of salted meats, hardtack and beans. Whenever possible, the crew caught and ate fish, turtles, seabirds and dolphins. When in port, crews were able to stock up on fresh fruits and vegetables. On longer voyages, it was not uncommon for ships to set sail with goats, cows, pigs and chickens aboard to provide fresh milk, eggs and meat at sea.

Traveling wives had opportunities to sample a wide variety of cuisines in the international ports they visited. They would try spices, fruits and vegetables that could not be found on the Cape. The women would often preserve in jars the foods they found abroad. In addition to helping supplement the fare on board, the preserves were also brought back home to to share with friends and family in Provincetown. Between ships bringing back food from abroad and ships landing here from all points of the globe, Provincetown, though a small, remote village at the tail end of a spit of sand, was introduced to more foods and flavors from around the globe than most rural towns of its size.

BLUE LAWS

During the era when this lovely old church building at 418 Commercial housed the reading room of the Christian Science Monitor, its members insisted the town enforce the Massachusetts blue laws in order to keep restaurants in the immediate vicinity of the church from legally selling alcohol. This meant that diners at nearby restaurants, such as Ciro & Sal's, had to bring their own liquor to have with their meal.

In the 1950s and into the '60s, there was a push by some in town to enforce a couple of somewhat ambiguous town regulations in order to deny entertainment and liquor licenses to establishments that had "gay overtones" or that openly catered to the growing portion of gay residents and visitors.

These days though, beer, wine and spirits flow freely in eateries and performance halls, all across town.

We've arrived now at Washington Street. While we are on the subjects of rules and regulations and Washington, I thought I'd include a few of the entries from a list of *"110 Rules of Civility & Decent Behavior,"* compiled by future-president George Washington when he was just a teen. These are a few of many that pertain to the table. The full list is archived by the Mount Vernon Museum.

FROM THE PEN OF YOUNG GEORGE WASHINGTON

9. Spit not in the Fire, nor Stoop low before it neither Put your Hands into the Flames to warm them, nor Set your Feet upon the fire especially if there be meat before it.

62. Speak not of doleful Things in a Time of Mirth or at the Table; speak not of Melancholy Things as Death and Wounds, and if others Mention them Change if you can the Discourse, tell not your Dreams, but to your intimate Friend.

90. Being set at Meat Scratch not, neither Spit, Cough or blow your Nose except when there's a Necessity for it.

91. Make no Shew of taking great Delight in your Victuals, Feed no[t] with Greediness; cut your Bread with a Knife, lean not on the Table neither find fault with what you Eat.

94. If you Soak bread in the Sauce let it be no more than what you [pu]t in your Mouth at a time and blow not your broth at Table [bu]t Stay till Cools of it Self.

95. Put not your meat to your Mouth with your Knife in your ha[nd ne]ither Spit forth the Stones of any fruit Pye upon a Dish nor Cas[t an]ything under the table.

100. Cleanse not your teeth with the Table Cloth Napkin Fork or Knife but if Others do it let it be done wt. a Pick Tooth.

105. Be not Angry at Table whatever happens & if you have reason to be so, shew it not but on a Chearfull Countenance especially if there be Strangers for Good Humour makes one Dish of Meat a Feas[t].

EAST END BOOKS, WHERE LANGUAGE IS A FOOD

East End Books is where we go to feed our minds. Jeff has books on most every topic, including a large selection of Provincetown and Cape authors. What he doesn't have on hand he can usually get for you. His is one of the few shops in town that, thankfully, stays open year-round. In the summertime, Jeff hosts weekly outdoor readings, signings and book events right behind the store, by the bay.

SOUTH OF THE BORDER WAY UP NORTH

We are lucky to have a growing number of Mexican restaurants, each bringing its own expression of Mexican culture and cuisine to Ptown's burgeoning food scene. We now have styles ranging from Rosie's Mexican street food to Big Daddy's Tex-Mex taqueria, and Chach, who serves up classic Mexican comfort food in her cozy diner, to various places serving different versions of Cal-Mex dishes. It's increasingly common to see Mexican and other Latin American dishes represented on menus at all sorts of restaurants around town.

Spindler's Restaurant, named for the shipwrecked rum-running schooner, offers a menu of select Mexican specialties (scallop and shrimp ceviche, shrimp *al ajillo, por ejemplo,*) alongside their classic French and Italian dishes. Chef Papi pulls out all the stops and presents a spread to rival any of the classy, top-notch restaurants from his hometown of Mexico City. And there's the Helltown Kitchen, owned by the well-traveled Venezuelan Chef Willy Garcia, who has a flair for a wide swath of savory flavors from equatorial regions around the globe. His menu boasts a zippy vindaloo in addition to dishes featuring a heady blend of spices and ingredients drawn from around Latin America and the Mediterranean.

With Provincetown's innovative Kitchen Captains at the helm, no ticket is needed, no passport required—simply step through their doorways to be transported directly to exciting culinary adventures showcasing local seafoods expertly blended with international flavors. *¡Buen provecho!*

THE WRECK OF THE *ANNIE L. SPINDLER*

The tale of the shipwrecked schooner, the *Annie L. Spindler,* is one of very few stories of a shipwreck that is amusing. It turns out that, during America's Prohibition era, a French-Canadian skipper was transporting a cargo of several hundred cases of Haig & Haig whiskey pinch bottles when his ship, the *Spindler,* ran aground during a horrific gale. As was common with rum-runners, the *Spindler's* papers indicated she was headed from Canada to the West Indies, which would have been perfectly legal as neither of these two regions was under Prohibition restrictions. However, it is strongly suspected that she was, instead, on her way to meet her illicit American connection off the coast of Plymouth when she foundered off the Cape's back shore, almost on the front porch of the US Coast Guard Station at Race Point.

Under international law the Coast Guard was required to render all aid possible to ships in distress, including safeguarding their cargo, regardless of the nature of its content. Therefore, in spite of the ship's consignment of booze's being illegal in the US, the Coast Guard set about helping the crew salvage as much of it as they could. The grapevine, being the fastest mode of communication known to humans, local citizens materialized almost immediately to assist in the whiskey recovery effort.

The rescued cases were initially piled into the basement of the Coast Guard Station for safekeeping. From there, a citizen-manned truck convoy was organized to transport the cargo from Race Point to the Provincetown Harbor, where a replacement ship was to come collect the stranded whiskey and crew.

Reports of the exact quantities involved vary, but they generally agree that, of the 600–800 cases of alcohol that the *Spindler* carried, only about 50 cases made it to the harbor to be loaded onto the backup vessel. One hundred or so cases had been lost overboard, and the remaining hundreds of wayward cases had managed to get themselves liberated somewhere between Race Point and the Provincetown Harbor. In her account, Mary Heaton Vorse wrote that for months following the sinking of the *Annie L. Spindler,* the town was practically afloat in pinch bottles of Haig & Haig.

The Rum-Runner's Lament, or the Pickle Poke Ballad

Light your pipe, top up your ale
Gather round to hear the tale
Of a girl as kind as her brother was cruel,
He a swindler, she a jewel.
That bonnie lass call MarySue,
Whose devilish brother earned his due.

She, a chandler of goods fine and fair,
of meat and fruit and chocolate eclair,
barrels of pickles and bags of flour,
sizzling pies, fresh by the hour.
That bonnie lass called MarySue,
With shining eyes of sapphire blue.

Brother Joe, he aimed to deceive
those who'd trust, and in him believe.

A scoundrel was he whom many did fear,
dogs ran away when he came near.
Bootleg Joe, a blackguard he,
Smuggling rum across the sea.

With a roving eye and a taste for rum,
Joe squandered away a staggering sum.
Brimming was he with spit and spite,
In bars by day, in jail by night.
Bootleg Joe, a blackguard he,
Smuggling rum across the sea.

Into the arms of the Devil Joe strayed:
When false coins to poor Tony he paid.
Barrels aboard, Joe sailed through the night,
His ill-gotten loot to shunt before light.
Bootleg Joe, a blackguard he,
Smuggling rum across the sea.

Tony's heart broke when he discovered
the trickery, treachery the coins uncovered.
With rage in his heart, to town he went,
To make the deceiver repay and repent.
Lo! There met he the bonnie lass MarySue,
With shining eyes of sapphire blue.

Together, the two concocted a plot
to avenge the wrong that Joe had wrought.
MarySue, dressed in men's apparel,
Sold the blackguard her pickle barrel.
That bonnie lass called MarySue,
With shining eyes of sapphire blue.

When rogues awaited for Joe on the strand
found pickles, not rum, they took Joe in hand.
They dumped the pickles, stuffed Joe inside,
And tossed the barrel upon the tide.
Bootleg Joe, a blackguard he,
In a barrel bouncing out to sea.

She, a chandler of goods fine and fair:
of meat and fruit and chocolate eclair,

barrels of pickles and bags of flour,
sizzling pies, fresh by the hour.
That bonnie lass called MarySue,
With shining eyes of sapphire blue.

She married Tony, he runs the pub,
with beer and wine and tasty grub,
and if you've got an itch for some
a knock at the side door will get you rum
from the bonnie lass called MarySue,
With shining eyes of sapphire blue.

And what became of Joe, you ask,
That wag set a-sea in a pickle cask?
Shed no tears, and raise your brew
For that devilish cad has earned his due
Boot leg Joe still floats about
with pickle breath in a barrel stout.

—Od.

FROM RUMBULLION TO REBELLION

In celebration of the Boston Tea Party (the tipping overboard of some 342 cases of British tea into the Boston Harbor to protest the untenable situation of "taxation without representation"), tea was considered by colonists to be the symbolic drink of the American Revolution. Especially popular were liberty teas, home-brewed concoctions of herbs and spices that were sipped in solidarity as a subsequent ban on British tea took hold. But it was objections to the tax on molasses, on which the colonists' lucrative rum industry relied, that finally ignited the sparks of war.

Initially called "kill-divil" or "rumbullion" (meaning a great tumult), this fierce, throat-scorching drink was likely first concocted by enslaved Africans using molasses residue from sugar production to create the fermented drink. As it grew in popularity, the spirit became better known as rum.

The tragic irony that ensued would certainly not have been lost on enslaved Africans who'd created the elixir, as rum soon became the very currency with which the colonists purchased additional enslaved Africans. African traffickers specialized in selling Africans to Europeans and colonists. The colonists then traded enslaved Africans in the Caribbean in exchange for barrels of molasses.

Once they arrived in the Caribbean, enslaved people were made to work the sugar cane fields and sugar refineries of the islands. It is estimated that a third of enslaved passengers died during the voyage to the Caribbean from Africa. The average life expectancy for those who survived the journey to the islands was only seven years, due to the inhumane living conditions and crushing workload.

Initially, rum was produced in the Caribbean and sent to America, but before long, colonists began importing molasses and distilling it into rum themselves, thereby earning an increased profit margin making several rum producers exceedingly wealthy. Barrels of rum were then shipped from America, particularly from New England, to Africa to be traded for more enslaved people, thus continuing the cycle. At one point, rum made up 80 percent of New England's exports. Trading cod, rum and humans as forms of currency served the colonists in their efforts to evade British tax laws. The British government had its tax-collecting fingers in as many taxable pies as possible, but its laws generally pertained to monies traded for goods rather than to the bartering of commodities. Each time the contumacious colonists adjusted their trading tactics, the British imposed more tax laws and trading limitations. These ever-escalating tensions over taxes and trade restrictions ripened conditions for the onset of the American Revolution.

"WASN'T THAT A MIGHTY STORM"

At the bottom of Pearl Street lies a parking lot and a beach where a proud Knowles Wharf once stood. It was named for its owner, George O. Knowles, a wealthy King Hiram Lodge member and owner of the ill-fated *Carrie D. Knowles* schooner captained by Collin Stephenson, whom we met earlier in the tour. The wharf housed the Casino, one of Provincetown's first dress-up dinner spots and night clubs. This wharf and others were destroyed in a fearsome gale in 1926.

THE *S.S. PORTLAND,* "*TITANIC* OF NEW ENGLAND"

As fearsome New England gales go, however, it's the Portland Gale that takes the cake. The palatial night boat *S.S. Portland* became the crown of the Portland Steam Packet Co. fleet as soon as she first set sail in 1889. This graceful wooden-hulled, side-wheel steamship cruised nightly between Boston and Portland, a trip of about eight hours. The *Portland* was designed to host large numbers of passengers at a level of luxury, elegance and service well above what most of her passengers experienced in their daily lives. Her well-appointed 167 cherry-paneled staterooms and 514 white-pine berths even ran hot and cold water. The rooms, halls and salons were electric-lit by the latest styles of lamps, sconces and chandeliers. Regular passage for the overnight journey cost $1 each way; the staterooms could be booked for an additional $1 to $3.

The *Portland* and other popular night steamers of the time were known for their scenic deck strolls, numerous dining venues, quiet libraries, lively card rooms and smoking rooms humming with conversation and the occasional handshake business dealing. As these stately ships glided through the night, passengers would while away the evening dancing on polished floors to a small orchestra or dining in an opulent salon, served by waiters in white, at tables topped with starched linen, embossed china, sparkling crystal and glistening silver.

Guests sipped wine, beer or champagne selected from an extensive menu. On the next page is a sample of menu choices and prices typical of night steamers of the time.

In addition to being outfitted with the finest furnishings, the *Portland* was run by an experienced crew made up largely of African Americans hailing from Portland, Maine, the ship's home port. Most African Americans worked as pursers, porters, waiters and on the kitchen and housekeeping staff. The hours were long but the wages were considered good in comparison to similar work on land. Coastline steamers attracted an array of passengers—presidents, politicians, professional and business travelers, as well as vacationers, honeymooners and clandestine lovers liaising for a romantic tryst.

THE PORTLAND GALE

A couple of days after celebrating Thanksgiving with family and friends, nearly 200 passengers and crew boarded the *S.S. Portland*. It was the 26th of November, 1898. Excited passengers dispersed into all corners of the boat to play cards, smoke, talk business, or bask in their luxurious staterooms. Others headed for one of several dining spots, or

Menu

Appetizers

Cape Cod Oysters on the Half Shell 35¢

Mock Turtle Soup 25¢

Escalloped Oysters with Red Peppers 50¢

Entrées

Roast Spring Lamb 50¢   Spaghetti a L'Italienne 30¢

Individual Pot Boston Baked Beans
and Brown Bread 45¢

Corned Beef Hash with Egg Sauce 60¢

Boiled Eastern Halibut with Poached Egg 50¢

Whole Broiled Chicken $2.00   Porterhouse Steak for two $1.50

Broiled Lobster in Drawn Butter $1.50

Desserts

English Plum Pudding or plate of Exotic Fruits
and Nuts with a Cup of Coffee 30¢

surged into a large salon to claim seats and order drinks in anticipation of enjoying the dance band. The crew, meanwhile, finished loading the last crates of freight into the hold—tobacco, cheese, oil, barrels of whiskey, tubs of lard and other goods.

As the 7 o'clock departure time approached, a fierce storm packing snow and nearly 100 mile per hour winds was hurtling toward Cape Cod, Boston and points north, directly into the path of the *Portland*. It remains unclear whether the captain was unaware of the coming storm or whether he disregarded warnings and sailed against orders. Be that as it may, Captain Blanchard raised anchor and set sail at 7 p.m., as scheduled.

During the 36-hour storm, which lasted through the night, all the next day and into the following night, houses along the coastline from the

Cape to Maine were wrenched to pieces or swept into the sea, telegraph lines were ripped down and rail lines washed out. As the telegraph cables between the Cape and Boston had been destroyed in the storm, the tragedy of the *Portland* had to be relayed by transatlantic cable first to France, then to New York by undersea cable, and from there to Boston. The timeline and events of the tragedy have been pieced together from reported sightings on land, from shoreline rescuers who heard blasts from a steamer's whistle calling for help, and from wristwatches found on passengers' bodies, believed to have stopped at the time they fell into the sea.

A good deal of the reconstruction of the wreck was determined from the clothing, life vests bearing the *Portland* stamp, steering wheel, cabin furnishings and crates of merchandise salvaged on Cape Cod and mainland shorelines. Only 40 bodies of the nearly 200 aboard the ship were ever recovered. Remains and wreckage continued to wash onto Cape Cod beaches over the coming weeks. Some 150 ships, large and small, were lost and around 500 people died in what came to be named the Portland Gale. The loss of the *Portland* was particularly devastating to the city of Portland, as most of both passengers and crew were from there.

The whereabouts of the wreck were not known until some 90 years on, when it was discovered lying in the Stellwagen Bank National Marine Sanctuary. At least 200 additional wrecks have come to settle there, too. A report from the Stellwagen Bank National Marine Sanctuary reads:

> … cultural artifacts lie scattered inside and outside the hull and remind us of the passengers and crew that lost their lives when the *Portland* sank. Stacked plates and cups lie exposed on the main deck in the kitchen, while other pieces of dishware, an electric light, a toilet, and a stack of glass window panes have fallen to the sea floor just outside of the hull. A single large mug or cup also rests amongst the tangled steam piping near the steering gear towards the bow.

In Provincetown, over 30 vessels sank or were blown ashore, several lives were lost, and the steeple of the Center Methodist Church (which now houses the library) came down. The storm's damage to the local fishing industry was felt for years afterward, and the profound impacts on the families and communities who lost loved ones still resonates today.

ON THE RADIO

I lived in Alaska (for eight hours short of a year—but who's counting?). Every winter morning on the radio, they'd report the outdoor temperature, along with the estimated "seconds-to-frostbite," so we'd know how many seconds we could be outside, scraping ice off the windshield, walking the dog or running from a moose before the exposed skin on our face and hands would begin to freeze.

Growing up in the rural mountains of Colorado, we used to hear the hog report in the mornings informing local ranchers of the going price for hogs, beef, sheep, chicken and eggs at market that day. They usually had a lost pet report, too, at the end of the news hour.

Here on the Cape and Islands, for the benefit of clammers, oystermen, mariners and beach-goers, some radio stations broadcast the sun and tide report—what time the sun will rise and set, the wind velocity, what time the high and low tides will arrive, and how high the sea level rise will be that day. We sometimes hear reports of the release into the wild of injured marine animals who have made a full recovery. The whales that frequent our waters have been given names by the scientists who observe them, and it is not uncommon, when one gives birth, for her happy news to be announced on the radio.

EUGENE O'NEILL

Several of Eugene O'Neill's plays were inspired by local figures. One such was Viola Cook, the reluctant Arctic traveler, who lived at number 376 Commercial. Although against her better judgment, and by some accounts, against her will, she accompanied her husband, Captain John Atkins Cook, on several multi-year trips to the Arctic, including a most agonizing one for which she dutifully left her child behind in Provincetown. All told, Viola spent nine harrowing winters in the Arctic.

The conditions were lonely and miserable and, for Viola, ultimately debilitating both physically and mentally. The elongated weeks of Arctic winters were sunless and gloomy, vacillating between dusk and dark for months on end. At times, temperatures slid down to −60°F, where they'd hover seemingly interminably. It was not uncommon for the ship to become, as O'Neill described in his play *Ile*, "stuck in ice like a fly in molasses" for weeks.

Eugene O'Neill based the play *Ile* on Viola's tragic story. "Ile" was the local fishermen's pronunciation of "oil," with which the character of the captain was utterly obsessed, to the destruction of many around him, especially his wife.

Captain John was a difficult and demanding man. He struck and flogged his crew, sometimes banishing them to isolation for months at a time as punishment. The crew, which had signed on for a one-year stint, attempted to mutiny when he insisted the ship would not return home until it had brought on a full load of whale oil, thus keeping them at sea for well over two years. In protest of his cruelty, Viola once locked herself in her cabin and refused to emerge for nine months. By the time Viola disembarked in Provincetown for the final time, she had reached a physical and mental nadir from which she never fully recovered. In addition to that, she was suffering from beriberi, a painful and serious food deficiency disease. For the remainder of her days, she'd putter about her house muttering nonsensically to herself.

Another of O'Neill's plays is based on the aforementioned librarian, Abbie Cook Putnam, who lived at the Figurehead House. O'Neill took umbrage with Putnam when she refused to break policy to let him borrow books. After she threw him out of the library for being drunk, he penned the play *Desire Under the Elms*. In it, O'Neill assigned the name Abbie Putnam to a cantankerous, duplicitous, adulterous character who kills her own baby. Though it became well-known, that particular play did not win O'Neill the Pulitzer Prize, whereas three of his other plays did; his body of work earned him a Nobel Prize in Literature.

We now find ourselves in front of our lovely town library, run by our wonderful librarians.

LIBRARY

Provincetown's first public library, located on Freeman Street, opened in 1874 with 2,202 volumes on its shelves. Before then, the only lending libraries in town had been private ones. That library was moved from its home on Freeman Street to this former Methodist Church in 2002. Today, the library contains 40,000 items, including not only books and media, but also 30 pieces of artwork and, as one might expect in Provincetown, there's a large ship inside.

In the center of the library stands a 66½ foot long, half-scale model of

Provincetown's most famous schooner, the *Rose Dorothea*, built by Provincetown's best-known boat builder, Flyer Santos, as would also be expected here. The coveted Lipton trophy the ship and her crew brought home in 1907 is prominently displayed here, too.

SIR LIPTON AND THE LIPTON CUP RACE

The Lipton Prize was created by Sir Thomas Lipton, who was born into the Scottish working class in a Glasgow tenement to Irish parents. He was knighted in 1901 by King Edward after making a mint both literally and figuratively in his own chain of grocery stores. He frequently made headlines for launching creative publicity stunts, among them, a Lipton currency he designed and printed, which could be tendered only in his stores.

Although he was the first to sell tea in individual serving packets and later incorporated the tea bag, Lipton did not invent the tea bag. His great success came from making tea affordable for the working classes by selling individual portions. Before he came along, only the wealthier classes could afford to buy tea, which was sold as loose-leaf, in large tins. In 1893 alone, he sold over one million small packets of tea.

His wealth afforded him the ability to promote one of his strongest convictions: that sport competitions provide cultural bridges and improve cultural understanding and cooperation. Sir Lipton sponsored sailing and other sports competitions around the world, awarding the winners with elaborately engraved silver trophies. The Lipton Cup, won by Provincetown's Captain Marion Perry and the crew of the *Rose Dorothea* in 1907, is the largest of Lipton's trophies ever to have been awarded. Second place in the highly competitive race was taken by a Provincetown ship, too: the *Jesse Costa*.

It's unfortunate that Sir Lipton could not visit Provincetown today. The dashing Lord Lipton was often referred to by the press as "the world's most eligible bachelor," although, more accurately he might have been described as "one of the world's most firmly confirmed bachelors," at least with regard to women's company. He and his aptly named companion of 30 years, William Love, or his later companion, the ostentatious Maurice Talvande, would likely feel right at home in Provincetown today. And, as marriage laws have changed since then, he'd have the option to marry his Love.

At the junction of Center and Commercial Streets, directly across from the library, is a red bricked alleyway, home to a handful of popular eateries and bay-view condos. The little complex was named for the daughter of a pilot who used to land his seaplane in front of their home, once located here.

ANGEL'S LANDING

Individually, the shops currently open at Angel's Landing have their own unique flare; collectively, they comprise something of a quiet alcove, just off crowded Commercial Street.

SCOTT CAKES

Scott Cunningham began by peddling his luminous pink cupcakes on the street corners of town at night to crowds of revelers wandering home after the bars closed. Town regulations prohibit hawking home-baked goods on the streets, regardless of how popular they are, and his enterprise was promptly shut down. But the clamor for his cupcakes did not die out. It wasn't long before a hungry funder helped install Scott in a shop where he could legally make and sell his cupcakes. His story made national news and a gazillion glaringly pink cupcakes later, he's still going strong.

BOX LUNCH

In 1977, Box Lunch invented a whole new sandwich. The "rollwich," a pita wrap stuffed with various sandwich fixings has become synonymous with summer on the Outer Cape for visitors. Year-rounders who are willing to travel to Truro in the off-season get to enjoy them through the winter months, too. Perfect for picnickers or local workers on the go, Rollwich sandwiches have become a staple on the Outer Cape. The sandwich names and ingredients reference nautical or American cultural influences. They sell a Gilded Lobster, Whale Watcher, Monument, Luau, Californian, Cousteau, Jaws and, of course, the ever-popular John Alden and Priscilla Alden classics.

THE FRENCH PATISSERIE ET CAFÉ PROVINCETOWN

When the breeze is coming off the bay just so, you can catch a whiff of her pastries baking, as the scent wafts gently up the alleyway onto Commercial Street. This alluring aroma is coming from the French Patisserie et Café. Follow that scent to the vanilla custard-colored cottage at bottom of the brick path. When you walk in you'll be greeted with Elsar's cheerful, *"Bonjour!"*

Open through both summer heat and winter blizzards, Elsar offers up European-strength coffees, hot cocoa, freshly baked pastries, and breakfast and lunch sandwiches, influenced by her time in France and her love for French and Italian pastries. In addition to what you'd expect to find in a good French pastry shop—light-as-mist meringues, festive-colored macaroons, pastries, croissants, pies and chocolates—many of the daily specials are drawn from the cuisines of France and Italy. As they say, if the choux fits… eat it!

COOL BEANS

Gargantuan, exhaustive volumes have been written on the long and complicated history of coffee, and for good reason. Its journey has been one of cultural, political, economic and environmental entanglement around the world. Over the centuries coffee has been celebrated, banned, revered, vilified; has been both a spiritual symbol, as well as suspected of being—simultaneously and conversely—satanic in origin. Coffee trees and seeds have been gifted, stolen, smuggled, traded and coveted around the globe.

One of the many adventures of the globe-trotting bean begins in 1723 with an officer of the French Navy, Gabriel Mathieu de Clieu, who was the Johnny Appleseed of coffee in the Caribbean. In spite of the flat refusal of King Louis XV to grant de Clieu's request for a few snips of his coffee plants, somehow the officer leaves Paris with several coffee tree clippings from the King's garden stashed in a glass container under his cloak. Having acquired his prize, he hops a boat back to the island of Martinique. It is not an easy voyage. The ship is set upon by pirates, there's a violent storm and the protective glass container breaks, exposing the fragile plants to the harsh and salty sea elements. When water supplies aboard the vessel run short, de Clieu shares his own water ration with his wilting sprigs.

Some say that, so protective of his precious coffee was de Clieu, that after arriving in Martinique, he hid the little shoots carefully among other plants so as not to draw attention to them while they took root. Take root they did, and before long, coffee plantations sprouted up all across Martinique and nearby islands. On Martinique alone, many millions of coffee trees thrived, soon producing more coffee each year than was consumed annually in all of France. Descendants of Gabriel Mathieu de Clieu's coffee sprigs continue to propagate throughout the Caribbean, Central and South America.

The coffee bean itself is actually the pit of a bright red, tree-borne fruit. The pit is extracted and prepared for roasting—and it's from this point forward that the process of roasting, grinding and preparing a coffee drink can vary wildly from place to place, country to country.

We need only to look at the menus of today's coffee shops to appreciate the impressive global trek the bean has made, and the innumerable, creative ways people enjoy drinking their coffee. There's macchiato, latte, mocha (not to be confused with moka coffee) and Portuguese galão, Turkish sweet coffee, café Cubano, Greek freddo, mazagran from Algeria, Indian beaten coffee, Korean dalgona coffee, café Touba of Senegal, Canadian double-double, Vietnamese egg coffee. Interesting new coffee concoctions are being cooked up all the time.

Across the street from the Land's End Marine Supply Store was, for a while, the To Be Coffeehouse, a quintessentially winter-in-Provincetown endeavor.

THE TO BE COFFEEHOUSE

Forged of a desire to get together with friends and neighbors, make new friends, beat one another at cribbage, share a copy of *The New York Times* and regale each other with stories, a handful of townies got together in 1970 to create a place to hang out over the winter when most public spaces were closed for the season. A local shopkeeper offered up his leather shop for the project. A few books, a couple of couches, some tables and chairs were dragged out of attics and odd corners, and the thing got off the ground. They covered the walls with their artwork. A house guitar inspired some to write songs or strike up spontaneous sing-alongs. There was the occasional poetry or book reading session.

Several participants in the To Be Coffeehouse were avid cooks and a few chefs in town jumped in to help out. No one made a profit or got paid; it was a group effort for mutual enjoyment. Those who popped by dropped money into the bucket to cover food and utility costs: the café asked 50¢ for the plate du jour, soup was a quarter, and hot coffee and tea could be had for 10¢. A collection of recipes was compiled and entries published in the local paper. The idea of putting them all together as a book was floated, but never made it into print. The To Be lasted a couple of winters and is still talked about with a hint of something like home-sickness among those who were there.

Now, on we go to the one-and-only Land's End Marine Supply Store.

LAND'S END MARINE SUPPLY STORE

Everyone in town eventually winds up at Land's End Marine Supply Store, whether or not they own a boat. Tourists stop through to pick up something they've left at home, to buy a gift or just to browse the bizarre mix of items on the shelves. Meanwhile, every fisherman/woman, restaurant owner, guesthouse owner, drag queen, artist, writer, pet owner, teen, retiree, butcher, baker and candlestick maker eventually needs light bulbs, batteries, a birthday card or a new coffee pot, and they come here.

This store, which was opened by Portuguese immigrants is still in the hands of the same family, generations later. And, it has a lot more on offer than light bulbs, batteries, cards and coffee pots. You can find aisles bursting with nautical whatnots—navigation charts, fishing lures and boat engine parts, of course—it's a marine supply store after all. But they also sell honey from the owners' own hives and make keys and customized bumper stickers. They stock pet stuff, patio furniture, plastic knick-knacks and novelties, wheel barrows, art supplies, space heaters, garden hoses, hardware thingies, egg timers, handsaws, rain gear, kitchen doohickeys, office necessities, electrical whatchamacallits, outdoor grills, snowblowers, giant rubber bands, plumbing thingamajigs, pest control gadgets, candles, clock gizmos, sweatshirts, house paint, bags of bird-seed and grass seed, rolls of chicken wire, clamming rakes, windshield wipers, candy bars and, well … you get the picture.

Probably my favorite thing about this store, though, is the enormous 4-foot-by-48-foot, not-quite-panoramic mural of Provincetown painted by Peter Macara, a member of the family. Its colors are clean, clear and youthfully optimistic. The perspective is the view you'd have if you were fishing in your dad's dingy just off Long Point, 'round about midmorning on a school day under a spring sky too achingly blue for a kid to be trapped inside a classroom.

The mural is a topic of discussion for customers who notice it, whether residents or visitors. Locals stand under the picture and pick out their homes or their childhood haunts. They reminisce about crazy things they got up to when they were kids, pointing out where it all happened and which alley they hid in to escape the cops. (Retired cops come in and point out spots where local teens used to hide while the cops turned a blind eye, so long as no one was getting hurt.) Something about looking up at this carefree view of the town brings bouts of wistful reverie to even the most hardboiled curmudgeons who take time to look at it. People enjoy working out where their favorite restaurant is, or where they first kissed. Although, inevitably the town has changed since this was painted in the early 20-aughts, people still get a kick out of standing under the mural, swapping stories and pointing up at the painting.

LUNCH, ANYONE?

"Hiya toots! Now let's see, what should I have for lunch today?"
— Donald Duck

We are coming into the section of town where most of the restaurants are located. Within these next few blocks you will be able to find most any style of cuisine you have a hankering for. Some restaurants are dedicated to one cuisine, while others offer menus with wide-ranging choices. Some restaurants have been around for decades, others are new to the scene, having filled a spot left by an establishment that closed down or moved across town. Some are high-end, others more wallet-friendly, which is helpful because, as Donald Duck likes to say, "Four dollars is very little money when you got 'em, but a heck of a lot of money when you ain't got 'em!"

What you won't find in Provincetown is a McDonald's, a Pizza Hut, an Olive Garden or any other restaurant chain. You may find that a restaurant you fell in love with the first time you come is no longer here the next time. This is part of the charmingly, frustratingly, transient nature of this town. Which is not to imply that restaurants, their chefs or owners are readily replaceable—quite the opposite. The distinctive personality of each owner, and the singular dining experience and cuisine each restaurant offers is precisely what attracts us, and we enjoy them while we can. When a business, restaurant or otherwise is gone, it is both a loss and an opportunity for something different to emerge. Whatever is next won't be the same; it may be better, it may not be. Like everything else in Provincetown, its food landscape is in constant flux. It's all part of the exciting world of food and culture that both delights and defines this town.

SPOILER ALERT!

So, what's the big idea with all the Donald Duck quotes, you may ask? Well, he's looking at us from the top of the Monument tower, so I thought I'd mention him.

I invite you to look at the Pilgrim Monument, as you see it now, from the corner of Freeman and Commercial streets, and admire it simply as a lovely Siena-esque stone tower, because after reading the next paragraph, the face of America's most famous duck will become visible to you, and you may never be able to un-see him. If you feel it will forever spoil your view of the Monument to see Donald Duck's face grinning back at you, you may want to skip to the next entry.

Donald Duck's face in the tower can only be seen from certain angles. The bay side of Commercial Street, where it intersects with Freeman, is one of them. See him there? The two tall arches are his eyes, looking down at the town. His beak pokes out just below, sporting that silly smirk for which he's so well known. The pointy bits on the top of the tower resemble his hat, sitting perky-like atop his head. And, as Donald said, "For me, it's all about the hat! Whaddya think? Nice, right?"

Wak! I'll be doggone, it's Donald Duck!

FREEMAN BUILDING

Freeman Street is named for businessman Nathan Freeman, once president of the Provincetown Bank and a philanthropist. He donated this building to be used as the town's first public library. The library opened in 1874, and in 2005 it was moved down to the old Methodist Church which had previously housed the Provincetown Heritage Museum. Since 2005 various civic organizations and nonprofits have taken up residence in the Freeman building.

In season, there are usually musicians, magicians or jugglers busking on this corner. The benches in front of the Freeman building are a terrific place to have a nosh, listen to the music and watch folks walking, cycling, skating, prancing and dancing by on a summer's day.

It's also a great spot for watching the famous drag brunch on parade at the restaurant next door. By the way, I am told that the collective noun for drag queens is an extravaganza of drag queens, whereas the collective noun for drag kings is said to be a dynasty.

ROSIE'S MEXICAN CANTINA

There are plenty of New England versions of Mexican food around, often taking the form of burritos gasping under a haystack of shredded lettuce, submerged beneath an avalanche of sour cream and splattered with bright red Tabasco sauce. But if it's south-of-the-border Mexican street food you're looking for—tacos, a fat burro or a couple of spicy enchiladas—you can find that here at Rosie's Cantina. Run by a friendly local family from Mexico, the aromas and flavors come straight from the streets and marketplaces of my memories of living in the heart of Mexico.

Maybe it's something in the water at this location, but restaurants that open here have continuously proved a good bet. Before it was Rosie's, we used to stop here for "great, cheap eats" when it was the Burger Queen. Before that, the Snack Attack was the place to get fat, affordable sandwiches and bump into friends. In those days, juggling four or five jobs at a time, my friends and I had little free time to sit down to eat and even less spending money. Eateries at this location always seem to fill the bill.

ARNOLD'S BIKE SHOP

Arnold's: whose unambiguous slogan is simply "Where you rent the bikes." This shop used to be Arnold's Radio and Cycle Shop. Back in the 1940s, you could rent a radio as well as a bike for just the day or for the whole summer.

OLD COLONY TAP

Opened in 1937, the Old Colony Tap has steadily ridden the highs and lows of Provincetown for nearly nine decades.

If you've ever wondered if you'll find a place where it is perpetually 5 o'clock, America's socially sanctioned hour to begin drinking, you need look no further. The tap starts flowing here from just after breakfast time. A flyer from a few years ago read, *"I'll meet you at the Old Colony Tap, where friendliness, fun, good fellowship prevail; Open 9–closing."* Back then it opened at 9 a.m. Night workers need a place to relax after a long shift, too.

Whereas women have always been welcome at the "O.C.," David Dunlap (*Building Provincetown*) writes that a nearby bar, the New Deal, banned women right up until 1959, at which time, "they took down the 'No Ladies Admitted' sign, replaced it with 'Ladies Cordially Invited,'" and changed the name of the bar to the Fo'csle. It's now the Squealing Pig, owned by an Irishman and a fantastic chef from Nepal, and is a popular watering hole welcoming all genders. The Pig also hosts a fun trivia night.

THE GOVERNOR BRADFORD BAR & RESTAURANT

Back in the day it was not uncommon to put a raw egg into your beer. It was/is supposed to help with a hangover, especially if you are drinking the hair of the dog. A basket of raw eggs sat on the corner of the bar and patrons would grab one or two and crack them into their beer. A few eyebrows might be raised if you did that in the Governor Bradford today, but it was commonplace in pubs of the distant past—and in some places it's never gone out of style.

For many decades, a steady flow of regulars and tourists migrated in flocks, swirling back and forth between the Old Colony and the Governor Bradford throughout the night, year-round.

NEW ENGLAND CLAM CHOWDER

While many might agree with Anthony Bourdain's claim that there is only one kind of chowder and that's New England clam chowder, not everyone agrees on exactly how New England clam chowder should be made. I won't wade into the thick of that fight here, but I will say that a strong argument can be made for the clam chowder they serve up at the Lobster Pot, which is one of the places Bourdain cooked in his early days working in commercial kitchens. Of his time at the Lobster Pot, Bourdain said in *Parts Unknown* that working at the Pot with his friends "started the tradition among my set that cooking was noble toil."

Recipes, like moments, are built one upon the other. The forerunner to today's New England clam chowder was a recipe taught to the colonists by Native Americans. Nasaump, shortened to "samp" by the colonists, was a stick-to-your-ribs dish made by cooking cornmeal and stirring in seeds, berries and nuts, and sometimes sweetened with honey or maple syrup. A whole host of hearty stews were created by starting with beans or corn, then adding herbs and a combination of root vegetables such as potatoes, onions and carrots. Whichever meats, shellfish or clams were on hand might be thrown in as well.

A few centuries of noble toil later, *et voilà*! You can now walk into the Lobster Pot in Provincetown and order an award-winning chowder that owes its existence to the concoctions first created and generously shared with colonists by Native Americans.

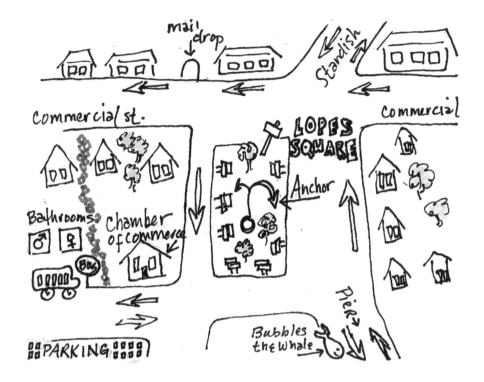

LOPES SQUARE

The Lopes in Lopes Square, is pronounced lōps. As in, the girls look up as he *lopes* toward the pier, fishing pole over his shoulder, humming a tune and eating the last of his linguiça sub roll.

This busy square is named for a young Portuguese-born American soldier who died in battle in France in 1917. Manuel N. Lopes had been a fish monger before being shipped off to war.

PROVINCETOWN'S DANCING COP

In a town blooming with people in eye-catching attire and unexpected color combinations, Donald Thomas stood out, even in his plain blue uniform. For years he stopped traffic with his dance moves—or more accurately, he stopped cars, cyclists and pedestrians pushing strollers, traveling in one direction while waving others safely across the intersection in the opposite direction. Officer Thomas directed traffic at the busiest intersection in town, at the height of the season, all the while gracefully blowing his whistle and gracefully pirouetting, dipping and bopping. Throngs of people would stop at the intersection to watch the show, eating their ice cream and linguiça sub rolls and taking photos of the "Dancing Cop" to show people back home.

Officer Thomas retired, then passed away a few years back; locals and tourists alike still talk about him. His joie de vivre is sorely missed. You can find videos of him online, though they barely do the scene justice.

LOOK WHAT THE CAPTAIN DRAGGED IN!

That enormous anchor in the middle of Lopes Square, forged in 1801, was recovered in 1959 by the crew of the dragger *Cap'n Bill,* and the trophy was placed here at the center of town. A plaque at the base of the anchor commemorates Captain George Adams and his crew.

On February 13, 1978, tragedy struck when the *Cap'n Bill* (sailing under a different crew) sank off Highland Light near Truro with all hands.

We now find ourselves at the foot of MacMillan Pier, in front of the Chamber of Commerce.

Inside the Chamber, you can find information on places to stay, maps of the town and the Cape, menus for local restaurants, flyers for various sightseeing tours, museums and points of interest. Bathrooms are around back.

From the Pier you can catch the ferry to Boston, go on a fishing expedition or a whale watch. In answer to a somewhat perplexing question someone once asked: "Are the whale watching tours round trip?" Yes, they are round trip. (Although I suppose other arrangements could be made ...?)

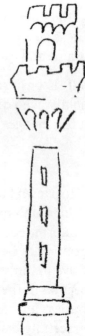

When you are ready to begin our second walk, let's meet back here at Lopes Square, near the benches and the big anchor.

INTERLUDE

Directly from the contagiously joyful repertoire of singer, Zoë Lewis, comes her song, "Bicycle." Hailing from Brighton, England, Zoë has been a townie favorite and an international phenom for decades.

BICYCLE

On my bicycle I can speak
to everybody on Commercial Street
I'm gonna ring my bell
'cos it's a sunny day
and the ocean's calling
Get out my way!

Hello seagull, hello ice cream
hello Ellie, hello Varla Jean
hello trolley, hello truck
hello poodle
don't push your luck!

On my bicycle feels so good
terrorizing the neighborhood
I'm gonna race the peddy cabs
dodge the cars
it's the middle of summer
Look, no handlebars!

Hello policeman, hello Pearline
hello fisherman, hello muscle queen
hello ladies, hello gents
Look, lemonade for sale for just 50 cents!

On my bicycle
tip of the land
riding around on a pile of sand
in a dizzy July and August bliss
all I know is it doesn't get better than this!

Hello stroller, hello car door
hello pizza, oops hello floor
hello honking, hello frown,
New York plates …
you'd better slow down!

On my bicycle I can speak
to everybody on Commercial Street
I'm gonna ring my bell
'cos it's a sunny day
and the ocean's calling
Get out my way!

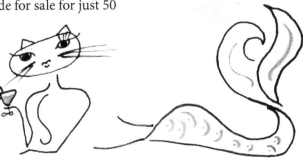

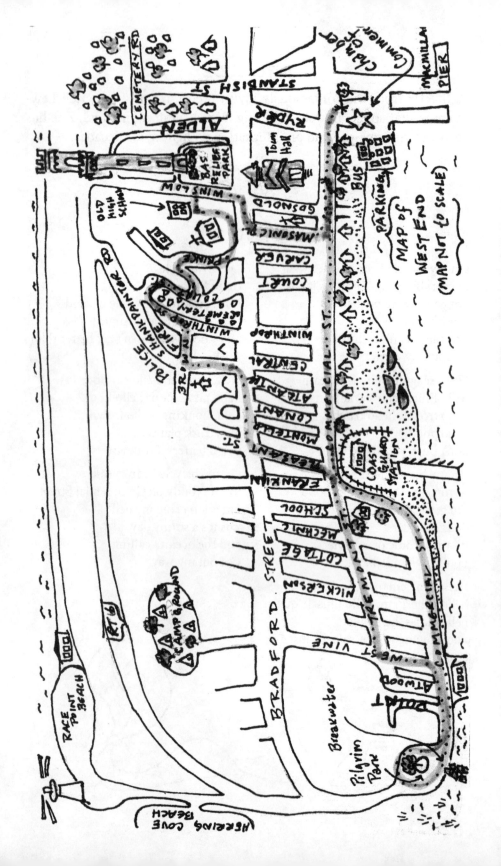

MAP of WEST END
(MAP NOT to SCALE)

WELCOME BACK!

Let's start the second tour by walking up MacMillan Pier.

Provincetown's most famous native son, Rear Admiral MacMillan, traveled by ship farther than the distance to the moon. He was accompanied on nine trips by his wife, who was widely recognized in her own right for her accomplishments. In 1908–09, MacMillan joined fellow explorers Robert Peary and Matthew Henson on their world record-setting expedition to reach the North Pole. In 1909, Henson became the first African American to stand "at the top of the world," the spot then believed to be the North Pole. He wrote of his life and adventures in a book he titled, *A Negro Explorer at the North Pole.*

According to the Peary-MacMillan Arctic Museum at Bowdoin College:

> Henson was excluded from receiving the many honors showered on Peary and the other white members of the expedition. Only near the end of his life did Henson receive recognition for his remarkable career as an Arctic explorer.

In 1937, Henson became the first African American inducted into The Explorer's Club as a life member and was promoted to its highest membership level. He was invited to the White House to meet with Presidents Truman and Eisenhower. Henson was presented with the Peary Polar Expedition medal in 1944, and in 2000, was posthumously awarded the Hubbard Medal by the National Geographic Society. Henson and his wife are buried at the Arlington National Cemetery. September of 2021 saw the International Astronomical Union name a lunar crater for him in recognition of the great heights he had reached.

As we walk along the right side of the wharf we come to a 10-foot-long concrete humpback whale named Bubbles, lounging on the boardwalk. As well as being photogenic, Bubbles is unfailingly patient with children and enjoys letting them sit on her back.

Bubbles is just one of a handful of sculptures scattered around downtown. Kids like to see if they can find them all: there's an oversized slice of pizza, a huge ice cream cone, a life-sized plaster shark dangling upside-down and, sweetly, a giant Hershey's chocolate kiss.

THEY ALSO FACED THE SEA

On one side of the Cabral Wharf, adjacent to the MacMillan Pier, hangs an installation of enormous black-and-white photos titled *They Also Faced the Sea,* an impressive exhibit of photographs of local Portuguese women whose husbands were fishermen. Initially, there were five images, but storms, wind and time are slowly taking them, one by one. The display was created by photographer Norma Holt and artist Ewa Nogiec to pay tribute to these and other Portuguese women's unsung contribution to the local community, Portuguese heritage and the lives of Portuguese fishing families.

"SITTING ON THE DOCK OF THE BAY"

In its fishing heyday, during the mid to late 1800s, 54 wharves served a mackerel fleet, 56 whaling ships, countless schooners, George's Bankers, Grand Bankers and the "Boston Boat," a ferry that carried passengers to and from Boston and Ptown. Back then, anywhere between 700 to 1000 ships vied for anchorage in the harbor at any given time. Provincetown was the wealthiest town per capita in the Commonwealth of Massachusetts, one of the wealthiest states, and it had the whaling and fishing industry to thank for that distinction.

Whether townsfolk were outfitting boats, hawking fish, selling canvases painted with triumphant or tragic stories of the lives of fishermen, performing plays about whaling ventures or feeding the fishermen and the tourists who came to look at the boats and play on the beach, all commerce in town was, in some way, dependent on the sea and on the success of the fishing trade. Much of it still is.

Today, from benches along MacMillan Pier, you can watch the comings and goings of draggers, trawlers, scallopers, clammers, long liners, lobster boats, ferry boats, party boats, house boats, sailboats, speedboats, dinghies and children floating in circles in candy-colored inflatable rings.

What a lovely way to spend a sunny afternoon.

PIRATES & SHARKS & ARTISTS, OH MY!

PIRATES

On the pier across from the Harbor Master's office, stands a large building that, for a couple of decades, was home to the Whydah Pirate Museum and the research vessel for underwater archaeological excavations of the shipwrecked pirate vessel, the *Whydah*.

The square-rigged, three-masted galley was constructed in London in 1715 and christened *Whydah* after the West African slave-trading port, the Kingdom of Whydah (Oidah). She sailed under the command of human trafficker Captain Prince who transported enslaved people from Africa to the Caribbean to be traded for precious metals, rum, sugar and spices like pimento and ginger, which he took back to England.

Enter handsome Samuel Bellamy. Born in Devon England in 1689, he took to the seas at a young age. His travels took him to Cape Cod in 1715, where he met the comely "Goody" Hallett, daughter of wealthy farmers who were none too keen on the prospect of having a seaman, poor as Job's turkey, as a son-in-law. So, Bellamy left the Cape in 1716, in search of fortune large enough to marry her on his return.

After he'd gone she bore his child, but it died shortly afterward, and she was accused of being a witch. When her sentence was up, she was banished to the outskirts of town.

Meanwhile, Bellamy was on his way to becoming the highest-earning pirate of all time, and at the same time, earning a nice-guy reputation. In 2008, *Forbes* magazine wrote that during the year or so that he was a pirate, Bellamy "plundered an estimated $120 million" from ships he captured. He became known as "Black Sam," because unlike most men at the time who wore white powdered wigs, Sam proudly sported his long, dark locks, tying them back with a satin bow. He and his men were quite proud of having captured a record 53 ships without killing a single person. His merciful reputation earned him a second nickname, the Prince of Pirates.

Captain Bellamy and his crew captured the *Whydah* in the Bahamas in 1717, on her return trip to England, her hold flush with more than four-and-a-half tons of gold, silver and other goods. Bellamy gave one of his smaller, slower ships to the *Whydah's* crew, set them free, and commandeered the *Whydah* as his flagship. By then, Black Sam captained a small flotilla manned by a crew of about 200 pirates made up of formerly enslaved Africans, displaced English sailors, Jamaican seamen, and men of various racial and ethnic backgrounds from Europe, Africa and the Americas.

Having captured the *Whydah* and made his fortune, Bellamy pointed his ship's bow north to return to Wellfleet and marry his lover, Goody. Just off the coast of Wellfleet the pirates were hit by a deadly April Nor'easter. At the time of its demise the *Whydah* was laden with the spoils of over 50 pillaged vessels—gold, silver and jewelry, some 60 cannons, and several barrels of Madeira wine they'd seized from the sloop *Mary Anne* earlier that same day. The storm sank the *Whydah* and damaged or wrecked the rest of the fleet. Bits of wreckage were strewn for miles along the coastline, drawing scavengers from several Cape towns.

Only nine people aboard Bellamy's vessels survived the gale. Six of the nine survivors were hanged for piracy. Two crew members who'd been previously enslaved were declared free, and the ship's young pilot, a 16-year-old Miskito Indian, was sold into slavery. Black Sam's body was never found.

Many of those who believed her to be a witch blamed Goody for conjuring up the storm in retribution for Sam's having left her pregnant and alone. By some accounts, she was seen gathering gold as it washed ashore and rumor has it she buried it somewhere near Wellfleet. Hopeful treasure hunters still seek it today.

The whereabouts of the sunken ship and her treasure of pirate gold remained unknown for more than 260 years until 1984, when it was discovered by underwater explorer, Barry Clifford. The wreck was authenticated by the finding of the ship's bell and a brass plate bearing the vessel's name and the date of her maiden voyage. The *Whydah* wreck is the first, and to date the only, Golden Age–pirate shipwreck to have been officially confirmed. In addition to the plaque and the bell, excavations of the ship's remains have uncovered a leg bone, several cannons, pistols, buckles and buttons, not to mention a raft of the stuff of pirate legends: gold, silver and pieces of eight.

WOMEN PIRATES

There were female pirates, too, of course, several of whom captained their own ships. They hailed from countries around the world. A few of the better-known include Lady Elizabeth Killigrew from England, as the Queen of Pirates, and Sayyida al-Hurra from Morocco. There were Anne Bonny and Mary Read who, separately, entered the world of pirating disguised as men. They ended up serving as shipmates aboard the same pirate vessel, and each took a pirate husband. The most successful woman pirate in history was Cheng Shih (one of several Anglicizations of her name), an attractive and ruthless former prostitute. At the peak of her reign of the South Pacific seas, she had more than 1,500 ships and 80,000 men under her command.

To date, there is only one woman from New England known to have been a pirate. In 1781, Rachel Wall, a housekeeper in Boston's Beacon Hill district, with the help of her husband, stole a ship, the *Essex*. Together with her husband's pals, the couple took to pirating the waters off the Boston coast. Their shtick had Rachel standing on the ship and hollering for help while her fellow pirates hid below decks. When passing sailors heard her calls of distress and rushed to her rescue, her co-conspirators swarmed up from below to rob and murder the good Samaritans before sinking the captive boat. All told, the Wall gang attacked 12 boats, absconded with thousands of dollars in valuables and cash and killed 24 unwitting sailors who'd generously offered their assistance. The pirates' boat was caught in a storm in 1782 and all aboard, excepting Rachel, were drowned.

Rachel returned to Boston, putting her sea pirating days behind her, adopting instead, a land-based method of thieving from boats. At night, she would slip nimbly aboard boats docked in the Boston Harbor and quietly plunder them while the crews slept. She was publicly hanged, in 1789, before thousands of onlookers on Boston Common and was the last woman to be hanged in Massachusetts.

SHARKS

Since 2021, the former pirate museum has housed the Atlantic White Shark Conservancy (AWSC), the leading nonprofit white shark research organization in the region. Their researchers track shark movements, including counting how many white sharks come to live seasonally off the shores of Cape Cod. The AWSC aims to raise public awareness in order to bring about a safer and more peaceful coexistence between humans and sharks. Being a keystone species, sharks are vital to the balance and maintenance of the marine ecosystems in which they live.

ARTISTS

The row of tiny shingled shacks lining MacMillan Pier are leased by local artists selling artwork you won't see on display in shops or galleries in town. The artists rent the shacks for a week or more at a time, so there's a constant changeover of work on display in the shacks throughout the entire spring, summer and fall. This arrangement offers a terrific opportunity to meet local artists and browse their work.

As we arrive back at Lopes Square, you can see that most of the eateries on the plaza offer quick to-go fare of ice cream, hot dogs, burgers, grinders and, of course, lobster rolls.

BATTLE OF THE LOBSTER ROLL

In this corner we have the lobster roll made with butter; in the opposite corner we have the contender, the lobster roll made with mayo. Fans of each have been known to come to blows vying for the titles of The Best or Most Authentic Lobster Roll.

Also entering into the fray are fans who toss celery, onion, or tomato into the ring, and those who top it with melted cheese. Still others add fire to the fracas by adding jalapeños or by venturing into the sometimes perilous territory of spicy curry or hot piri-piri. There are those who argue fervently whether or not a lobster sandwich should be served on a sub roll, a pita or in a wrap, and none can agree on whether a lobster sandwich of whichever sort should be served hot or cold. There is no end to the variations and opinions on the lobster roll, nor the raging debates they incite.

In his day, Governor William Bradford and the colonists were apologetic when they had no meat or fowl for the table and had only lobster on hand to serve guests. It was considered the "cockroach of the ocean" and was generally used for fishbait and as fertilizer in the fields. For ages, lobster was regarded as a poor man's protein. Served plain without a side of warm garlicky butter, of course, lobster was commonly fed to prisoners and indentured servants. Once the railroad was able to carry seafood to New York and inland destinations quickly, lobster began to be marketed as exotic—and priced as such. Lobster became eminently fashionable, and only the wealthy could afford to eat it. During WWII, the demand for high-end foods dropped and, once again, lobster was regarded as a cheap, readily available protein suitable for the masses—and military. Soldiers deployed overseas during the war were issued tinned lobster in their rations.

It was not uncommon in the past for lobsters to be three feet long and weigh as much as 40 pounds. In contrast, most lobsters on menus nowadays weigh between 1 and 2 pounds. Lobsters weighing 3–4 pounds are considered to be large. The largest lobster on record reached 3.5 feet long and clocked in at 44 pounds. It was estimated to have been 100 years old.

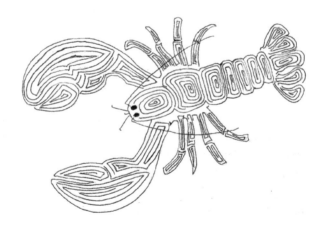

IF YOU DON'T LIKE FAST FOOD, EAT SNAILS

There is quite a range of local sea snails eaten on the Cape, and they have such fun names! We have moon snails, periwinkles, slipper shells, abalones, Kellet's whelk, channeled whelk and common whelk. Snails are voracious predators of quahogs, mussels, oysters and other shellfish, so our eating them helps protect the shellfish population, as well.

PORTUGUESE BAKERY

Pete Seeger once wrote a song about the Portuguese Bakery inspired by their tasty pastries. He performed the song live at the Town Hall one summer, alongside townie musicians of the Linguiça Band.

The original owners of the bakery brought with them the flavors and recipes of the Azores when they came over, so several of the pastries at this shop are more commonly found in the Azores than on mainland Portugal. When you taste these malasadas, rabandas, linguiça rolls, bolinhos de bacalhau or pasteis de nata, perhaps you, like Mr. Seeger, may find yourself wondering, "How can I keep from singing?"

KUNG FU DUMPLINGS

They have come and gone over the years, but from at least the 1940s there has nearly always been at least one Chinese restaurant operating in town. For the past many years, the Chinese dumpling restaurant at the end of this alley has been warming the cockles of locals, even through the long, frigid winter months and satisfying cravings of those looking for authentic Chinese food.

THE MAYFLOWER CAFÉ

In a town where it's hard to find a children's menu charging less than $15 for a simple bowl of buttered spaghetti or some fish sticks, this long-standing restaurant offers a whole array of kids' meals for a fraction of that. It's run by the friendly Janoplis family, the first of whom arrived in Provincetown from Greece in 1908 and opened this place in 1929. This cheerful little restaurant clearly has families in mind, with its long tables and broad menu aimed at pleasing diverse palates. From Portuguese specialties to Italian dishes, tacos, burgers, Southern fried chicken, pizzas, all sorts of hot and cold sandwiches, as well as salads, chicken, pork, beef, seafood, beer, wine and cocktails, this coach hits all the stops. Oh, and did I mention desserts? They're big on desserts.

The decor is pure Provincetown. There are Nancy Whorf murals on the walls, framed Jake Spencer caricatures around the dining room, and a proud Greek flag reigns over the bar. Its central location makes it easy to get to for families of hungry fishermen and visitors alike.

Just a tiara's throw away, across the street, is the Post Office Café and Cabaret. This is one of the venues in town where you can enjoy a truly-Provincetown experience: diners can get traditional Portuguese cuisine, sip Provincetown beer brewed just around the corner and watch a world class drag show, all at the same time.

TALL DRINKS, TALLER HEELS AND EVEN TALLER HAIR

"Drag doesn't change who you are, it reveals who you are," said RuPaul, who is perhaps the world's most famous drag artist. "I do not impersonate females. How many women do you know who wear seven-inch heels, four-foot wigs and skintight dresses? I don't dress like a woman, I dress like a drag queen."

The art of drag performance has been around in various iterations since ancient times. Although most drag queens are men, there are ever more transgender and cisgender women in the drag scene, some of whom belong to the growing dynasty of drag kings. Drag performers come from around the globe to perform in Provincetown, and each has their own take on the art form. Drag shows are usually comedy, often musical and, while some are family-friendly, many are bawdy enough to make Chaucer's Wife of Bath blush crimson. Performers may sing live, lip sync, dance, play instruments, do impersonations, or showcase any number of laudable talents. Performances are made up of something like a vigorous shake of Las Vegas, with added hints of burlesque or opera, and maybe some Moulin Rouge or Bollywood stirred in for good measure.

During the afternoons in high season, Provincetown's drag queens promote their shows on Commercial Street, donned in full regalia. Like an ostentation of peacocks, drag queens sashay up the street, enrobed in violescent dresses, constellations of rhinestones swirling across the bodice, singing show tunes and exchanging raillery with passersby, while a gathering crowd of curious tourists looks on.

It was also RuPaul who said, "We're all born naked, and the rest is drag."

Food for thought.

PENNY PATCH CANDIES

The same family of confectioners has been making small-batch fudge in this shop since 1973. They also sell saltwater taffy, and a carnival of candies whose flavors will transport you straight to a New England–penny-candy childhood—Coconut Long Boys, Bit-o-Honey, Lemon Heads, Sweet Tarts, Mary Janes, Razzles, Bazooka gum. Remember those?

CABOT'S CANDIES

Directly across the street is the famous Cabot's Candy factory and store. Cabot's began making candy in 1927 and, despite changing hands over the years, they're still pulling taffy on the same, reliable, German-made Hansella-Werke machine (just short of a century old!) and whipping up brittles, crunches and fudges in the traditional, tried-and-true ways. Their assortment of candies, some old-fashioned, others of a more recent vintage, come in more colors than there are names for. Oooo, those enticing smells!

TOWN HALL 2

We again find ourselves in front of Town Hall as we head up-along Commercial.

It was in Provincetown's Town Hall that the married lives of 900 gay and 25 straight couples began in 2004. The previous year, 19 marriage license applications were submitted, all for straight couples. Massachusetts was the first state in the country to legalize gay marriage and the sixth jurisdiction in the world to do so. After the closely followed Massachusetts Supreme Judicial Court Ruling on the 17th of May, 2004, regarding equal marriage, same-sex couples arrived in droves, from across the nation, to tie the knot and feed one another slices of rainbow-colored wedding cake in political-trend-setting Provincetown.

AHOY THERE, MATEY!

Although pairing pirates are not likely to have fed one another cake during their commitment ceremonies, it was not uncommon for them to exchange rings and drink jugsful of 'bumbo' (rum mixed with water, sugar and nutmeg or cinnamon).

"Matelotage," or civil unions between male pirates, was most common during the 17th and early 18th centuries. The unions were generally not recorded in logbooks, so just how many pirates paired up is not certain. In such a dangerous occupation it was useful to have an arrangement with a fellow shipmate to protect each other during shipboard brawls and in battles with other vessels. The civil unions also offered financial security, allowing for the sharing of income and the assurance that one would inherit property of his partner in the event of death. These lifelong, committed companionships were inherently intimate, and while some were platonic or fraternal rather than romantic, others were overtly amorous bunkmates. Being matelot lovers did not imply monogamy. In addition to sharing plunder and property, matelotage partners were known to share male lovers, female lovers or wives with one another, as well.

The civil union ceremonies were witnessed, supported and celebrated by their pirate shipmates. Upon the death of one of the men, the captain of the ship was responsible for upholding the inheritance agreements and ensuring his property was distributed accordingly. When a pirate in a matelotage arrangement was married to a woman, it was not uncommon, upon his death, for his belongings to be divided between his wife and his matelot partner.

Although among men at sea close friendships and sexual relationships existed, publicly declared unions such as these, especially romantic ones, appear to have been conducted exclusively between male pirates rather than between men (or women) in other seafaring occupations. During the period of time that matelotage was most prevalent, the majority of the world's navies, as well as the governments of many countries and churches around the globe, forbade homosexuality outright, oftentimes declaring it punishable by death.

"THOSE LAZY, HAZY, CRAZY DAYS OF SUMMER"

In the words of Michael Cunningham, from his book, *Land's End:*

> Among the strollers and shoppers on a summer afternoon, it is not unusual to see, within a fifty-foot radius, all of the following: a crowd of elderly tourists who have come for the day on a tour bus or have disembarked from a cruise ship anchored in the harbor; a

pack of muscle boys on their way to the gym; a vacationing mother and father shepherding their exhausted and fussy children through the shops; a pair of lesbians with a dachshund in a rainbow collar; two gay dads in chinos and Izod shirts pushing their adopted daughter in a stroller; a dread-locked and ostentatiously tattooed young woman who works at the head shop; a man dressed, very convincingly, as Celine Dion; elderly women doing errands; several closeted school teachers from various parts of the country who come to Provincetown for two weeks every year to escape the need for secrecy; several weary fishermen coming home from their stints on a scallop boat; a bond trader in three-hundred-dollar sandals, up for the weekend from New York; and a brigade of furious local kids on skateboards, seeing how close they can come to the pedestrians without actually knocking one over, a stunt that is usually but not always successful.

KING HIRAM MASONIC LODGE

When we eat with our Brothers, we digest more than the meal.
— Bryce's Law

We come now to the corner of Masonic Street and the home of King Hiram Masonic Lodge. Over the years, local men—tavern keepers, innkeepers, grocery store owners, chandlers, ship owners, mariners, carpenters, church wardens, bank presidents, salt producers, lumbermen, purveyors of foods and goods of all sorts, politicians of various stripes—have met on the first Monday of each month since the Lodge was first chartered by famed nightrider Paul Revere in 1795.

REVERE, HIS RIDE, HIS RUM TODDY

In Henry Wadsworth Longfellow's poem *The Midnight Ride of Paul Revere*, which immortalized the ride in anapestic tetrameter, there's no mention of rum. By other historic accounts of the evening though, young Paul may have been sailing three sheets to the wind by the time the British caught up with him that night.

As the British laid course from Boston toward Lexington, intent on capturing American revolutionaries John Hancock and Samuel Adams before heading to Concord to destroy the rebels' stash of military supplies, Paul Revere was dispatched to raise the alarm and thwart their plans. Revere stationed himself down by the river with a clear view of the church tower so he could see the lamps as they were lit, signaling to him which way the British were traveling: "One if by land, two if by sea."

Once he saw the second lamp lit, Revere set off on his steed at such a speed that "the spark struck out by that steed, in his flight,/ Kindled the land into flame with its heat," according to the poem. That night, Revere's compatriot, William Dawes was sent on the same mission, though along a different route toward Hancock and Adams in Lexington.

Also not mentioned in the poem is that the pace set by his steed apparently gave Revere such great confidence in his lead on the British that, despite "the fate of the nation riding that night" on the outcome of his precarious mission, he stopped off for a couple of quick ones at his friend's tavern in Medford town. Isaac Hall's Medford tavern was famous for the potency of his rum, which was "strong enough to make a rabbit bite a bulldog," writes historian Rebecca Rupp.

Longfellow's poem says Revere's mission was to travel through the night, calling out his message of warning to "every Middlesex village and farm" between Boston and Lexington, and across the land as far as Concord. In the poem it is Revere who is given complete credit for bellowing out across the countryside, "The British are coming!" thus, saving the day. But, as we know, that's not quite how things turned out.

As planned, Revere and Dawes met up at Lexington and alerted Hancock and Adams that the Brits were on the way. After a fortifying meal and more drinks, Revere and Dawes and Dr. Samuel Prescott, another comrade, hopped on their horses: destination Concord. Unfortunately, before they'd gone far, they were detained by a roving British patrol. Dawes and Prescott escaped but Revere was marched, horseless, back to Lexington at gunpoint.

Of the three men, only Prescott managed to reach Concord in time to give the warning. But the mission was a success! By the time the British marched into town, a hearty contingent of rebels was assembled, armed, and awaiting them. That night, the Battles of Lexington and Concord began, kicking off the American Revolutionary War.

REVERE'S RUM TODDY

"Rum, sugar and water, heated by plunging red-hot poker into the mixture."

— Rum toddy as Paul Revere may have had it in Medford, from
History of the World in 6 Glasses by Tom Standage.

SPEAKING OF BRAVE NIGHTRIDERS

A few nights after Revere's legendary ride, 16-year-old Sybil Ludington was entrusted by her father, General Ludington, with a similar mission–though double the distance (and she didn't get caught). She set out on a night ride of over 40 miles round trip to alert the rebels of Danbury, Connecticut, of the imminent attack on their town by British troops. The British managed to set the town ablaze, but having received her advanced warning the colonists were successful in gathering enough rebels to force the Redcoats to retreat from the area. For her courage and bravery, Sybil received commendation from George Washington, and a statue of her was erected along her route of the night of April 26, 1777.

THE BATTLESHIP *SOMERSET*

Incidentally, the night of Revere's famous ride, the British warship *Somerset* was in the harbor. Longfellow describes the ship in his poem about that night:

> Just as the moon rose over the bay,
> Where swinging wide at her moorings lay
> The *Somerset*, British man-of-war:
> A phantom ship, with each mast and spar
> Across the moon, like a prison bar,
> And a huge black hulk, that was magnified
> By its own reflection in the tide.

The *Somerset's* night watchman didn't notice him row past however, and Revere was able to carry on with his mission unimpeded. After the battles that night at Lexington and Concorde, the *Somerset* was instrumental in helping British forces escape.

Later that year, the *Somerset*, which was helping to enforce the British blockade of Provincetown and the Cape, sank in the waters near the tip of the Cape during a brutal gale. Of the 400-plus crew members, 21 died in a lifeboat that capsized as they tried to make the shore. According to the New England Historical Society, the rest of the enemy forces were housed and fed in the homes of Truro's 250 families that night.

Massachusetts officials offered the ship's officers a lift by ship to Boston, but forcibly marched the remaining 400-odd lower-ranking men, though many of them were injured, 120 miles into Boston in the November cold. They were kept under armed guard provided by towns along the way—Eastham, Harwich, Yarmouth, Barnstable and Sandwich. It fell to the towns to shelter and feed the captives, as the crew's food stores had been lost or drenched in seawater. Due in part to the British blockade of food and goods to the Cape—in which the *Somerset* had participated—many of those who were called upon to feed and house the British prisoners didn't have enough food on hand to do so. When he was asked how the townsfolk were to feed the prisoners, the Governor's Council responded, "If you have not bread for the prisoners let them live without, as many better men have done before them."

Some of the prisoners managed to escape along the way, but most were brought all the way into Boston, where they were detained aboard a ship in Boston Harbor. Several were exchanged for American prisoners and a dozen or more who opted to swap sides and fight for the rebel cause were inducted into the American forces.

THE A-HOUSE

As we walk down narrow Masonic Place, it is easy to imagine this as the stagecoach stop and inn that it was, back when the stagecoach made the trip all the way out to Provincetown.

The business and patronage at the Atlantic House (usually shortened to the A-House now) has continued to change with the times. Its stage has hosted luminaries the likes of Ella Fitzgerald, Billie Holiday, Ertha Kitt and Stella Brooks, and its list of past guests includes Tennessee Williams and Eugene O'Neill. It is now a collection of several disparate bars, each with its own particular mood and clientèle. Most of the patrons are gay men and other members of the LGBTQ+ community.

At the end of the lane we'll go up the handful of steps that let onto the sidewalk on Bradford Street. Our route turns right now and leads downhill toward Gosnold Street. As we approach the intersection, you may catch a wave of appetizing smells drifting from the tall cream-colored building across the street at the AIDS Support Group.

THE AIDS SUPPORT GROUP OF CAPE COD

The AIDS Support Group originated in Provincetown in 1985, formed by a team of townsfolk who came together to provide meals and life-sustaining support services to locals with HIV/AIDS. In its early days, the organization's founders delivered meals and necessities out of the back of a Ford Escort. The organization offered education about the illness with the goal of reducing further spread. The support group now serves about 400 people across the Cape and the islands of Martha's Vineyard and Nantucket. The group's ongoing efforts assist people who are living with HIV to live longer, healthier lives.

The small kitchen produces hot, chef-prepared meals five days per week, as well as managing a food box–delivery program so clients can prepare nutritious meals themselves at home.

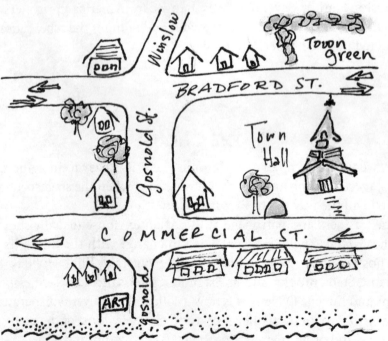

We cross at the zebra here and start up the hill on Winslow Street.

WINSLOW STREET

Edward Winslow, a former salt-producer from England, along with his family and servants, sailed from Delft Haven aboard the *Speedwell* to Southampton, England, where the *Speedwell* rendezvoused with the *Mayflower*. From there, the two ships planned to convoy across the Atlantic. After several false starts, the *Speedwell* was declared unseaworthy, and 20 circumspect *Speedwell* passengers opted to give the ocean crossing a miss and decamped for home. The other 11 passengers, including the Winslow household, piled onto the already-cramped *Mayflower* for the slow, snug journey across the wide Atlantic. As for the *Mayflower* passengers, in the characteristically optimistic words of William Bradford, "Now being compact together in one ship, they put to sea again with a prosperous wind."

That winter, most of the passengers and crew of the *Mayflower* took ill and half of them died. Winslow's wife, Elizabeth, was among them, as was the husband of Susanna White. Susanna was the mother of baby Peregrine (meaning "traveler" or "pilgrim"), who was born aboard the *Mayflower* while the ship lay anchored in the bay of Provincetown. He was the first of the colonists' children to be born after the ship had made landfall. One sunny day in May, Edward married Susanna; theirs was the first wedding to be celebrated in the new colony.

Winslow wrote prolifically of the events and the explorations of the colonists. It is his and Governor William Bradford's written accounts that lend us the only surviving first-hand insights into the happenings and lives of those who settled Plimoth Colony and their interactions with Native Americans they met there. Winslow served three terms as Governor of Plimoth and was in great demand for his diplomatic skills and his ability to liaise between white settlers and local Native Americans, as well as between the colonists and their financial backers in England. He made several trips back to England to negotiate on behalf of the colonists.

Oliver Cromwell, after overthrowing the monarchy, took a shine to Winslow and appointed him to various parliamentary committees, including one overseeing the confiscation of property from dethroned royalty. In 1655, Cromwell, with the goal of colonizing the islands, assigned Winslow to go on a military expedition to the West Indies. For his efforts, Cromwell offered to make Winslow Governor of Jamaica. The trip proved a fatal decision for Winslow, who died en route to the Caribbean.

"WAMBLING" HOUSES

The benefic migration of the house now roosting at number 4 Winslow was mentioned during our walk in the East End. *Mayflower* descendant, abolitionist, Freemason and Universalist minister, Reverend Ryder, and his family, donated their land for the construction of the town's new administrative building, and relocated their home here.

Some accounts have it that this house became one of several in Provincetown to offer a safe haven for people fleeing slavery. There's said to be a kitchen, including a stove, in the cellar where people cooked meals while in hiding.

As generous as it was for the Ryders to move their house to make way for the construction of Town hall, moving one's home was not unprecedented—or even unusual—says Mary Heaton Vorse in *Time and the Town*. "Formerly, every summer one saw houses moving cumbrously down the front street." Not only were many houses ferried across the water from the Long Point settlement to take up a new postal code in Provincetown, but even houses on shore moved about more than is customary in most places. Vorse goes on to write:

> People in Provincetown do not regard houses as stationary objects.
> A man will buy a piece of dune land above the town and a cottage
> on the front shore, and presently up the hill toils the little house.
> Or he buys a piece of shore front and a cottage on the back street,
> and presently the house is wambling along to take its place on the
> water.

Our walk now takes us uphill for a stint, and I cannot think of a better way for getting us up a hill than the lively, upbeat dance tune called "Provincetown Rag" by John Wiley Nelson, more widely known as The Rev.

Provincetown Rag

Well there's a place that you should go,
it's out at the end of the earth;
Gotta travel both east and west
if you wanna get your money's worth;
You gotta go across the canal, thru the pines,
over the sand dunes, too;
You'll find the time of your life
is out there waiting for you.
Isn't it time to dance the night away, hey, hey;
Move your feet to the beat,
you gotta feel it swing and sway;
You know it, Come on now,
teach 'em how, Mama's got a brand new bag;
So show it: 1, 2, 3, 4, Doin' the Provincetown Rag.

Once you get there you're gonna find,
this is where the rainbow ends;
You're gonna count Portuguese fishermen
and drag queens among your friends;
You'll throw away your coat and tie
and your dress up clothes, and put on a laid back style;
And the food and the music and the people
are all gonna make you smile.
So what are you waiting for, come on out,
we'll be looking for you;
There's clams and oysters and mussels and cod
cooking in a stew;
We got Billy on bass, Jerry on guitar,
Rev's brought his mouth harps, too;
We're planning on keeping it going
till we give the Devil his due.

— From the 2022 album, *Another Day in Paradise.*

PROVINCETOWN HIGH SCHOOL

The clock above the entrance to the former high school is stopped at 10:30, a time when students would have been in morning classes back when the high school was still open. At its peak in 1967, a couple hundred kids, give or take, passed beneath this clock every school day. There are far fewer families with children in Provincetown these days; the neighborhoods are quieter now than they once were. The graduation of the final senior class in 2013 saw eight girls take the stage at Town Hall to receive their diplomas before a packed audience of family members and alumni.

At one point the school was the target of a serial firebug, whose obsession was a terrifying threat to this town built of wooden buildings. When the high school was set on fire, firefighters from four towns raced to help put it out. The whole community pulled together and were able to rebuild the school in time for the start of the school year the following fall.

The hallways in the building are now filled with the pitter-patter of feet belonging to children in kindergarten through the eighth grade. Upper classmen travel up-Cape to attend high school.

HIGH POLE HILL

Provincetown's VFW was named for 22-year-old Lewis A. Young, who died during the 1918 flu epidemic while serving in France in WWI. He died 27 days before armistice. Lewis Young's father was the first president of the Provincetown Art Museum. His mother, Anne, was president of the Nautilus Club and a founding member of the ladies' Research Club of Mayflower Descendants. The Nautilus Club was originally organized in 1907 by seven women whose mission was both civic and personal progress and development. The club was active for over 100 years. For decades it was headquartered at the location that is currently the Boatslip. The Nautilus Club sign is still nailed to the wall where there is now a bar.

During its long, productive history, in addition to installing a water fountain and horse-watering trough downtown, the club helped children impacted by both sides of the Spanish Civil War. They set up a local visiting nurses association and worked to prevent cruelty to animals. The women hosted lectures, sponsored an annual flower show and held a bake sale fundraiser on the front lawn of the Unitarian Universalist Church every summer.

The Research Club of Mayflower Descendants was formed in 1910 and made up of women who could adequately demonstrate the appropriate genealogical lineage. The original mission of the club was to restore the Winthrop Street Cemetery and to research local history in order to erect commemorative markers around town. With this latter goal in mind, they began to collect historical items and documents. As the pile of historical artifacts began to grow, they resolved to open a museum. They purchased the Lancy Mansion (a four-story, 23–room mansion near the center of town) and moved in. Rear Admiral MacMillan contributed items from his expeditions, not the least of which were a musk ox and a white wolf, the preserved head of a walrus, and, curiously, one and a half polar bears. The Research Club opened its museum doors in 1924.

Eventually, the collection grew beyond the club's ability to manage, and the whole lot was entrusted to the Cape Cod Pilgrim Memorial Association, the entity also responsible for the Pilgrim Monument. When a new building was erected atop High Pole Hill to house the Museum, the combined collection of the Research Club and the Cape Cod Pilgrim Memorial Association was installed, going on public display in 1962.

THE MUSEUM

"We are all pilgrims here," observes K. David Weidner, Ph.D., the current Executive Director of the Pilgrim Monument and Provincetown Museum. The Pilgrim Monument, founded in 1892 as the Cape Cod Pilgrim Memorial Association, is the oldest nonprofit organization on Cape Cod and was created to educate the public about Provincetown's unique place in American history, including correcting common misconceptions surrounding the landing of the *Mayflower*. As Provincetown-phile Harry Kemp wrote (and promptly mailed to the governor of every state, to further make his point), "Not on Plymouth Rock but on Provincetown Sand,/ The Pilgrim Fathers first came to land."

The museum is currently being reimagined and renovated to reflect more comprehensive perspectives of Provincetown's history, including the vital roles of the Native American and LGBTQ+ communities. In collaboration with local Wampanoag leaders, the Museum works to better represent and honor Wampanoag history and Native American presence from before the *Mayflower's* landing on Native lands, up through the present day. In conjunction with LGBTQ+ townies, museum displays are being created to discuss the AIDS epidemic and the cultural, political and historical influences and achievements of the LGBTQ+ community.

THE MONUMENT

PRESIDENT THEODORE ROOSEVELT LAYS THE CORNERSTONE

Speeches were made, patriotic songs were sung, babies were kissed and a time capsule was laid in the foundation of the Monument. Arriving that day to lay the cornerstone of the Monument, as part of an elaborate ceremony arranged by Provincetown's King Hiram Masonic Lodge, was fellow Freemason President Teddy Roosevelt. He glided majestically into town on his splendid presidential yacht (named the *Mayflower*, of course!) on August 20, 1907.

The US Navy's entire Atlantic Fleet crammed into the Provincetown harbor to welcome him. Fifteen hundred Marines in spiffy uniforms were dispatched to control exuberant crowds lining the streets. The entire town was festooned in American flags and red, white and blue bunting. Cocktail and tea parties were in full swing on front porches along the parade route as the President and his wife passed by in a carriage, winding through the streets and up the hill to the building site of the Pilgrim Monument.

A variety of items were placed within a copper time capsule and cemented into a cavity in the cornerstone. Among them: a copy of the Bible, copies of the Mayflower Compact, William Bradford's *Of Plimoth Plantation*, the town's bylaws. Also added were several souvenir booklets and historic stones—one from the quay in Delft Haven from which sailed the *Speedwell*, one cut from the ancient church at Austerfield where William Bradford was baptized. And, interestingly, an annual fiscal report of the United Fruit Co. (now Chiquita Banana). This last document would seem unusual to include, were it not for the fact that the company's exceedingly wealthy owner, Lorenzo Dow Baker, had contributed pots of money toward the construction of the Monument. (He is credited with introducing bananas to Boston and the Cape, earning him a gilded crust or two, along with the nickname, Banana Baron.)

Even so, the document stands out as an odd choice given that the President's speech that day was, in essence, a vigorous tirade against the greed and misdoings of corporations. At full-throttle into his trust-busting phase at that point, TR denounced the "malefactors of great wealth" that subject employees to low pay and poor treatment. The President also lambasted the blatant disregard for the health of the environment by corporations single-mindedly intent on the pursuit of riches. The United Fruit Co., by that time operating banana plantations in Jamaica, the Dominican Republic and Latin America, was already on its way to becoming a veritable poster child for the type of corporate gluttony and misconduct the President's speech condemned. One wonders if TR was aware of the document in the copper box and the actions of the corporation that the papers represented.

The time capsule was duly embedded into the foundation in accordance with Masonic ritual and tradition, using a trowel that, to this day, resides in the archives of Provincetown's Masonic Lodge. To wrap up his trip to Provincetown, President Roosevelt, his wife and their extensive entourage, were honored with a lavish luncheon, more pomp and more speeches. Author Debra Lawless details the meal in her remarkable account, *Provincetown: A History of Artists and Renegades in a Fishing Village*:

> Appropriately, the meal began with chowder and breadsticks and moved on to fish au gratin and chicken à la Maryland with green peas and Delmonico potatoes. A lobster salad, cold boiled ham, cold turkey and smoked tongue followed, along with rolls. For dessert, there were assorted cakes, ice creams and sherbets; watermelon, cantaloupe, grapes and plums; and, finally, coffee and iced tea.

PRESIDENT TAFT DEDICATES THE MONUMENT

Upon the completion of the Monument three years on, the dedication celebration became an entire "Monument Week" jammed with festivities, culminating in the arrival of President Taft on August 5, 1910. To tiny Provincetown for the grand event that day, were delivered over 3,300 people by special trains, 1,500 more via steamship, as well as 1,000 by automobile, and one American President and his wife, by yacht.

Like President Roosevelt before him, President Taft traveled to Provincetown aboard the presidential yacht, the *Mayflower*. On this occasion Taft, too, was greeted by a contingent of Marines in Dress Blues and the entire Atlantic Naval Fleet. Street vendors hawking kitschy souvenirs and salted peanuts, plus an organ grinder and his monkey added to the carnival-like mood. Just as the presidential yacht entered the harbor, the town was rocked by an absolutely thunderous 21-gun salute, let loose simultaneously from eight enthusiastic battleships. As one voice, an approving cheer of thousands on shore went up, accompanied by a wild flurry of flags.

The dedication ceremony was held in front of a crowd of 2,500, crammed into bleachers at the base of the Monument. The dedication ceremony, as with the laying of the cornerstone, was orchestrated by the Mason Lodge, after which Freemason brother Taft and his wife were swept off to the Town hall to have a lunch with hundreds of guests. The sumptuous, flower-bedecked banquet was served by daughters of the town dressed in frost-white dresses. The meal was followed by a ball which lasted well into the night. Once again, I defer to Debra Lawless's comprehensive rundown of the memorable evening:

> The meal opened with lobster stew. The diners continued at a leisurely pace, nibbling iced olives, small sweet pickles and small dinner biscuit crackers. They waded through salmon cutlets and peas with sliced cucumbers and tomatoes, salmon and peas being a traditional Fourth of July dish. A *vol-au-vent au salpicon* followed. This, sometimes served with a Duff Gordon sherry (although in this case it was not), was a favorite dish on the banquet circuit at the time. It consisted of diced meat mixed with a sauce fed into a baked patty shell that was then covered with more sauce. The main course was yet to come: cold roast tenderloin, a vegetable salad, roast turkey with chestnut stuffing, potato salad, smoked tongue and thin-sliced ham. The fifty-two-year-old Taft chewed through it all, occasionally dabbing his walrus mustache with a napkin. More crackers and cheese, a harlequin—vanilla frozen pudding with burnt almonds and cherries—a bisque glacée, sherbets, assorted cake, fruit and coffee followed.

UP THE TOWER

Built on the spot where the first Town Hall ("Town House") burned down in 1877, the Pilgrim Monument is the tallest all-granite structure in the country. Its design was inspired by the Torre del Mangia, built in the 1300s in Siena, Tuscany. Some 116 stone steps and 60 stone ramps whorl dizzily, ever-upward within its walls, eventually letting onto a wide stone deck.

From high atop the tower, we get a surreal view of Provincetown usually reserved for passing clouds and osprey on the hunt. We can clearly see that the tower beneath our feet rises, straight and proud, from the center of a ginormous cake. The edges of the cake are sculpted in vigorously whipped blue and white icing. Off to our left, a sun-sand alchemy forms a herd of huge golden-haired camels in slumber, hump to bump, covering about half of the cake, from the foamy edge of blue frosting inland. The breeze ruffling the camels' tawny fur looks remarkably like sand blowing across great, heaving sand dunes. The center of the cake, just below the tower, as well as the rest of the cake, is swirled in green frosting, right down to the frothy blue edge. Below us, tumbling off to our right, to the edge of the cake, lies a jumble of discarded giant's teeth, carelessly strewn along the ground, some crooked, some pointy, some square, and looking for all the world like clusters of ivory-white wooden houses clinging to one another at the very edge of the would-be sea. I don't know about you, but I'm feeling a bit lightheaded; let's descend.

THE *SPEEDWELL*

Some historians reckon the *Speedwell* may not have been the lemon it was purported to be. They suspect that the Dutch government, having its own eye on the piece of land (now Manhattan) to which the *Mayflower* and *Speedwell* were headed, may have engaged in dilatory tactics, intentionally scuppering the English venture by encouraging the *Speedwell's* captain to hobble the ship in order to delay or divert the journey. Whether intentional or not, the lag-time in setting out played a part in the outcome of the *Mayflower's* voyage—and resulted in the Dutch, rather than the British, becoming the first Europeans to settle the territory that is now home to The Big Apple.

Given the erratic route of the *Speedwell* and her sister ship *Mayflower*, it is easy to see why Provincetown's Pilgrim Monument is only one of several monuments dedicated to the *Mayflower*, her passengers and crew. Each of the port cities from which the *Speedwell* and/or *Mayflower* departed—Delft Haven in The Netherlands; as well as London, Southampton, Dartmouth and Plymouth in England—have put up markers commemorating the voyagers. In Shropshire, England, there's a marker in honor of the four little More children who were taken from their mother and shipped overseas, without parents, and without their mother's knowledge or consent. British towns where other *Mayflower* passengers and crew had lived, as well as cities and towns around the world that have connections to those aboard the *Mayflower* have erected memorials of various sorts.

Heading back across Winslow Street now, we'll follow the path in the front of the high school, around the building and across the lot, to a marker near the fork at the top of the hill.

RESIDENT REVENANT IN THE KITCHEN

From her position at the crest of Mill Hill reigns an elegant captain's mansion, now the Crowne Pointe Hotel and Spa. The house was built by the son of a whaling captain who, it's said, still haunts the place, along with a ghost who potters about the kitchen, opening and closing cupboards. Occasionally, a worried female spirit comes to guests in the night begging them to tell her where her husband, the Captain, has gotten to.

THE GIFFORD HOUSE

Across Bradford from the Crowne Pointe Hotel, stands the Gifford House, an old inn rife with legends of its own, which have stacked up during the 150-plus years of guests rooming, dining and clubbing here. Visiting presidents Ulysses S. Grant, Theodore Roosevelt, and William Howard Taft are said to have been among the guests who have come to the Gifford, adding to the lineup of prominent guests who've made their appearance and presence felt in Provincetown.

Taking the street to the right of Crowne Pointe and going a ways down the hill on Prince Street, we come to the Roman Catholic Church of St. Peter the Apostle. It was named for Saint Peter, the patron saint of fishermen, locksmiths, builders and stonemasons, ship builders and shoemakers.

ST. PETER THE APOSTLE CATHOLIC CHURCH

Unlike many churches that have been ministering to their flock for almost two hundred as this one has, the church building itself is only a few

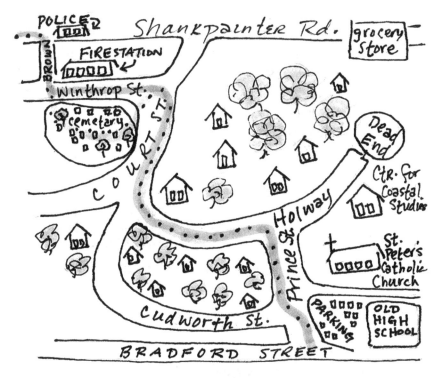

years old. Well before the Church of St. Peter the Apostle was built here in 1874, Catholics in town held mass at the King Hiram Masonic Lodge. The building standing here now is much newer than 1874, however. The church had to be entirely rebuilt after a devastating fire in the winter of 2005. Local firefighters, many of whom were themselves parishioners here, fought desperately in the freezing cold for hours to save the church, alongside firefighters from several Cape towns. In spite of their heroic efforts, the building was lost. The old church bell was cracked in the fire and now stands as a silent witness on the cement pedestal near the front door.

ABOLITION AND CROSS-BURNING IN TOWN

Two abolitionist groups sprang up in Provincetown in the 1830s, one run by and for women, one by and for men. The Provincetown Abolitionist Society met once per year, held public lectures and handed out flyers to aid in their anti-slavery efforts. They created a library to house relevant anti-slavery publications and materials. The group's goal was "to petition congress to put an end to the domestic slave trade and abolish slavery in all those portions of our common country."

These efforts toward racial equality did not mean that the Outer Cape became free from racism and inequality. In the mid-1920s, both Provincetown and Truro saw cross burnings by Klansmen—one right in front of this Catholic church. Catholics and Jews, local Portuguese, Greeks, Irish and Italians, as well as other immigrants and people of color, were frequently targets of slurs and racial bias.

Several Klansmen participating in cross burnings were suspected to be members of influential families in town, including some holding elected office. The cross burnings set the towns of Truro and Provincetown on edge. Neighbor became suspicious, fearful, resentful of neighbor. Lines were drawn as to where to shop, dine and socialize along racial, religious and ethnic lines. This was followed by a push-back to these tactics. After the KKK burning of the cross in front of the Saint Peter's Catholic Church, the Portuguese community rallied and formed the politically minded Saint Peter's Club. They actively registered voters and organized their community behind Portuguese candidates. As a result, the 1925 election saw unprecedented numbers of Portuguese residents elected to top policy-making posts.

FOOD AS SYMBOLIC

In the Catholic faith, as in many other faiths, the Eucharist offered at Mass is one of many examples of how food is used in ways other than to provide physical sustenance. The body and blood of Christ, in the form of wafers/bread and wine/juice, are blessed and then eaten to nourish the soul, rather than the body. As the name Holy Communion implies, the ritual serves to strengthen spiritual bonds between participants, as well as with the Divine. Communion, not calories, is the purpose.

WATER, PRECIOUS WATER

"Thousands have lived without love, none without water."
— W.H. Auden

One of the two operational water towers in town stretches 90 feet above Mount Gilboa, upon which it stands. It holds 2.6 million gallons of Pamet Lens aquifer water. The second, located on Winslow Street, has a capacity of 3.8 million gallons. Together, they meet the town's current (2022) demand of 650,000–700,000 gallons per day, on average, according to the Provincetown Water Department. Combined, the two towers contain a 3-day water supply.

HOLWAY STREET

The building just below St. Peter's church was formerly a Catholic school run by Cuban nuns who were brought in by St Peter's church. It is now the world-renowned Center for Coastal Studies, founded by Stormy Mayo (father to Josiah, whom we met earlier hoisting his lobster-man friend back in the boat after encountering a whale, and whose family runs the Cape Codder guesthouse we saw in the East End.) The Center's focus is on researching sustainable solutions to challenges facing coastal communities and marine ecosystems, as well as the rescue of entangled marine animals. They also educate the public about stewardship of marine coastal environments. Their work is vital to the health of the fishing and tourism industries on Cape Cod, as well as to the waters that sustain them.

From here, we will make a left, taking us along Holway toward Court Street, where we'll turn a right to make our way toward the Winthrop Cemetery.

As we meander through these quiet streets in this picturesque neighborhood, we pass the homes of workers who have long been the very backbone of Provincetown: librarians, grocers, construction workers, fishing families, wait staff, firefighters, whalers, dairy farmers, shop keepers, cooks, musicians, police officers, house painters, school teachers, nurses. We pass unassuming houses, abuzz within—a beauty parlor around the corner from a barber shop, a handyman's garage, a small guesthouse, a former package store, the Old Shirt Factory, a carpenter's workshop, a weaver's studio and a journalist's office.

COURT STREET

In the large house on the rounded corner of Holway and Court lived a prominent judge and his family of future judges (whence the name Court Street perhaps?). Judge Welsh was the first of multiple generations of Welshes to sit on the bench in Barnstable County, altogether spanning more than 100 years. Two of the many recognizable faces who appeared before Judge Welsh included Eugene O'Neill and Harry Kemp. Known to the rest of nation as the "Tramp Poet," and the "Freight Car Poet," in Provincetown, where he preferred to sign his name with the feather of a seagull, Kemp went by "Poet of the Dunes." Neither O'Neill nor Kemp was a stranger to the inside of a court room. Generally, O'Neill was hauled in for disorderly conduct during drinking bouts. Kemp, in addition to appearing before Judge Welsh, appeared in an English court, making international headlines for his arrest as a stowaway on an ocean liner.

Harry Kemp had a knack and a penchant for self-promotion. He liked to stand out and actively cultivated a reputation for being eccentric. He lived in a shack in the dunes and would wander over the sandy hillocks and into town, dressed dramatically in a swirling black cape. In 1913, wanting to travel to England, but without the money for the fare (or perhaps looking for a hoboing adventure on a boat similar to those he'd had on rail cars out West), Kemp snuck aboard the *Oceanic*. He was discovered, ticket-less, in a first-class cabin, detained, confined to the galley and forced to wash dishes for the duration of the trip. Once ashore in Southampton, England, he was tried and convicted of embezzlement of first class passage. He was sentenced to solitary confinement for three weeks at hard labor, waxing thread at Winchester Prison. Having previously made his name as a vagabond poet, his image was only further enhanced by his stowaway stunt. Kemp's internationally publicized arrest on the *Oceanic* and subsequent imprisonment hijacked headlines and helped to further spread his name around the globe. He died in 1960, at age 76, while living at Tasha Hill in the East End of Provincetown.

Court Street wanders past Judge Welsh's former home and arrives at the back side of Winthrop Cemetery before gently curving around to the entrance on Winthrop Street.

WINTHROP CEMETERY

About 600 headstones are cradled in quiet crevices and corners on the wooded hillsides of Winthrop Street Cemetery, the oldest cemetery in town. The graves of town founders, Revolutionary rebels, and townsfolk from faded eras lie here, along with the town's oldest permanently marked grave, that of Deseir (Desire) Cowing, dated 1723. Prominently placed on a gentle slope within the cemetery and encircled by a small fence is a brass-on-stone marker dedicated to *Mayflower* passengers who died en route and while in the harbor at Provincetown.

SMALLPOX

Near the Court and Winthrop entrance is a memorial dedicated in 2015 to those who succumbed to smallpox. Killing many millions around the globe, it was one of the deadliest diseases in human history. It was also one of the oldest, dating back at least 3,000 years. Smallpox made several passes through Provincetown in the 1800s, each worse than the one before. Although a vaccine was developed as early as 1796, it was not widely available nor readily embraced, allowing the disease to continue to spread, taking its toll here and elsewhere.

The worst bout of smallpox in Provincetown arrived in 1872. As people were fearful of social repercussions after reporting the illness, an accurate number of cases was not documented. Twenty-two infected people were banished to the "Pest House," which was no more than a rudimentary shack built off in the woods for that purpose. Fourteen of the patients died and were immediately buried, without religious rites or mourning relatives in attendance, for fear of spreading the illness. Given the appalling conditions in the shack and the limited food and medical supplies on hand, it is remarkable that Dr. Horatio Newton and his nurse were able to save even six lives.

So stigmatized was the illness, that numbers rather than names were assigned to those who died. Near where the hut once stood, six of the original 14 stone markers, each, eerily, about the length and size of a forearm, rise from the ground, with only a number etched into the stone. More recently, thanks to the work of diligent local residents, the names and stories of those who died have been recovered and publicly commemorated, and a marker was placed at the site.

In 1980, as a result of comprehensive worldwide vaccinations, smallpox was declared by the United Nations to be eradicated. It is the only infectious disease in humans to be successfully eliminated thus far.

1918 FLU

According to a 2020 article in the *Ptownie Magazine*, when the 1918 flu epidemic came to Provincetown a century ago, masks were mandated and weekly dances and social gatherings were reduced or canceled. Over 800 fell ill in Provincetown and at least 55 people died within just a few weeks—an average of one person every four days. Local doctors were worked off their feet, sometimes making as many as 70 house calls in a day to tend to the ill. The Unitarian Universalist church became the town infirmary. The church provided cots, medical care and meals for many of the 829 town residents who fell ill.

The outbreak and rapid spread of the 1918 flu coincided with the time that Americans entered World War I. The close quarters of military personnel on trucks, trains and ships and in damp trenches exacerbated the spread of the illness among service members and managed to kill more troops during the war than died in battle.

HIV/AIDS

Because of its role as a haven for LGBTQ+ people, long before many other places, people came from around the globe to live here as openly gay. Beginning in the 1980s, people with HIV came here to live as openly HIV-positive. Which is not to say that there was no fear, stigma and discrimination surrounding the illness here—there was, but it was usually less pronounced than in the places people came here from.

In Provincetown, people found the emotional and practical support lacking elsewhere. In addition to the Provincetown AIDS Support Group, which still provides meals and support services to People Living with AIDS, local churches and civic organizations stepped up to help. Education and outreach helped to quell fear of transmission, while the treatments, though far less effective than today's, helped lend hope to the Provincetown community, including its HIV-positive residents. It was a remarkable time—remarkably awful and remarkably heartwarming to see the progression from stigma and fear and death to one of care support and successful treatments.

COVID-19

Neither the Provincetown Health Department nor the Barnstable County Health Department provides a public, readily accessible count of coronavirus illness and deaths in Provincetown, so it's hard to know the scope of its impact in numbers. Its impacts on our daily lives, though, were and are measurable in a multitude of ways. In general, the response among town residents to COVID-19 was one of cooperation with mask mandates and vaccine requirements, although like everywhere else, the initial news of the disease was met with uncertainty, fear and even some stigmatization of people known or suspected to be infected.

Many in town strove to be mindful not to repeat the mistakes of alienation and stigmatization that were made during past illnesses, like smallpox and HIV/AIDS. People stepped up to help elders and immune-compromised neighbors with shopping and errands. Churches, civil organizations, various food banks and meal service programs adapted quickly and robustly to the new and ever-shifting landscape. Restaurants and other businesses had to adjust their business practices according to local and national requirements. With each rise and fall of the coronavirus caseload, residents have responded collectively, enabling the town to mitigate spread while still carrying on with life as normally as is safely feasible.

Provincetown resident David Rodriguez, who wrote and acted under the name David Matias, was living with AIDS at the time he visited the remnants of the cemetery at the smallpox Pest House. David felt a strong affinity for those who'd been sent there. The following excerpt is taken from a poem he wrote after he visited the site in the 1990s. People living with AIDS and those with smallpox often endured a debilitating and life-threatening illness in addition to the painful stigma that came along with it. This stigma was heaped upon those who fell sick, as well as on their families and friends who associated with them. His full poem, "Eyes to the Sun," was published in 1998 in his book titled, *Fifth Season*.

EYES TO THE SUN

I step outside and Orion's Belt
twinkles fierce on this cold October night.
Dionysus threw The Hunter
into a deep sleep and blinded him.
An oracle said he could regain his sight
by letting the rays of the rising sun fall on his eyes.
My vision is also restored
as I look at his constellation pierce the blackness
fire-white just as it did over a century ago when
another epidemic spread through Provincetown.
I want to visit the Smallpox Cemetery
but I'm not sure where it is.
Locals claim the graves are east of Clapp's Pond.
Simple granite markers,
tucked in layered moss. Eroding.
Some broken off. Only 5, 6, 9, and 10 legible.
Families ashamed to display surnames
picked numbers instead.
All their possessions burned.
Disgraced of any identity.
This is being gone.
No record, no trace,
no name on a tombstone.

II
Polly takes me there.
It is a May morning.
Warmth flirts with our skin as we walk.
Tree buds hold back their summer canopy
so the sun can still touch the ground.
Down a steep hill we lose our footing,
stepping on stacked leaves
damp from melted snow.
Thorns tug our clothes
Branches scratch our hands.
We only get lost for a minute…
then find a natural amphitheater of hills.
Nestled in the valley the modest cemetery sleeps.

At the sighting of the first marker
our excitement is curbed.
We are here. Graves have been found.
A squirrel dashes in the distance.
Curious black-capped chickadees
perch above us.
All is sacred.

We count aloud—
one, two, three, four, five, six …
There are seven visible.
Buried in sequence after each death,
they curve away from a grassy crater.
The foundation of the shack
has long sunk into this piece of wetlands.
This was their last home.
No bigger than a room.
Diseased outcasts.
We sit across from each other
at this well of Spring motion;
small pastel-blue butterflies skirt
inches above the leafy pit,
large black ants scramble oblivious of giants.
My friend's voice blends with the wind,
It must have been peaceful here.
Time stretches the air
as we contemplate their lives.
On *this* morning they are not forgotten—
our eyes stare at stars beyond the blue skies.
The town's noon whistle breaks our quiet,
bringing us back to this century
to these decaying, undated stones.

        — David Matias

WINTHROP STREET

Winthrop Street was named for Governor John Winthrop, who is best known for being the first governor of Massachusetts Bay Colony, and for his oft-quoted "City Upon a Hill" speech, delivered as he readied to sail on the good ship *Arabella* to the Colonies. He and his compatriots departed Southampton, sailing on a fair spring wind in March 1630. His mission was to settle and govern Boston. In his famous speech he declared that Boston would be "as a city upon a hill, the eyes of all people upon us" as the world scrutinized the community's success or failure as an exemplary Christian fortress.

Winthrop served 12 terms as Governor. He did not approve of democracy, labeling it "the meanest and worst of all forms of government," and he worked tirelessly to restrict voting and civil rights to those few whose religious mettle had been proven and approved by him and his appointees. Winthrop sternly resisted the acceptance of non-whites into the Christian fold. A holder of enslaved Native Americans and Africans himself, Winthrop helped draft legislation legalizing the ownership, trade and sale of human beings. Massachusetts became the first of the colonies to legalize slavery.

Winthrop met a stalwart rival in Anne Hutchinson, a formidable proponent of civil liberties and religious tolerance. Initially thinly veiled as tea socials, she hosted meetings for women (later permitting men) at her home to discuss religion and straying, possibly inevitably, into discussions on politics and the future of the colony. Her beliefs and increasing stature were regarded as the worst sort of influence for the colony by some (Winthrop et al) and the best sort by others (who, to Winthrop's alarm, were growing in number). The final straw for Winthrop came when Hutchinson testified in court that God had revealed directly to her that she and fellow believers could read and interpret the Scriptures themselves, without needing a church leader as an intermediary. In short order, she and her family (a husband and 15 children) were banished from Massachusetts.

As we leave the calm of Winthrop Cemetery, we will cross Winthrop Street to follow Brown Street to Shankpainter Road.

SHANKPAINTER CHILDREN'S ZOO

Near where Brown and Shankpainter meet, a children's petting zoo once stood. From artists to zoologists, Provincetown has had it all. Locals who visited the Shankpainter Children's Zoo on school trips, in the early 1970s, recall that the zoo owners let the kids feed and pet the goats, geese and pigs. The children loved seeing the exotic menagerie accrued by Ruth Dutra, the owner. David Dunlap's *Building Provincetown* lists an extensive inventory of critters at the zoo:

> … an anteater, sloth bears, a black bear, a cinnamon bear, a 7½-foot boa constrictor, fallow deer, English spotted deer, sika deer, jaguars ("probably our biggest handful," Ruth told me), llamas, mongooses, spider monkeys, squirrel monkeys, a macaque, macaws, toucans, parrots, peacocks, pheasants, Barbados sheep, timber wolves, and a mountain lion named Kitty, three months old in this picture, whom Ruth walked along Winthrop Street on a leash.

FIRE STATION CHOWDER

At the corner of Brown and Shankpainter is now the Provincetown Fire Station. The squad is made up of volunteer firefighters. Most fire stations have at least one person on the squad who likes to cook for the others. In many American firehouses it's chili. On the Cape, the recipe given to me is for clam chowda. No surprise there!

A former Cape Cod firefighter was kind enough to share a recipe with me for a clam chowder he used to make for his crew. His instructions are below. I added garlic to the recipe when I made it at home. As it was not in his recipe, I put the (garlic) in parentheses.

Clam Chowder

1 qt soft-shell clams, chopped finely
3 oz salt pork, diced
A handful of potatoes, diced
A white or yellow onion, diced
(A clove or two of garlic, minced)

A pint of milk
A Tbsp of white wine
Butter
Salt, pepper and bay leaves

Plunk the onions, (garlic) and potatoes into a skillet with a bit of warmed olive oil and add some salt and pepper. Sauté them together until the onions are soft. Add in the chunked pork. Cook a few minutes (5 or so) longer, then pour in the juice of the clams and wine and let them all get acquainted for a while, until a prodding fork tells you the potatoes are done. Add the clams and a lump of butter and cook about 10 more minutes. While this is cooking, heat up your milk, with a bit of salt and pepper in it, and the bay leaves. When it's good and warm—but not boiling!—pour the milk into the chowder. Taste to see if it needs more salt before serving. (The guy who gave me the recipe shuddered when he told me he once saw a Texan add Tabasco to a clam chowder— that's not something he would tolerate in his own kitchen. He says it would taste like all the ingredients were having a family feud.)

THE BLESSING OF THE FLEET

Clem Silva was a former Provincetown fire chief. He was also an ambulance driver, Navy veteran and fisherman, famous for his passion for cooking and especially for the boisterous annual block parties he and his wife, Ursula, put on for Provincetown's Blessing of the Fleet. A few years into it, their extended family affair became a huge, jubilant celebration with food, music, dancing and hundreds of guests.

Though blessings of the fishing fleet have been happening for ages, Provincetown's first official Blessing of the Fleet began in the late 1940s, complete with a parade and marching band. The procession departed from downtown at the Knights of Columbus and made its way to St. Peter the Apostle Church. Then, as now, a mass was held before everyone reconvened at MacMillan Wharf where a long, colorful ribbon of fishing boats loops in front of the Catholic Bishop to be blessed, one by one, then sails off to anchor at Long Point for parties lasting long into the night.

An annual celebration, dubbed the Portuguese Festival & Blessing of the Fleet, now lasts several days and takes place in June during Massachusetts's Portuguese Heritage Month. Provincetown's festival attracts thousands of people to town every June to feast on Portuguese cuisine, dance to live Portuguese music, play games and watch the blessing of boats, large and small, zig-zagging through the harbor. A special draw is the wide variety of Portuguese food to be had—squid stew, *vina d'ahlos* tuna, sea clam stuffed with linguiça, linguiça sub rolls, flippers, spicy fava beans, and a host of sweetbreads and pastries.

Directly across the street from the Fire Station sits the Police Station.

POLICE STATION PUMPKINS

For years now, the police station has been *the* place to get your free Halloween pumpkins. You can choose your large, small, perfectly round or charmingly misshapen pumpkin from the parade of them waiting to be picked up in front of the station during the month of October.

SOUP KITCHEN OF PROVINCETOWN

One of the most successful "very Provincetown" food stories is that of SKIP—the Soup Kitchen in Provincetown, which has operated out of the United Methodist Church building since 1992. In its infancy, it rotated year-to-year between St. Mary's of the Harbor, the Unitarian Universalist and Methodist church kitchens.

SKIP fosters a "culture of community, kindness and caring." The chef-made food is excellent, healthy and varied, and, to top that off, it's one of the best places to socialize in Provincetown in the wintertime. Rich, poor, youth, seniors, wash-a-shores, old-timers, and everyone betwixt and between, all are welcome.

Hot meals are served family style at long tables. Everyone is welcome to enjoy a meal at no cost. In addition to being a lively place to catch up with friends, SKIP has been a life-saver for the many Outer Cape folks who are without work over the winter months. The kitchen serves lunch on weekdays from November to April and offers to-go meals on weekends. They serve 15,000 meals each winter, around 125 meals per day. During the COVID lockdown, SKIP remained in full operation, making more than 100 meals per day available to-go, more than a third of them vegan.

Donated foods that cannot be used by SKIP are passed along to the on-site Food Pantry. They paired up with the Provincetown Library to create Crop Swap, a program that accepts garden vegetable donations, allows people to swap fresh produce, or to simply come take home the food they need.

Innovative SKIP menus showcase a variety of cuisines, reflecting the ever-increasing call for dishes of diverse culinary traditions, as well as a call for diverse ingredients, some with meat, some vegetarian, some vegan. By way of example, menus offered during a recent week included a variety of soups: Thai Coconut Curry Soup one day, Butternut Squash the next, followed by Avgolemono (Greek Lemon Chicken) Soup, and Rick's Homemade Pasta-and-Piselli Soup. Side dishes ran the gamut, too, from Beef and Pork Meatballs, Caesar Salad, Mac and Cheese, Edamame Salad, Fajita Style Chicken with Peppers and Onions, Red Beans, Shopska Salad, Falafel with Tahini Sauce, to Baked Tofu with Pineapple and Red Peppers. The dessert menu featured Blueberry Cobbler, Yogurt with Fruit, Smoothies, Lemon Cake.

You never know who will turn up at SKIP; it's never the same twice, and it's always a hoot! Come join in, there's always room for one more!

As we come to the intersection of Shankpainter and Bradford, we'll turn right, up the gentle hill and come to the lovely old schoolhouse on our right, with an ever-changing sculpture garden out front. This is the Commons, a community hub, a place to learn, teach and to get inspired, all year long.

THE COMMONS

In this former schoolhouse, the learning and growing has never ceased. The hallways are lined with fresh-off-the-easel artwork by artists, both emerging and established, and the collaborative work spaces hum year-round with the contagious energy of creatives of all stripes. You may see people participating in workshops, teaching classes in art, writing or business, attending lectures or art receptions, holding meetings or just popping in to see what's going on—because there's always something interesting going on at The Commons.

There is a large co-working space with workstations, comfy chairs, meeting rooms, and a multi-functional printer for use by the diverse, intergenerational community who comes here. Artist studios are available to emerging, mid-career and established artists on a rotating basis.

Inevitably and importantly, there's a communal lounge where various factions cross paths while making a cup of coffee, grabbing a snack or making a bit of lunch. Not surprisingly, this is a room where serendipitous interactions spark unexpected opportunities. The brewing of ideas here, which start out as casual banter over coffee, just may end up as a collaborative art exhibit or Ptown's next new start-up.

The uncommon possibilities here are endless.

CONANT STREET

Some branches of the Conant clan can trace their lineage to Richard More, the only child of the four young More siblings to survive the first winter at Plimouth Colony.

Richard More grew up to travel the world as a sea captain, dealing in tobacco, grains, lumber, furs and salted fish, and trading in ports around the Atlantic. When he set aside his sailing days, he became a publican, opening his own tavern in 1674 in Salem, Massachusetts.

EATERIES AS CULTURAL OUTPOSTS

Since their inception, restaurants have served as cultural outposts of a sort. Some represent the local cuisine and characteristics of the people of the geographic region they are in, others feature dishes and ambiance from another place or even another era. Dining in certain restaurants may remind some diners of places they've traveled, whereas for other diners, the restaurant experience may be the closest they will get to visiting some parts of the country or the world.

The function of restaurants as cultural outposts was never more evident than during coronavirus lockdowns. When travel within the country and abroad was limited or unavailable, many got their travel fix by ordering take-out from places that serve food from far flung places.

Once people returned to eateries to dine indoors, simply stepping over the threshold into certain restaurants felt to some like a mini-getaway. The combination of distinctive music, décor and ambiance, in addition to culturally specific cuisine helped people feel they were experiencing a sample slice of destinations in other regions of the country or the globe. We traveled through taste.

Between Conant and Pleasant Streets, directly across from The Commons, sits a busy little café with moth wing–yellow awnings.

LIZ'S CAFÉ AND ANYBODY'S BAR

This was Tip for Tops'n—and so much more than a corner Portuguese diner. It was a homey, feels-like-family spot for decades. Its breakfast menu remains embedded in the heart and appetite of Provincetown. So much so that several items from the Tip for Tops'n menu hold a permanent spot on the menu of Liz's Café. Liz (whose Angel Foods Deli we saw on our walk through the East End) is an Italian foodsmith whose culinary roots meld well with Yankee and Portuguese flavor profiles to create a singularly Provincetown dining experience, breakfast, lunch and dinner, year-round.

For the busy summer months, Liz puts out cheerful yellow picnic tables which match her yellow awnings to accommodate diners outdoors. When the cold of winter arrives, up pops attractive, see-through igloo bubbles, complete with piped-in music, amber lighting and heaters in each igloo. So creative, convenient, cozy and romantic! It's a bit like catered glamping.

For those who miss(ed) hanging out at the dory bar at the Flagship restaurant, you can still enjoy a cocktail seated at a dory bar here at Anybody's Bar. Unlike many bars in town, this was where both East and West Enders came together: this was Anybody's Bar. By the way, if you're looking for a drink suggestion, I'd say you can't go wrong with a tall Spicy Sailor!

Just past Liz's, we'll turn left for a pleasant walk down Pleasant Street, past the row of houses where many a fishing family has lived, within easy walking distance to the wharves. Most of the workers at the various fish-packing and cold storage operations at this end of town lived on these West End streets.

When we pop out onto Commercial Street, we come upon 133 Commercial Street. Cat-like, this little building has had multiple lives, most of them as restaurants.

A RESTAURANT OF MANY HATS

This was, for a good long while, Cookie's Tap, run by Friday and Clara Cook, where, for some 50 years, fishermen and townies gathered, knowing this was the place to get the best homemade fava beans, stuffed sea clams and squid stew around. Actually, Clara did the cooking in her home kitchen next door and her sons carried the dishes over to the restaurant. For the most part, Friday ran the bar.

Though the generously portioned fare and the neighborly welcome gave the taproom a down-to-earth feel, its interior décor of handcrafted "mahogany inlaid with maple and ebony" lent a nautical air suggestive of a ship captain's fine quarters. Brass ship lanterns suspended on tiller wheels added to the aboard-ship feel.

This was a favorite hangout of chef Howard Mitcham, who incorporated his experiences at Cookie's Tap into his *Provincetown Seafood Cookbook*. Cookie's menu changed depending on the catches of the day, the seasons and whatever odds and ends its fishing clientèle brought in. Mitcham wrote that fishermen would bring to Cookie's what they didn't sell of the various fish, crab, lobster quahogs, tinkers and blinkers (young mackerel of different sizes). Clara and her boys would swoop it all up, disappear with it, and return the offerings cooked into a plethora of fragrant dishes. The sumptuous spread was laid out for the taking, at no charge.

The place took on a new personality under Italian-Bostonian David Gallerani, who opened Gallerani's in 1986. David was a much-beloved figure in town, known not only for his exceptional cuisine, but also for his kindness, humor and generosity. He gave liberally of his food and his time to support locals struggling with poverty, living with HIV and other challenges. After "The Perfect Storm," the deadly hurricane that hit in 1991, David fired up his gas stove and dished up free meals to those in town who remained without power or access to warm food for days on end. I queued up with my roommate, appreciative friends and neighbors, all glad to have a hot meal and camaraderie.

The little building took a spin as yet another eponymous restaurant, Lorraine's. Lorraine Najar, who had been Gallerani's "Mexican Night" chef, opened up her own restaurant here to serve the Mexican cuisine she'd grown up with. She filled the walls with rotating art exhibitions.

Several years later, Lorraine's was followed by the Joon Bar & Kitchen, bringing to Provincetown a seasonal menu featuring familiar seafood choices and a variety of tasty Persian dishes. When the kitchen closes up for the evening, the after-dinner cocktail and wine social hour begins.

We'll continue up-along Commercial Street, passing Whorf's Court on our right, named for the famous Provincetown family of fishermen and artists. Shortly after, we arrive at the junction where Franklin and Tremont streets converge with Commercial. Commercial Street veers hard to the left here, lending this intersection its name, The Turn.

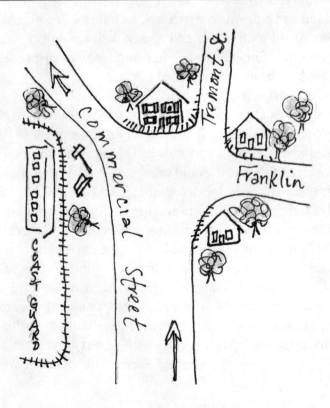

There are several things, historically speaking, going on at this intersection. Let's take a seat on the comfy bench here while we look around. The marker above our bench was erected to remember the service and death of Luis Ferreira, the son of Azorean immigrants. He died in World War I during the 1918 flu epidemic, at 21 years old.

Across the street from us is Perry's Liquor Store, still bearing the name of Captain Perry of *Rose Dorothea* fame, who ran a liquor store here.

THE *ROSE DOROTHEA,* PRIDE OF PROVINCETOWN

The sleek, Lipton Cup–winning, two-masted schooner was named for her Portuguese captain's own Irish Rose. His wife, Rose Dorothea, was born in the US to Irish immigrants. Young Rose Dorothea married her Azorean beau two years before the big Fishermen's Race in 1907, which brought world-wide attention to Provincetown and well-placed pride to its Portuguese community and Captain Perry. The course ran from Thieves Ledge to Davis Ledge and back, a 42-mile stretch through challenging Atlantic waters. In spite of suffering a broken fore topmast, she brought home the cup, besting her strongest competitor, Provincetown's *Jesse Costa,* by over two minutes.

After winning the Lipton Cup, the *Rose Dorothea* sailed the Atlantic carrying fishery salt and other commodities between various countries. In 1917, off the coast of Portugal, a German U-boat forced the *Rose Dorothea* crew to abandon their ship in lifeboats. The Germans then peppered the legendary schooner with torpedoes, sending the beautiful ship to the bottom of the sea. The crew had to row to the nearest island and plead a ride on the next ship heading back to Provincetown.

FRANKLIN STREET

Franklin Street was named for founding father Benjamin Franklin. It is believed to be near here that unmarked graves, possibly belonging to *Mayflower* passengers, were found in 1873, when the land was prepared to make way for Bradford Street.

THREE FOREFATHERS WALK INTO A PROVINCETOWN BAR

So, three *Mayflower* shipmates, John Alden, William Bradford and Miles Standish, walk into a pub in Provincetown. It is the year 2022.

Adventurous, strapping young Alden orders a large plate of Dragon's Breath Buffalo Wings and a double IPA. Bradford, also adventurous, but older and more health-conscious, goes for the chicken sandwich, the chicken breast grilled, not fried, on wheat bread not white, hold the mayo, add guac and jalapeños. And a lager, please. Standish loudly commands a rib-eye steak, rare enough to squirm, with two hunks of baked potato and a tall boilermaker, which he chugs straight down and belches, immediately calling for another.

The three forefathers glance around the place and notice George and Martha Washington at a cozy fireside table, tucking into a piece of cherry pie chopped into two thick wedges. They are sipping their favorite Barbadian rum from warmed snifters and discussing their whiskey-distilling business. In particular, they are wondering whether they should join the latest craze: infusing spirits with fruits, vegetables and spices. At present, they're weighing various suggestions from their customers: grapefruit & garlic, ghost pepper & cucumber and banana & basil. The very thought of these is sort of putting me off my feed, to be honest, George is telling her.

At a nearby table a rowdy gathering of confirmed bachelors is offering a champagne toast to the marriage, tomorrow, of two of the bachelors to one another. George Washington's highly-decorated General von Steuben and his handsome aide-de-camp, along with a few of their close friends, have come to Provincetown to celebrate the wedding.

Thomas Jefferson and Benjamin Franklin enter the pub and take stools at the crowded bar. Jefferson, nostalgic for France, orders quiche. When the bartender asks what he wants to drink, Jefferson says, Good wine is a necessity of life for me! The bartender pours him a glass of Bordeaux and turns to Franklin. What'll it be today, Ben? Franklin, having only just got back from France, says he's now got a hankering for ye goode olde New England fare. How about a cold Sam Adams and some Boston Baked Beans. But! Franklin says, have them make that with kidney beans instead of navy beans!

The bar falls silent. You could've heard a quill drop.

Heresy! yells someone. Who ever heard of Boston baked *kidney* beans? Sacrilege! shouts another.

Why, I oughta ... mumbles a third, rising to his feet, fists clenched, as his friends egg him on.

Sensing tensions reaching a boiling point and fearing a food fight on his hands, the bartender says, Keep your powder dry, gentlemen. I've got this. Turning to Franklin, the bartender says, Sir, are you *certain* you want kidney beans in that?

Franklin stands up and moves closer to the stove, carefully wiping his bifocals. He puts them back on and peers long and intently at the bartender before replying, Young man, in this world nothing can be said to be certain except death and taxes! And—the fact that those damned navy beans disagree with my constitution!

Bemused, Jefferson shakes his head and says, Once again, Ben, you are on the money! But even though I'd be the first to say that information is the currency of democracy, all that about your constitution is more information than I care to digest! Chuckling and raising his glass Jefferson adds, Ben, dinner out with you is always enlightening!

"IN BOSTON, EVEN BEANS DO IT"

They are very attached to their Boston Baked Beans, those Bostonians. The above story about the three forefathers was inspired by a culinary experience I once had in Boston. When we ordered nachos at a restaurant there, to our surprise and horror, they arrived with Boston Baked Beans on top, rather than chili. Truly a travesty in my (cook)book!

Pilgrims at Plimoth Colony learned to make baked beans from local Native Americans. Over time, folks in Massachusetts adapted the recipe to create the dish that lent Boston the nickname, "Beantown." The dish is generally made with navy beans, slow-cooked with salt pork, black pepper, (some add onions, too) and, for that special, caramel-y gooeyness, Bostonians add molasses (in place of the maple syrup used by Native Americans). Some cooks today substitute hot dogs for salt pork.

As the religious practices of some of the colonists restricted cooking on the Sabbath, a batch of these beans could be cooked up on Saturday and kept warm overnight, supplying them a hot meal on Sunday, without breaking rules of the Sabbath.

We will now make our way up Tremont Street to Cottage Street.

THE NORSE WALL

An excavation to build a home on the corner of Cottage Street created a stir in 1853 when workers uncovered an uncommon, stone-walled fireplace. Uncommon in that it was reported to have been constructed of stones not native to Cape Cod, suggesting they may have been brought here as ballast by voyagers from afar. Among the ashes in the fireplace were the leavings of the bones of seabirds believed to have been cooked and eaten here. Based on these findings, this was considered possibly to be the site where Thorvald Ericson (brother of Leif) and his crew stayed while they repaired the keel of their boat, sometime around the year 1004. Later, when Thorvald sustained a mortal wound, he asked to be buried in the place where they had mended their boat's keel, leading to the theory that he may have been laid to rest at what is now Long Point. The notion remains speculative, but intriguing.

> If the Vikings did come to the Cape, they may have gathered sweet gale here, also called bog myrtle, a plant they'd have recognized from home. Norsemen used to steep sweet gale to make a stimulating drink they enjoyed in moderation to lift their spirits, and in larger quantities to rev themselves up for battle.

No further physical evidence has been discovered so far to confirm the presence of Vikings at the outermost reaches of the Cape, and the wall that was discovered in the Provincetown excavation has not been accessible since a large house was set on top of it. Some historians, including Frederick Pohl, have connected Cape towns with traveling Norsemen, possibly Leif Erikson, Thorvald's brother. Eastham, for example, may have been the place Vikings called "Wonderstrand." Norse "mooring holes," (mooring pins driven into rocks in order to tie up boats) were said to have been found in rocks in rivers and ponds. Some suggest these may have been sites of Viking settlements. The jury is out as to what conclusions may be reliably drawn by the findings, and research continues.

Next along Tremont is Nickerson Street, followed by Soper.

SOPER STREET

According to the Logs of the King Hiram Masonic Lodge, fellow member Captain Samuel Soper was master of the whaling brig *Ardent* when it collided with a hurricane off the Azorean Islands in 1823. Three men and both masts were washed into the sea. The remaining crew retreated to the afterdeck, the only bit of the boat still poking above water. For the next 26 days the men hovered ever closer to starvation, having only rainwater from passing showers to drink and nothing but barnacles and the occasional small fish to eat. Exposure, hunger and thirst began to take their toll. As the crew members began to die, one by one, the Logs read, their "bodies furnished the rest with their only food until there were only five left."

The five survivors were finally rescued by a passing British ship, the *Lord Sudmouth*. One of the rescued men died before reaching shore, and two others died not long after returning to Provincetown. Captain Soper refused to speak of the suffering and deprivation he'd endured. He returned to the helm undeterred, commanding whaling voyages for years afterward. The other survivor, lodge member Phillip Rich, lived to a ripe age and spoke of the shipwreck only to his granddaughter, who was given the middle name of Sudmouth, in honor of the ship that had plucked her grandfather from the sinking remains of the whaling brig.

We come now to West Vine where we'll turn left toward Commercial Street.

WEST VINE

This slender, paved way is reportedly named for grape vines that were cultivated along the pathway many decades ago. To our right, at the top of West Vine, once stood a Dairy Queen run by the local Provincetown High School principal. It may well have been the only Dairy Queen in the country where customers could order a cup of hot Portuguese kale soup with a side of fries.

Gale Force Bike Shop at West Vine and Bradford has been going strong since opening in 1977, providing bikes and basic picnic supplies to locals, tourists and campers (from the campground just beyond) heading to and from Herring Cove Beach. The name of the bike and sundries shop is a tip of the hat to the Gale Force Farm, which was the very last of Provincetown's five dairy farms; it closed in 1952.

WAS THAT A COW I SAW GRAZING ON THE BEACH?

During the 1880s, according to the Bulletin of the US Fish Commission, local farmers brought their cows down to the shoreline to graze on discarded fish bits among the boats. I have not come across any reports on how this diet affected the flavor of the milk or beef they produced, but the practice helped feed the cows, cleared the shoreline of fish leavings and makes for an off-beat quiz question on trivia night at the Squealing Pig pub.

"A JUG OF WINE, A LOAF OF BREAD AND THOU"

Picnicking has long been a popular pastime in Provincetown, but perhaps never more so than during COVID lockdowns, when restaurants reduced or closed their indoor dining. Picnicking reached a crescendo during the initial lockdown phase, when eateries began serving to-go meals only. This inspired new start-ups, like Perfect Picnic Ptown, which capitalized on this fun dining trend and that hopes it will continue to grow now that diners have the option to eat indoors again.

These days, picnicking on a Provincetown beach means tasting salt in the breeze, wiggling bare toes in clean, sugary brown sand, collecting fragile, pinkly gray shells—a quintessential Cape Cod affair. But it was not always like this, and we have Mary Heaton Vorse and fellow enlightened activists in town to thank for fighting for the clean beaches we play on today. There was a time, right up until the late '30s to early '40s, in fact, when multiple sewage pipes spilled directly into the harbor. Garbage was dumped in reeking mounds onto the town beaches; flies and creepy-crawlies, as well as pigs, dogs, cats and rats scavenged the rotting debris and piles of fetid offal in search of dead animals and scraps of food.

FLOATERS

Where West Vine comes out onto Commercial Street, we'll take a right. Just ahead is a neighborhood rich in blue-plaqued houses. These plaques proudly pronounce these homes as "floaters," believing them to have arrived in town from the Long Point settlement aboard small barges called scows. So commonplace had the practice become, it was frequently joked that a Long Point woman could carry right on cooking and tending to children while her house glided lightly across the harbor, never spilling a drop of soup, which she dished into bowls just as her house came to a gentle rest on the Provincetown shore. In 1818, John Atwood was the first to build his home out at Long Point; the last building to leave Long Point departed the outpost 1865.

It's been pointed out that there are now more houses in town with blue floater plaques than had existed at Long Point. Even though most of the houses at the settlement did, in fact, make the journey, only a portion of the houses in Provincetown currently bearing blue tiles could have been among the floaters from Long Point. That aside, the Long Point provenance is well-established for several of the houses along this upcoming stretch of Commercial, as we head into the far West End.

ATWOOD STREET

Captain Nathanial Atwood's house was one of the last to migrate from Long Point to nest in Provincetown. Born into poverty, Atwood began fishing at age 10 and became a Master Mariner, a member of both the Massachusetts House of Representatives and Senate, and one of the founders of the Museum of Comparative Zoology at Harvard University. As a self-taught ichthyologist, he discovered a man-eating shark that was then named after him.

Once, during a raging gale, Captain Atwood rescued a crew of nine men and a dog from their sinking ship, the British brig *Lone Star*. For this, he received a commendation from the Consul General of the United States to Britain, as well as an inscribed spyglass from Her Majesty,

Queen Victoria. The spyglass now resides in the collection of the Heritage Museum of Provincetown.

Captain Atwood's interest in ichthyology led him to research fish and fish oils, with an eye on the possible medicinal uses of cod oil. He opened a cod liver oil factory downtown. Summertime generally found Atwood fishing for bluefish, dogfish, halibut and lobsters; in the winter he'd manufacture cod liver oil. Eventually, he sold his boat and stuck to making oil and smoking halibut. He would sell somewhere between 400–700 quintals of smoked halibut per year. (A quintal is just over 220 pounds.) Even so, most of his wealth flowed from producing his highly-prized cod liver oil.

We come now to a parking lot at one of the Town Landings. Let's stroll over to the bayside benches and have a sit-down while we take in the views.

TOWN LANDING

The light out here is not segmented into morning, midday, and evening; rather it's a continuous shifting of contrasting shades and a fragmenting of unexpected combinations of color. The benches here at the edge of the bay are an ideal place to sit and watch the light show as it unfolds throughout the day.

The air is filled with the ceaseless bickering of gulls scrabbling for mussels. Sea gulls live in colonies, but they don't fly in flock formation as many birds do. They are fiercely competitive with other animals and one another. When one finds food, others follow, often trying to steal one another's finds. From where we're sitting, we can see the gulls snatching mussels off the beach, swooping upward to a point high above the concrete landing then, suddenly, dropping the mussel, clack! onto the ground. Before a rival gull can get to it, the gull hurtles down, beelining for the fallen shell. There, the bird struts around its prize for a bit, cawing at the world, daring any to challenge its claim, before finally slurping up the sweet, soft meat from the broken shell.

On the strand across the bay, the lighthouse you see on the left is Long

Point Light, which takes its name from the stretch of sand it stands on. A bit farther along to the right you can see Wood End Lighthouse. If you had happened to be sitting out at Wood End, looking out to sea in 1951, the eye peering back at you through a periscope may well have been that of future president, Jimmy Carter, who was serving as a lieutenant in a submarine just off the coast at the time.

Behind us, seated along Commercial Street, we can see a neat row of well-coiffed homes gazing with contented pastel primness at the rise and fall of the tides, the competitive air dance of the gulls and, off across the bay streaked with purples and gold, blues and greens, they watch the dutiful, indefatigable little lighthouses guiding boats into and out of the sheltering harbor, by day and by night.

SETTLEMENTS, IN A NUTSHELL

The Wampanoag, Nauset and Paomet tribes were the first to settle in this area. The Cape became a stopover for explorers of various ilks long before the *Mayflower* stumbled upon it in 1620. The remote location, with its calm harbor and ready access to the ocean, drew pirates, smugglers and traders of illicit goods, looking for a hideout from which they could quickly come and go by sea. Drinking, fighting and gambling were the order of the day. The land stretching from the town of present-day Truro out to the tip of the Cape was incorporated as part of Truro in 1709. Puritans living in the town of Truro proper, nicknamed this fledgling town of motley shacks and troublesome inhabitants Helltown. As more people came to settle in the outermost reaches, many began living year-round, fishing, farming and raising families. In 1727, Provincetown split from Truro and incorporated as Provincetown.

LONG POINT & HELLTOWN

Looking out across the water, it's not hard to imagine the tidy cluster of buildings that once freckled the outstretched arm of sand at Long Point. From this vantage point, however, we cannot quite see Hatches Harbor, where the shacks of Helltown sprang up, haphazardly patched together farther along the shoreline.

Though sometimes conflated or mistaken for one another, these two settlements, Long Point and Helltown, were not one and the same. They inhabited different locations, eras, attitudes. The Long Point settlement was populated in the early to mid-1800s, while Helltown was in full swing from the 1880s right into the 1960s. When the residents of Long Point vacated, they picked up their houses, and took them with them across the bay. Once the usefulness of the clapboard shacks at Helltown had run its course, they were simply abandoned, left to wither and die away. Their tattered remains were eventually carted off by the winds and the sea.

The first house at Long Point sprang up in 1818 and by mid-century there was a close-knit community of about 200 women, men and children living there. Most of the men fished or worked in the saltworks. The settlement consisted of about 35 homes, a post office, a bake house, a general store, several saltworks, a wharf, a lighthouse and a school in which children attended classes and the community gathered for church services.

Helltown was made up of thirty-odd shacks, where a new generation of troublesome inhabitants seem to have carted the discarded nickname of Helltown out to the ocean's edge with them, then tried with all their might to live up to the name. Life in the little settlement proved to be rough, resembling the wild frontier, with its gambling, boozing, fighting and rabble-rousing. In addition to being a shoreline base for about 125 fishermen, it was a hideout for pirates, smugglers, ne'er-do-wells on the lam and, sometimes, women with whom men conducted illicit business. Helltown's story has been the inspiration for generations of poets, songwriters and artists partial to tales of nonconforming rebels, mavericks and odd ducks.

HELENA RUBINSTEIN COMES TO PROVINCETOWN

Being an art collector, perhaps it is not surprising that Helena would add Provincetown to her list of homes dotted round the globe.

As a young woman in Poland, Helena Rubinstein learned, from a Hungarian chemist, the secrets of making face cream from herbs, essence of almond and the extract of the Carpathian fir tree. At 18, she left home to escape entering an arranged marriage. She landed on the doorstep of relatives in Melbourne, Australia, with her recipe, 12 jars of herbal face cream, very little money and a minimal command of the English language. Women she met there were quite taken with her soft, pale complexion and promptly purchased all of her jars of face cream. She made more and promptly sold them, too.

Until as recently as 1971 in Australia, women were not permitted to take out a business loan in their own name from a bank. An affluent woman who had faith in Helena's product and in the marketability of her herbal creams lent her enough money to set up a shop from which to sell her products. Before long, Rubinstein made enough money to move to London to introduce her line of creams and her newest concept, the day spa.

In 1908, Rubinstein finally married an American businessman, having chosen to delay her wedding long enough to make the money she needed to fund her own business ventures. In 1915, she moved to New York City, opened salons there and soon after, around the country. When her husband left her for a younger woman, she married Georgian Prince Archibald Gourelli, some 20 years her junior.

Rubinstein and her prince husband came to Provincetown in 1942. She was active in the art scene here and was an avid fan of Peter Hunt's folk art furniture. Her parties in Provincetown were reportedly attended by local notables, as well as international celebrities.

(As a point of interest, Australia was three years ahead of the United States with regard to institutional lending practices. It wasn't until 1974 that an American woman could get a line of credit from a bank solely in her own name. It took until 1988 that women in this country could get a business loan without needing a male cosigner.)

STANLEY KUNITZ

Provincetown's gardening poet Stanley Kunitz won a Pulitzer Prize, Bollingen Prize, National Medal of the Arts Award, National Book Award and served as the nation's Poet Laureate.

Kunitz lived in Provincetown half of his life, much of it here at number 32, before dying at age 100. Kunitz wrote, "Be what you are. Give what is yours to give. Have style. Dare."

The daring and delightful poet Kate Wallace Rogers now resides in this house and tends this garden.

Our walk has brought us to one of the most special sections of town. Compared to downtown, here in the far West End, you can hear fewer human noises and more of the ocean, birds and breezes around you. The pace is slower out here, too; there is more room to swing your arms, skip and dance up the street.

THE red INN

The red Inn has been serving the well-heeled and well-known for well over 100 years. The menu changes with the seasons and features a raw bar and traditional New England seafood alongside dishes with touches of English, Nova Scotian, Asian and Latin as well as Creole and Southern influences. It is a place people come to see and be seen, or a place to hole up and get away from it all, if you prefer.

LANDS END INN

Nesting high atop Gull Hill is Lands End Inn. The original structure was built by wealthy fishing captain Jonathan Nickerson, a descendant of Peregrine White, who was born on the bay just below this hill. Peregrine was the first baby born to the *Mayflower* colonists after arriving on this side of the Atlantic. Lands End Inn has been a guesthouse for many decades, hosting the gens du monde, movie stars, celebrities, writers and artists seeking an elegant hideaway. David Schoolman owned and ran the Lands End Inn from 1972 until his untimely passing of AIDS in 1995.

David had an outsized impact on the cultural calendar of Provincetown. Invitations to David's garden and Christmas parties were usually dispatched by word-of-mouth, and David graciously welcomed all-comers to his architectural marvel of a mansion filled with artwork and antiques, stained glass lamps, richly-colored drapes, fringed lampshades, luxurious carpets and bric-à-brac from around the globe. A polygonal, roofed porch wraps around the house and an octagonal turret soars above it all. At Christmas, he would bring in an enormous pine tree, from Maine or Vermont or somewhere, and open the Lands End doors to anyone in town who wanted to share canapés and sip cocktails before bundling up to go caroling around town. The price of admission was simply an ornament for the tree. Most guests made theirs by hand. We'd place our ornament onto a tree branch, then search out ornaments brought in years past, hanging high on branches already decorated.

The Schoolman Trust, established in his name, helped found and support the Provincetown Theater.

PROVINCETOWN INN

Best guess by historians is that the *Mayflower* landed right about here, in front of where the Provincetown Inn sits now. The inn opened in 1925 and has been celebrating the *Mayflower* narrative ever since (even putting in a swimming pool in the shape of a Pilgrim man's hat in the 1950s).

You're welcome to come in to take a look at the series of murals on display here, which were painted by Don Aikens in the 1960s. Several of the images feature historic points in the town's history, many of which are part of the American story learned by school children across the nation.

One of the paintings illustrates Washing Day, the Monday when *Mayflower* women came ashore to wash clothes for the first time in months. This led to a tradition of washing laundry on Mondays among New England's colonial housewives for generations to come. Another painting depicts the arrival of a second ship called the *Mayflower*. In this image, the presidential yacht has just docked in Provincetown, ushering President Taft and the First Lady to the gangway for the dedication of the Pilgrim Monument on August 5, 1910. Subjects of the paintings aim to capture special events as well as daily life of Provincetown's past.

The inn's restaurant, too, looks to the past for inspiration, offering "traditional" Cape Cod seafood cuisine (clam chowder, fish and chips, Wellfleet mussels steamed with Portuguese chorizo) in addition to offering pastas and chicken tenders.

THE LEGEND OF THE COD AND THE HADDOCK

A common legend has been handed down that explains how to tell the cod from haddock by looking at the markings on their skin. Massachusetts forbears claimed it was the cod that Christ used to feed the multitudes. He left marks of His thumb and forefingers on its skin as He held the fish. When the Devil attempted to do the same, the codfish wriggled free and swam away. The Devil's scorching fingers burned two dark lines down its sides as it escaped his grip. Thereafter, it was known as the haddock. In Massachusetts, the cod is sometimes referred to as "Sacred Cod."

FROM THE NOTEBOOK OF ZOË LEWIS

Let's go SQuidding

In a town they call moonlight
away from the bustle of tourists
and taffy and pizza and beer,
there's a place that I go
where the water is swimming with stars
by the fishing boats down at the pier
* I'm not one for clubbing I really must say
I feel much more like dancing
when I'm underneath the milky way
Hold my hand and my heart if you like me OK

(C) Let's go Squidding
    with the grandpas and boys
    I'm really not kidding
    It's full of summertime joys
    I got ink on my hands
    and a jig on the line
    and enough in my bucket for dinnertime
    Let's go squidding
    with the grandpas and boys

· Well, the night gulls are squabbling
  over a fish head
  and Topknot's one legged instructions
  begin

there's a splash of a bass
and the lines start a crossing
and zoo tentacles run for their skin
if you tease them a little from out of the deep
You will find that your heart's beating fast
for the rest of the week
wide awake when the trolley cars
and the dancing cops sleep

                 ~ C H O R U S ~

• And slowly I open my eyes in the morning
with the silver mink, the Liberty and
Sweet Josaphine
what a night to remember
Still damp with the ripe smell
of seaweed and anchors and
fisherfolk dreams
              repeat *
              CHORUS x2

WEST END BREAKWATER

A walk across the breakwater should be carefully timed to ensure you are not stranded by the tide as it comes in. Sometimes, at high tide, the waves wash up and over the top of the rocks making traversing them dangerous if not altogether impossible. Sturdy shoes and a sturdy balance are also recommended for crossing this rough stretch of rocks. The top of the breakwater is uneven and can become slick with water, seaweed and slippery sea detritus.

That said, the breakwater is one of the most alluring places in Provincetown. I love to take a picnic out to a spot a little more than halfway across, plop down on the rocks, and lose myself in watching the sea creatures going about their busy days beneath the glass-green water, oblivious to me and the rest of our human mess-of-a-world above the waves.

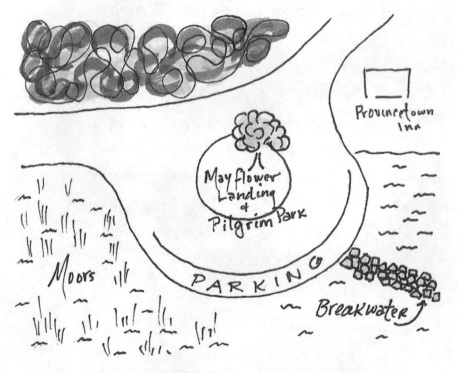

THE PILGRIM'S FIRST LANDING PARK

A marker denoting the site of the *Mayflower's* landing is located at this traffic circle. Under this spot sits a time capsule, too. The stainless-steel container was buried by the 375-year commemoration committee to be opened 100 years hence. The benches and engraved bricks that make up the terrace pay homage to loved ones who lived in or simply loved spending time in Provincetown.

Jack Kerouac hung about in Provincetown in the 1950s while working on his novel *On the Road* in which he wrote:

> [T]he only people for me are the mad ones, the ones who are mad to live, mad to talk, mad to be saved, desirous of everything at the same time, the ones who never yawn or say a commonplace thing, but burn, burn, burn, like fabulous yellow roman candles exploding like spiders across the stars and in the middle you see the blue centerlight pop and everybody goes 'Awww!'

THE MOORS

I need only to feast my eyes on these moors to satisfy a hard-to-feed hunger in my soul. The light out here is moody and impishly fickle. One moment a bouquet of beguiling, luscious greens appear, the next, it splinters into an audacious array of purples, shot through with shards of scarlet and orange, before seeping into a deeply pensive brown softened with flecks of gold. Within a span of a few minutes, glistening strands of grass, caught in a passing breath of sea air, flutter in ribbons of burnt yellows, striped in rakish pink, flicking aside glittery droplets of water like a spray of rogue sparks.

After sundown, a gauzy vespertine mist flutters over these moors, unveiling glimpses of a thousand tide pools, black as squid ink, in which float a thousand reflections of the moon, like handfuls of incandescent garlic cloves scattered about.

HERRING COVE BEACH

The beaches at both Race Point and Herring Cove are public and are under the protection and care of the Cape Cod National Seashore. Herring Cove Beach is the closest public beach to town; Race Point is farther out, just beyond the airport. The bus goes from Truro out to Herring Cove and Race Point, and there are paved bike trails to both beaches.

Once or twice a week on summer afternoons, throngs of locals and visitors of all ages come to Herring Cove to dance to live music and enjoy food and drink on the beach. You are welcome to bring your own food and beverages to the beach, but for safety reasons, nothing in glass containers, please. These town dance parties have become one of Provincetown's favorite summer pastimes, come join in!

PROVINCETOWN'S SEA SERPENT

Provincetown and its Town Crier at the time, one George Washington Ready, were the talk of the entire nation in 1886, when Ready reported seeing a huge sea monster just beyond these moors, near Herring Cove beach. Crier Ready's friend, Herman A. Jennings, a journalist on Cape Cod, quickly dispatched the story, elbowing out more humdrum headlines around the country. Ready announced that early that morning he'd witnessed an enormous serpent, 300 feet long and 12 feet in diameter, raising its scaly head from a whirlpool offshore and shooting great jets of water into the air. Ready, who was lying cozied up with a bottle of rum on the shore at the time, vigorously maintained that "he was not unduly excited by liquor" and went so far as to sign an affidavit attesting to that.

The creature was not only mind-bendingly large, but colorfully bedecked in red and green scales. Its head was the size of "a 200-gallon cask" from which grew six long, strong stalks, topped with roving eyes the "size of dinner plates" which moved independently of one another—enabling the serpent to look in all directions at once—side to side, fore and aft. Three of its eyes glimmered green and three blazed red. In its gaping mouth, Ready could see rows of sharp teeth glistening. A tusk eight feet long jutted out from its scaly nose. Ready ducked behind a beach plum bush and watched the serpent lumber out of the waves and undulate erratically across the sands. It left a trail of singed foliage and burnt grass in its wake, along with a pungent, sulfurous odor. It then slithered to a freshwater pond in the dunes nearby and disappeared headfirst into it, leaving behind only a deep, dry hole, 20 feet in diameter. Once it was gone, no trace of water or the creature could be found.

Ready's story resurfaced for a brief while in 1939 when an 18-foot skeleton with 71 vertebrae washed up on a Provincetown beach. The excitement was squashed by a Harvard scientist who broke up the party by identifying the skeleton as being that of a basking shark, an extraordinary creature in its own right, but miles less exotic than a sea serpent to many minds.

The Hatches Harbor Monster.
To Odale — drawn from reported sightings
Bill Fitts

Drawn specially for this book by artist Bill Fitts, a member
of the inaugural class at the Fine Arts Work Center and
the author of the acclaimed *An Artist's Cookbook*.

Let's turn around here and walk back down-along Commercial, into the
center of town.

THE MURCHISON HOUSE

Atop the hill to our left stood a mansion called "The Castle," purchased in 1936 by Carl and Dorothea Murchison. At the time they bought the place, it would have looked out over the tail end of Commercial Street, where the road halted at the impermeable bosk below. It was not until 1937 that the tangled brush was tamed and the road was extended out to the beach (then called New Beach, now Herring Cove Beach).

The Castle went up in a tower of flames in 1956, along with a collection of important artworks worth a fortune. Among them were works of well-known local artists, as well as pieces by Rubens, Gainsborough and Tintoretto. The blaze could be seen way up-Cape and far out to sea.

The new structure you see in its place is a model of mid-century modernism. Its walls of 8-foot-tall windows and wraparound verandas lend water views spanning from the sandy gold of the cliffs on the left to the polished ripples of the sea to the right. Frank Sinatra is one of many luminaries to have tripped the light fantastic on the terrazzo terrace, sipping cocktails at pool-side parties here, way back when.

KALE SOUP FOR THE SOUL

Tennessee Williams camped in a shack behind the house at number 8 Commercial in 1944 while writing *The Glass Menagerie*. Regarding William's time here, local journalist Steve Desroches recounted in the *Provincetown Magazine*:

> Although Tennessee Williams spent only four summers here in the 1940s, they were incredibly influential experiences for the young writer on the cusp of fame and success. At that time he may have been regarded as a starving artist, quite literally, as his skinny appearance elicited the concern of his Portuguese neighbors, who fed him fish and kale soup.

Kale soup recipes generally call for beans, onions, potatoes, kale, salt, pepper and vinegar. Cooks can be tenacious when it comes to recipes, and the "right" amount of each ingredient is vigorously debated. Local award-winning kale soup maker Ruth O'Donnell called this traditional soup "Portuguese penicillin."

THE FIRST ART SCHOOL IN PROVINCETOWN

Three years before there was Charles Hawthorne, there was Dewing Woodward. She and her life partner lived in the house at 18 Commercial Street, in what is believed to have served as a home and the bake house at the Long Point settlement. This was one of the last buildings to bob across the bay to join the rest of the floaters in town.

Woodward swapped out her given first name for Dewing so that her artwork might be taken more seriously in her male-dominated profession. Woodward came to Provincetown to practice and teach what she'd learned at the Academie Julian in Paris. She opened the first art school in Provincetown in 1896, as the Dewing Woodward Cape Cod School of Drawing and Painting.

Her work brought her acclaim far beyond Provincetown. In her *New York Times* obituary, she was praised as "one of the nation's leading painters." The theme of many of her paintings was everyday life in Provincetown. Her work offered a glimpse into Cape foodways and traditions, as in her piece "Clam Diggers Coming Home." After leaving Provincetown, Dewing Woodward opened the Blue Dome Fellowship Art School near Woodstock, New York. Several of her pieces belong to the Provincetown Art Association collection.

PROVINCETOWN'S BEACH PLUM QUEEN

Known as the Beach Plum Queen, Ina Snow lived at number 36. She was the secretary-treasurer of the Cape Cod Beach Plum Growers Association, and an enthusiastic proponent of advancing beach plum production beyond simply selling jam to tourists. In beach plums, she saw untapped environmentally-friendly, economic potential for the Cape, and especially for Provincetown. In addition to being made into jams and jellies, she used beach plums to make syrups, wines and liqueurs, as well as adding a tart zing to pies, breads, muffins and scones. In her yard she grew plum, apple and quince trees, as well as raspberries and assorted vegetables. I think she'd be pleased to know that today on the Cape, beach plum is integral to many foods that make up "Cape cuisine."

DANCING WHALE

The deft hand of Conrad Malicoat strikes again, at 64 Commercial Street, only this time, you can see his brick handiwork on the outside of the house. Among his many talents, Malicoat became known for his style of sculpting wavy, asymmetric fireplaces in houses all over town. Here, you can see his bricked whale on the outside of the chimney. Some describe the whale as breaching, others see it dancing on its tail.

On a side note, comedian Kate Clinton, to whom this house was bequeathed, observed:

> Gays have always been in the military. Alexander the Great was originally Alexander the Fabulous. A gay man invented C-rations. He claims he could never talk anyone into the cilantro garnish. Obviously, gays were not allowed to design the outfits, because we never would have stayed with the earth tones so long.

NAPOLEON'S WILLOW?

We now come upon a slight bend in the sidewalk (in front of house number 68) where an enormous willow tree, more than five feet in diameter once stood, forcing the sidewalk to go around it. Amy Whorf McGuiggan, a chronicler of history, tales and cultural traditions of Provincetown, added this intriguing story on David Dunlap's *Building Provincetown* web pages:

> Legend has it that the willows that once graced Commercial Street were all grown from cuttings taken from Napoleon's grave at St. Helena. During his exile, Napoleon is said to have spent many hours beneath the shade of a majestic willow, an emblem of sadness and sorrow. Near the time of Napoleon's death in 1821, the willow was blown down and cuttings from it were planted around his grave. American whale ships calling at St. Helena, including those from Provincetown, took away cuttings of the tree and planted them back home.

ALICE'S RESTAURANT

"Tomatoes and oregano make it Italian; wine and tarragon make it French. Sour cream makes it Russian; lemon and cinnamon make it Greek. Soy sauce makes it Chinese; garlic makes it good."

— Alice Brock

Alice May Brock, self-taught in the arts of cooking, painting and storytelling, makes her home in Provincetown and has done so for ages. You might recognize her name from her hilarious books *My Life as a Restaurant*, *How to Massage Your Cat* and *Mooses Come Walking*.

She is the "Alice" of Arlo Guthrie's 1967 hit song, *"Alice's Restaurant Masacree."* But, as Guthrie says, the song is not about a restaurant. It's the story of Arlo's arrest on Thanksgiving Day when he was visiting Alice. The tale unfolds in eddies of verse over the course of his twenty-minute ballad, sung in a looping, satirical, talking-blues style, as he recounts the time he and his friend were booked, tried and sentenced for littering. Seems they tossed bags of trash down a cliff when they found that the town dump was closed for Thanksgiving. In high-spirited, tongue-in-cheek rhyme, Arlo shares his thoughts and opinions on the shortcomings of the government in general, and the police and military, in particular. The song, now something of a national Thanksgiving anthem, is still broadcast on radio stations across the country every year at noon on Thanksgiving Day.

In 1969, a spin-off movie titled *Alice's Restaurant* was released at the same time as the book *The Alice's Restaurant Cookbook*, written by Alice, dishing up Alice's delightful, insightful folk wisdom along with her recipes and photos of her and Arlo. Vinyl recordings titled *"Italian-type Meatballs"* and *"My Gramma's Beet Jam,"* accompanied the book.

THE OLDEST HOUSE IN TOWN

By some estimations, the oldest house still standing in Provincetown is the one at 72 Commercial. It's built of bits and pieces of old shipwrecks that Seth Nickerson, a skilled ship's carpenter, scavenged and incorporated into its structure. The next owners became part of Provincetown's enduring cultural tradition of cottage industry creatives. F. Coulton Waugh and Elizabeth Waugh, made his/hers creative workspaces in their home and invited the public in to buy the hand-carved ship models he made, and the hand-hooked rugs crafted by Elizabeth and her friend, Edith.

CAPTAIN JACK'S WHARF

Captain Jack Williams built this long pier, topping it with a clamor of brightly-colored wooden shacks, cobbled together, cheek-by-jowl, and stacked astride one another. Captain Jack rented them out to estivating bohemians and creatives who came to Provincetown for the summer on a word-of-mouth whim and a shoestring budget. One of his tenants was Tennessee Williams, who'd come to this "frolicsome tip of the Cape" (as he called it) to write.

Some 125 years on, the rustic piggy-backed cabins, though wind-and-sun-embattled, valiantly persevere. Two tall, dark rows of pilings, like parallel squads of sentinels, patrol the waters beneath the wharf. Bearded in scraggly moss and clad in a chainmail of barnacles, they wade from the shallow, sandy shoreline into the depths of the bay, shouldering the wharf between them.

SAL'S PLACE

In the early '60s, Sal del Deo, one half of the East End Ciro & Sal's duo, struck out on his own, opening Sal's Place at 99 Commercial in the West End, at the opposite end of town. Sal became known for his generous portions of both hospitality and pastas. A fine painter himself, Sal supported emerging artists by displaying and selling their work on the walls of his restaurant. Occasionally, budding musicians would drop in and sing for a bit. Gillian Drake wrote in her book *A Taste of Provincetown* that Sal maintained that "Good artists make good cooks." For both Sal and Ciro, that has certainly proven to be the case.

The restaurant has since changed hands, but the current owners work to keep Sal's signature, homey atmosphere and Italian seafood menu alive in the West End neighborhood. During recent winters, when most restaurateurs shutter their shops and up-stakes for sunnier climes, the staff of Sal's has run a pop-up version of the restaurant downtown to serve locals during off-season months.

COAST GUARD STATION

In this collection of white buildings is the current Coast Guard Station. The first one was built out at Race Point in 1872, where the tides, rip currents and shifting shoals are particularly treacherous. In the waters between Truro and Provincetown alone, more than 1,000 ships are estimated to have been lost, along with countless thousands of lives on board. Of the nearly 100 ships which have wrecked off the outermost tip of the Cape since the life-saving station at Race Point was built, rescuers have saved over 600 lives, tragically, sometimes at the cost of their own.

When ships flounder or sink, it is not uncommon for crates and barrels of commodities—foodstuffs, textiles, tobacco, booze—to wash ashore. In 1928, the *Robert E. Lee* wrecked near Boston, resulting in piles of pie filling and bubblegum showing up on the beaches near Provincetown. Sometimes a crew would toss crates of cargo overboard if rough seas threatened to capsize the vessel—or, as was often the case, if the cargo they were carrying was illegal and they were under pursuit by authorities. In either case, word would quickly get around, and locals would swarm to the beaches like magpies to an open jewelry box, to gather up crates as they landed.

These fenced-in white buildings were opened as the new Coast Guard Station in 1979, which is run by a couple dozen or so service members working in rotating shifts. For the most part they live off-base and report here for a few days' duty at a time, bunking and eating on-site during their rota. One of the service members is a Culinary Specialist (CS) whose job it is to cook meals for the others. The present CS told me her Cincinnati Chili is a big hit with the crew, who have an affinity for comfort foods like biscuits and gravy for breakfast and Cincinnati Chili for supper. This particular chili is a meat sauce flavored with Mediterranean spices. She writes:

> Don't be fooled though—it is not to be eaten as a soup! It is eaten instead over a steaming pile of spaghetti noodles, cheddar cheese, and other accoutrements OR you can use it to make chili dogs AKA "Cheese Coneys"! Oh and don't forget the oyster crackers!

THE REAL McCOY

This Bill McCoy and his story are not the origin of the phrase "the real McCoy," but his fame popularized the saying, and he was proud to bear the nickname given him. Bill McCoy's rum-running adventures (along with the wave of smugglers he inspired) frustrated the government, ultimately reshaped the US Coast Guard and ignited the imagination of the nation, according to the 2012, award-winning documentary, directed by Bailey Pryor, and created to tell of McCoy's life and enterprise.

McCoy was responsible for having kept a river of rum and other spirits flowing into the country during Prohibition, in spite of efforts by Congressional politicians, the police and the FBI to thwart his enterprise. The Coast Guard, which had been a small fleet of boats primarily geared toward saving lives at sea, was expanded and reconfigured to become a drug and alcohol enforcing arm of the law. The spirited retelling of his antics made him a hero of Robin Hood stature and proportions and "Bill McCoy" became a lionized household name.

McCoy is credited with cooking up the first Rum Row scheme. In January of 1920, he and his crew stocked his boat with liquor in the Bahamas and sailed it to the very edge of the international waters boundary, three miles off the coast of New York City. There, he set up shop as an off-shore liquor store. Small boats from the mainland came out to his ship to purchase cases of liquor—legally, as the boats were anchored outside of US jurisdiction—to smuggle back and sell, illegally, on land. Other rum-running ships came alongside McCoy's, growing into a row of boats selling every sort of spirit available. While many smugglers increased their profits by diluting spirits they sold with prune juice, or dangerous ingredients like turpentine and wood alcohol, McCoy did not. Because his clientèle trusted his liquor to be unadulterated, he and his rum earned the nickname "The Real McCoy."

Other mariners, sensing there was money to be made from the public's romantic notion of Rum Row, began ferrying liquor-thirsty tourists by night out to the rum-running ships where they enjoyed a bacchanalian adventure on the sea. The fleet became bobbing speakeasies, with multi-course dinners, fancy rum cocktails, jazz bands, scantily clad dancing women, the works.

Rum Rows inspired by McCoy sprouted up along the entire length of the eastern seaboard. The tip of Cape Cod was no exception. Provincetown had its own Rum Row, its own audacious rum-runners and its own fleet of smuggler-busters. Probably the best-known rum-runner in town was the "Sea Fox," Manuel Zora. His exploits are the subject of a book by Scott Corbin, titled *The Sea Fox*. (Zora was also a fisherman and an actor and starred in a play put on by the Wharf Theater called *Fish for Friday*, based on his own life. A portion of the proceeds went to help fishing families struggling during the Depression.)

Although legally-speaking, Provincetown was dry long before the passage of Prohibition, there had always been booze to be had by those who knew how to find it. And here, as in other places where it was enacted, Prohibition failed to stem the consumption of alcohol to the full measure intended. During Prohibition, the Race Point Coast Guard Station was manned by townies tasked with the job of curbing not only the illegal rum-running activities of international players, but also those of their own neighbors. The stakes were raised as rum-running escalated from being sort of a small-time, mischievously daring venture to being a dangerous racket operated by mafia-style networks of armed thugs, financed by big money. Both rum-running and smuggler-busting became increasingly perilous throughout the remainder of Prohibition, pitting competing local factions against one another and leading to strongly divided opinions among town residents.

THE TURN

We find ourselves back at The Turn on Commercial Street. I didn't mention last time we stood at this intersection, how "The Turn" came to be. The story goes that when the town wanted to continue the path of the road straight across his property, which would mean removing his house and his saltworks, Benjamin Lancy, Sr. refused to permit it. The town relented and routed the road around. His home from that time is no longer standing but his legacy, in the form of Commercial Street's abrupt swing to the left, remains.

AT JOHN'S

The large white house with the wind-chapped green shutters on the corner is that of landscape painter John Dowd. John is best known for his artwork, and his house is known, in part, for the white marble bust of Shakespeare in the upper window, quietly studying the square below.

(Speaking of Shakespeare, here's a slice of trivia connecting the Bard to *Mayflower* passenger, Stephen Hopkins. Literary historians believe a shipwreck in Bermuda that Hopkins had narrowly survived, was the inspiration for principal aspects of *The Tempest*. After their ship wrecked, Hopkins and several others were sentenced to execution, accused of inciting mutiny, when they refused to continue following orders of their captain. However, Hopkins managed to talk his way into being banished to another part of the island, instead. Hopkins and other surviving would-be mutineers were able to craft two small ships and stock them with fresh water and food such as salted pork, dried fish and vegetables from the fertile woods of Bermuda. Thus fortified, they set sail once again for Jamestown, where their original ship been headed before being wrecked on the island.)

But back to John's place.

I twice spent winters at John's. One winter I spent my days helping him refinish the interior of his house. During a second winter I lived upstairs in the room next to silent Mr. Shakespeare.

One of my favorite memories of John's house was an evening when John, his friend Michael and I, returned in the early morning hours after a night out dancing at the A-House and pizza-ing at Spiritus. We made mugs of lava-thick cocoa and curled up under fields of flowered quilts to read David Sedaris's "Santaland Diaries" aloud. (At the time, reading aloud was one of our favorite pastimes on a summer afternoon at the beach or draped in shaded chairs in his back yard. In winter, friends huddled in his drawing room or, as we were that night, flopped atop a huge ol' mahogany sleigh bed.) Reading and laughing kept us up all night, and I had to drag myself off to work, long before breakfast, to bike through the snow to my job selling gas, coffee and lottery tickets at the Cumby's convenience store up the road. Michael turned up to my work around midday to help me keep awake for the rest of my shift, entertaining me with strange and exciting stories of life in NYC. The store was otherwise empty; no one was buying gas or coffee or lotto.

It was the still, life-lorn middle of winter, and snowing.

THE FORMER BLUES BAG COFFEE HOUSE

Arlo Guthrie came to town in the '60s to sing at the "folk coffee house," the Blues Bag at 120 Commercial, as did other folk singers who defined the era: Leonda, Son House, James Taylor, Richie Havens, John Lee Hooker, Dave von Ronk, Tom Rush among them. Apparently, its being a coffee shop, alcohol was not permitted to be served so patrons would buy a soda pop and slip into it booze they'd brought with them (quite possibly purchased at Perry's liquor on the nearby corner).

COLD STORAGE PLANTS

With the advent of the ability to keep massive amounts of fish fresh by refrigerating or freezing it in large, cold storage facilities, the fishing industry was able to provide fresh and freshly frozen fish to customers located even great distances from where the fish was caught. Instead of the cod and haddock's being sold in its original form, fish began to be sold in loaves, brick-shaped chunks of frozen fish meat, which were easier to package, store and transport than fish-shaped fish. The ability to quickly freeze and widely distribute large quantities of fish helped further stabilize and expand markets, increasing wages for fishermen. Both women and men were employed in the cold storage facilities. The work was grueling, but year-round, which presented an opportunity for steady employment—as rare as hen's teeth (then and now) in Provincetown.

This meant that in the early 20th century, the lovely shop-lined waterfront we enjoy today was, instead, nearly chock-a-block with giant, loud, ugly industrial buildings, from Howland Street in the East End all the way to Atwood Avenue in the West End. Each was topped with an agglomeration of smokestacks coughing up smothering black smoke and noxious fumes, amidst reboant whirring, clanging and banging at all hours. Work inside the plants was backbreaking and brutally frigid. In winter it could be even colder inside the facilities than outside, notes author David Dunlap.

FLYER'S BOAT RENTAL

Flyer Santos and his team built the lovely replica of the *Rose Dorothea* ship on display at the Provincetown library. His boatyard was a frequent subject of many an artist looking for a dose of nautical flavor to paint,

Norman Rockwell, Don Aikins, John Whorf and Harvey Dodd among them. The painting of Flyer by Sal Del Deo (of Sal's restaurant) may be the best known of the lot.

Flyer himself is sadly no longer sailing on this plane of existence, but his boatyard is thriving and run by one of his grandsons, Noah. (What better name could there be for a boat guy than that?)

From Flyer's Boatyard you can rent pontoon boats, speedboats, a sail-boat, sloop, skiff, kayak or paddle board. Flyer's also teaches sailing les-sons. If you don't care to sail under your own steam, you can hop onto their Long Point–bound shuttle in the summer months. On your way from pretty much anywhere in town, you are sure to pass one of the many little markets with sandwich delis where you can pick up a picnic lunch—or whatever floats your boat—as you head to Flyer's for a day out on the water.

PEARLS OF WISDOM ABOUT OYSTERS

The legendary Chef Greg Atkinson wrote:

> Pacific oysters reflect the taste of the waters in which they are grown. Pondering this phenomenon, [Jon] Rowley and I coined the term "merroir," after the French "terroir," which describes the way certain foods and wine grapes bear the detectable flavors of their home soil. To christen the new word, we shucked another oyster and poured another glass of wine. We were so pleased with our-selves that, had we been a little bolder or a little less sober, I think we would have burst into song.
>
> — *Seattle Times*, March 2003

Although here Chef Atkinson mentions Pacific oysters in particular, since the coining of the word by Atkinson and Rowley, oysters around the world are now discussed in terms of their merroir/meroir.

LUCKY LIPS OYSTERS

Although there are oysters in Provincetown waters, Wellfleet oysters are generally considered to be the cream of the crop. I had the privilege recently to tour the charmingly named Lucky Lips oyster farm located in Loagy Bay, in Wellfleet. As each oyster processes anywhere from 50 to 60 gallons of water every day, the flavor of the meat reflects its meroir, the variations in water salination, temperature and other conditions in which the oysters live. For example, even within the small portion of Loagy Bay, where Lucky Lips farm is located, the meroir of the oysters varies. Those oysters living on the side of the farm closest to where the freshwater of Blackfish Creek flows into the bay, taste noticeably different to those oysters raised in the deeper, brinier waters, just yards away, in this small bountiful patch of sea.

FORMERLY RICK'S

When I first moved to town, number 149 was Rick's Pub & Tavern, a bedimmed, smoke-choked piano bar. (Remember when people smoked indoors, even in restaurants? In Massachusetts, that was right up until 2004.) Rick's was where singer songwriter Peter Donnelly and several other notable musicians got their start in town. The location is now home to the lively Johnny Thai Monkey Bar, the only restaurant in town at the moment specializing in Thai food. Their signature drink is a sushi martini, perhaps the only sushi-based drink in town.

A SNUG HARBOR

On the bay side of Commercial, where Atlantic Street spills onto the intersection, sits a tall-ish building rich in lore and legends.

Past owners and guests have reported that the place is haunted by ghosts of an African-American family who found food and shelter here after escaping their captors. A cavity in the chimney is said to have provided a "snug harbor" for people fleeing the South for Nova Scotia. In a bedroom upstairs, a sea captain's wife and a young African-American girl occasionally make their appearance. From time to time, the ghost of a sea captain has been noticed sitting at the dining room table in his uniform.

Perhaps the captain is waiting to be served by one of the array of restaurants that have been here over the years. There was a classy French restaurant serving classic French cuisine; Chez Romain Bistro, which preceded a popular Cajun-meets-Cape restaurant, Snug Harbor. Snug Harbor's tenure was followed by the widely-praised Martin House, which described its menu as "cuisine embracing a whole world's worth of cultural influences." Each restaurant offered its own spin on seafood, chicken and other dishes, in response to the ever-expanding desire for diverse cuisine in Provincetown.

FROM TEA DANCE TO PIZZA SLICES

After busy days crammed with whale watching, hiking the dunes, shopping, playing on the beach, nursing a hangover or hopping from one job to the next, a mostly gay crowd of visitors and locals converges upon the Boatslip beginning at 4 o'clock every afternoon for the time-honored tradition of Tea Dance. Throngs of dancers swarm to the harborside deck and bar for the three-hour outdoor dance party. By the time it wraps up at seven, most are ready to get something to eat, or grab a cocktail and put up their feet before heading out for more dancing or to catch one of the many comedy, drag or music shows in town.

When the bars close at 1 a.m., the night is far from over; it's merely on to the next phase of Provincetown's hopping late-night social scene: Spiritus. A boisterous, predominantly gay, predominantly male crowd gravitates to Spiritus for pizza, ice cream, cruising, carousing or just for a chance to catch up with friends. This oft-repeated, yet never duplicated routine, beginning with afternoon tea dance and ending at Spiritus, is a ritual that, for many, embodies the very essence of summertime in Provincetown.

PROVINCETOWN DOUGH

In the unobtrusive brick building set back at the corner of Winthrop and Commercial, where you can now get both fresh coffee and legal pot, was once a bank that issued Provincetown Bank bills used as legal tender in many of the world's ports. The crews of whaling and merchant ships, which often spent a year or more abroad, frequently docked in international ports and needed to be able to readily buy provisions and sell commodities in foreign lands. The Provincetown Bank provided the solution: it printed its own money.

The Provincetown Bank, founded in 1865, continued to print money for 71 years, up until 1935. During that time, it printed $2,216,210 worth of currency in 22 different denominations. Occasionally, you can still find collectible bills for sale floating around shops that deal in old currencies. A word to the wise: the earliest $2 bill that the bank printed, nicknamed "Lazy deuce," due to the angled printing of the number "2," is particularly rare and much sought after by collectors in the know.

SIMONA'S SOUPS

"Memories and dirty dishes are the only parts of a meal that exist once the last of the food and drink are gone," Simona, told me once. Simona is a young Bulgarian woman I met one summer, when she was at the docks trading a loaf of fresh Bulgarian bread for a bucket of fish heads from a fisherman she'd befriended. Most nights, after the restaurants and bars had closed and the bike taxis had dropped off their last fares, Bulgarians in town would head for Simona's bayside balcony. They were mostly students who came to the States for the summer to wait tables, tend bar or pedal bike taxis to help defray the cost of their college education. At Simona's, they got the chance to speak Bulgarian freely, listen to the latest Bulgarian music, drink rakija and, best of all, eat homemade Bulgarian food.

Simona used her bartered fish heads and other edible leftovers for her soups and stews. She'd make Ribena Chorba of fish bits, fish heads, chunks of potatoes, carrots, onions, peppers, garlic, tomatoes, eggs and sour milk. Sometimes she cooked up Kavarma stew, made of pork and vegetables, or to heal hangovers, Shkembe Chorba, a spicy stew of tripe, garlic, paprika and hot chili peppers.

After finishing off a pot of one of these hearty stews, along with a hunk of pitka (her delicious bread) and a few glasses of beer or rakija, her friends would bring out their guitars and sing traditional Bulgarian folksongs. Simona liked to say that a meal lasts, not just until the plates are empty, but until all the stories are gnawed off the bone and all the sweet is wrung from the songs. From the little balcony, their voices would rise into the night, mingled with the strains of Pasha Hristova singing "Take with you, on this lovely day/ One Bulgarian rose from me/ Let it remind you/ With its aromatic voice/ About the Balkan range, about the sea/ And about all of us, all of us …"

JIMMY'S HIDEAWAY

Descend the narrow brick steps into a cool room beneath a bayside store and enter what once was the stomping ground of Chef Howard Mitchum. This underground retreat was his domain when he ran it as Howard Mitchum's Seafood Restaurant. David Dunlap describes Mitcham as "the most influential figure in Provincetown cuisine during the latter 20th century because he advocated doing more of what the town's Portuguese cooks were doing in the first place: fixing fresh seafood simply and flavorfully."

Mitchum wrote what many consider to be the quintessential Provincetown cookbook and, even better, it's chock-full of Provincetown stories. My own garlicked-thumb–smudged, sauce-splattered, wine-ringed, torn and battered copy of his book waxes both humorous and poetic on the delights of Portuguese cuisine, its simplicity and complexity. Within its pages are secrets on everything, from how to open and stuff a quahog, to hints on boiling swordfish in beer, to detailed advice on making Cape Cod Gumbo and preparing Periwinkles Italienne. Mitchum's recipes are not only a good guide to making great food, they were written, I suspect, with a twinkle in his eye and a glass of rum in his other hand. Anecdotes splashed liberally throughout, as sweet-tart-spicy as a good vinaigrette, recount Mitchum's escapades among Provincetown fishermen, farmers, artists and fellow foodies.

One of his anecdotes tells of two local fishermen, Captain John Santos and Vic Pacellini, who would fry small squid on the muffler of their boat's engine while at sea. It's not something I've ever tried, but he claims the technique makes the squid come out "brown and crisp as a potato chip."

The book finishes with a recipe for cooking George Washington Ready's sea serpent. (Not a recipe recommended for a first date due to the lingering, sulfur-escent smell it leaves on one's breath.)

A few years ago one of Provincetown's favorite bartenders, Jim McNulty, opened one of Provincetown's favorite restaurants in Mitchum's old "subterranean haunt." Jimmy's menu satisfies the longings of those craving familiar Cape fare—grilled Wellfleet oysters, clam chowder, fried calamari and shrimp—as well as the hankerings of those craving local seafood with a bit of European flair. A patio out back rewards diners respite from the noise of Commercial Street and a crab's eye view of the sparkling sunlit/moonlit harbor.

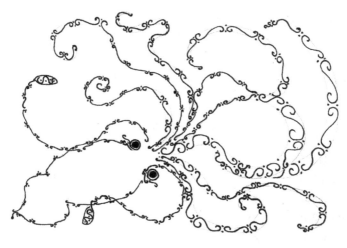

THE CLUB

The lesbian bar with the longest life-span in the country operated here, where The Club is now, until just a few years ago. The "After Tea Dance" social at the Pied Piper was the next stop down the street for the boisterous Boatslip Tea Dance crowd—a joyful mix of orientations and interests, agendas and genders—before everyone dispersed for dinner and more dancing elsewhere. In a town where there were once several women's bars, there are currently only mixed venues.

Since 2019, The Club has been a jazz lounge serving brunch, lunch and dinner. It's frequented by a diverse mix of patrons and performers and is owned by lesbian musician-comedian-actress, Lea DeLaria. You may have seen her on *Orange is the New Black, Will and Grace, The Jim Gaffigan Show, One Life to Live, Reprisal,* and she even solved mysteries on *Matlock.* Now you can see her singing smoky jazz tunes and performing her naughty, bawdy comedy show here in Ptown.

Lea DeLaria notes, "What do you mean you don't believe in homosexuality? It's not like the Easter Bunny, your belief isn't necessary."

THE AQUARIUM MARKETPLACE

This squat, wooden building takes its name from its stint as the summer home of three Atlantic bottlenose dolphins and a smattering of other marine animals in the 1960s-early '70s. The dolphins, Jackie, Lady and Lucky, relocated to Florida each winter before the snow arrived on the Cape.

These days, this a fun spot to check out the range of New England and international take-out food venues. You can take your Tex- Mex burrito, gelato, a slice of cake, Chinese bowl, vegan lunch, Jamaican jerk, or other take-out food out back to the harborside deck of the Aqua Bar, where there's a deck-full of picnic tables on which to sit and eat, order an adult beverage and, in the summertime, listen to live music in the late afternoon.

THE STATE OF THINGS

Fun facts: The Massachusetts state muffin is the corn muffin. Our state bean is the navy bean; the state berry is the cranberry; and the state dessert is, of course, Boston Cream Pie.

The state dog is the Boston Terrier, the state cat is the tabby. The state insect is the ladybug, a group of which is a loveliness of ladybugs—how perfect is that!

One of our state birds is the wild turkey, the collective noun for which is a gang, whereas a group of domesticated turkeys is a rafter. Our second state bird is the black-capped chickadee. Given the black masks across their little faces, a group of them is known as a banditry.

The state marine mammal is the right whale, a group of which is a gam or a pod.

GARDEN COCKTAILS IN A BEER GARDEN

It used to be that beer sold on the Cape came entirely from off-Cape breweries. It is a sign of the cultural shift, nationally and locally, toward small craft brewing that you can now find several breweries on the Cape, including one in Provincetown. The Nor'easter Beer Garden, for example, serves up several of these beers, as well as cocktails made with fresh-from-the-garden ingredients. Their cocktails feature South Hollow Spirits, hand-crafted at the nearby Truro Vineyards, and include unexpected, but surprisingly, tasty fresh garden ingredients in their signature Arugula Mojito and Rhubarbarita cocktails.

POST OFFICE

Time was when you could hang about on the front steps of the post office, drinking coffee, discussing newspaper headlines (long before internet/cell phones), and watching all of Provincetown passing by. Anytime before midday, you could see delivery trucks making their rounds, shopkeepers biking to work, and stragglers dragging themselves home from last night's escapades, some hungover and looking much the worse for wear. Some might be missing a shoe or have their wig on backwards and occasionally someone would go by wearing nothing at all, their clothes having been mislaid somewhere in the night. In the end, it was deemed there were too many of us coffee-sipping street-watchers loitering on the steps, and the kibosh was put on porch perching.

THE CANTEEN

The Canteen claims to have introduced the Frosé—a sort of rosé wine slushie—to Provincetown. Though this restaurant is one of the more recent arrivals, it hit the ground running and hasn't stopped. Their summer menu offers clam chowder, lobster rolls and the like, as well as a few dishes with international twists and additions. The Canteen is one of the few restaurants in town that stays open year-round. To the delight of all, they host an outdoor Holiday Market in December, reminiscent of German Christmas Markets. Local artisans peddle their arts and crafts, which patrons browse while sipping steaming peppermint cocoa, warm mulled wine, spiked nog or hot cider. Pretzels and chocolates, schnitzels and currywursts, potato salad and sauerkraut are on hand for those wanting to get into the full *Weihnachten* swing of things.

VORELLI'S STEAK HOUSE

Since 1987, though passing from one owner to another, this has remained a reliable, family restaurant serving steak and seafood, burgers, sandwiches and soups. Both regulars and tourists in search of cozy, old-Cape charm in Provincetown, still find their way here, as folks have been doing for decades. Note: its window tables are coveted viewing spots on Halloween night, which is considered a major holiday in Provincetown, so go early!

FRONT STREET

Next door to Vorelli's is another Provincetown stand-by that's been around nearly forever, offering one of the most comprehensive Italian seafood menus in town. It was opened by Howard Gruber (who later opened Gruber's, across the street). He was a true Provincetown character and a highly-regarded restaurateur who brought a friendly, enthusiastic face to elegant cuisine. Howard was also a generous man who derived pleasure from introducing people to food he loved. I'll never forget an evening long ago when he introduced my friend and me to Belle de Brillet. He didn't charge us for the luscious, golden elixir, likely knowing I couldn't have afforded it back then. He simply enjoyed watching our faces light up at the taste of it.

WHALER'S WHARF

This kaleidoscope of food shops, art galleries, a bay-view restaurant and the town cinema was rebuilt on the ashes of one of the largest fires in the town's history. People as far away as Dennis, 30 miles across the bay, reported seeing the late-night flames on the 10th of February, 1998. The fire claimed a good deal of the neighboring Crown & Anchor complex on one side, and damaged the Marine Specialties store on the other. Although no lives were lost in the fire, sadly, the guard who was on watch that night took his life, apparently blaming himself for not having been able to stop the blaze.

The destruction of the nearly eight decades–old building was an emotional blow and an enormous loss culturally and historically for the

town. After the long-running Provincetown Theater had stopped showing movies there years before, the place had been kept alive by artists
and other creatives who sold their wares in small shops and spaces they
rented on the cheap.

These days, in addition to the multitude of artists' and artisans' shops,
the Water's Edge Cinema hosts the annual Provincetown International
Film Festival and the Jamaican Film Festival among other events.

TIM'S USED BOOKS

It's easy to miss unless you're looking for it. The chipped yellow sign
announcing the bookstore's quiet presence swings gently above a mossy,
bricked path leading away from the rowdy crowds of Commercial Street
to the door of a small cottage crouched in a yard shaded by elms. Open
the crooked wooden door and step into a book lover's paradise. The
place feels a bit magical, not least because it doesn't seem at all possible
for this many books to fit into a place this size. Having been a food writer, Tim has a terrific collection related to the subject, but there's a bit of
everything in here. If Tim doesn't have what you're looking for, he may
be able to recommend something you'd like instead. Even in the depths
of winter the lure of this trove of books can pull me out of my own book-
lined nest and induce me to traipse clear across town, just to spend a
warm, quiet hour or so wandering amongst these shelves.

Leaving the calm haven that is Tim's Books, we walk back out to Commercial Street, and right in front of us is one of the happening-est places in town, The Crown & Anchor.

Lady Fin, drawn specially for this book by Provincetown
artist and illustrator, Daniel Trotter.

THE CROWN & ANCHOR

A glittering asterism of drag queens in wind-billowed dresses and hip-hugging, flared-leg pantsuits the realm in front of the Crown & Anchor, each shooting to be the one fulgent quasar ablaze in a field of shimmering stars. Several of them have mastered the delicate illusion of appearing to be aloof and almost disdainfully oblivious of onlookers, all the while remaining keenly aware of who's watching.

Although some drag artists may perform under their own name, most adopt a catchy stage name that is playful, punny, or dripping with "insinuendo." Some of my favorite drag names are Anne DeTwa, Bertha Venation, Bang Bang La Desh, Anita Cocktail, Anita Procedure, Barbara Seville, Barbie Que, Esther Gin, Hedda Lettuce, Rhoda Dendron, Ania Bangcocks, Dixie Normous, Heidi Haux, Paige Turner, Eileen Dover, Helena Handbasket, Liza Lott, Koco Caine, Miles Long, Robin Kradles, Misty Meaner, Anna Misty Moanin.

The Crown & Anchor boasts bay view hotel rooms, a restaurant with an international menu, a cabaret, leather bar, nightclub, poolside bar, video bar and multiple performance venues where LGBTQ+ entertainers come from all over to perform.

At the corner of Commercial and Gosnold is Adams Pharmacy—no, not that corner, the opposite one.

ADAMS PHARMACY

Adams Pharmacy used to be on one side of Gosnold, but after 146 years there, it got the itch to travel, gathered its skirts and took itself to the other side of the street. In its place is now Vin's Liquor Store, a vendor of that age-old cure: liquor. During Prohibition, it was possible, and not uncommon, for people to go round to the doctor complaining of a head cold in order to receive a prescription for a pint of whiskey, which could be filled at Adams Pharmacy. In its new digs, Adams Pharmacy still sells over-the-counter medications but no longer dispenses prescription drugs.

When I first arrived, Adams Pharmacy, at its original location, still had its old-fashioned soda fountain and long Formica counter. Early mornings at Adams saw fishermen in feed caps bantering, elbow-to-elbow, over coffee mugs. They'd shove off to work and give way to swirls of women popping in to meet for a cup of tea on break from work or between errands. Day tourists stopped by for over-the-counter remedies or an ice cream float. When school let out, the place teemed with kids spending pocketfuls of change on a soda fountain drink and a Snickers bar.

And here we are back at Town Hall, where I will leave you now to enjoy the town on your own. In any direction you go from here, cultural and culinary history lies embedded in every bite, every sip, every street name and every view, waiting to be uncovered.

Both in its non-edible and edible forms, the foods and cuisines around us speak to us. Images of pineapples offer us a warm welcome, baskets of fruit carved into a stone gate impart wishes of good health and abundance. Artists' and writers' depictions of farmers and fishermen at their work, families clamming together, cooks in kitchens, waiters serving tables and children selling lemonade immortalize the stories of the people of this particular place, now and over the centuries.

The ups and downs of various food industries are evident in the architecture of the town. From stately homes built by wealthy fishing captains during their heyday, to fishing shacks, abandoned when the industry collapsed, becoming the cheap cottages and studios of artists who created Provincetown's world-renowned artist colony. From historic churches that work together to feed the souls of parishioners and the bellies of the hungry to the enormous ice house, obsolete as storage for ice and cranberries, now boasting waterfront condos with incomparable views, and to the towering Pilgrim Monument, the construction of which was funded by fortunes garnered by fishing and whaling, dairy and crop farming—even by the sales of bananas grown in foreign lands.

China plates and crystal glasses resting at the bottom of the sea tell of lives interrupted by a fateful Nor'easter, a chocolate bar celebrates the story of a lobsterman's grapple with a whale, the tale of the mocha latte of today may be traced back to stolen coffee plant clippings of 1723. The specific spices and ingredients in the various cuisines found in Provincetown reveal the complicated and colorful histories of the people who have lived or spent time here over the centuries.

It's time now for me to grab a bite, my beach hat, a good Donna Leon mystery and head to the beach!

A FINAL WORD

CACOETHES

The Oxford Lexico defines the word *cacoethes* (kak-oh-ee-thees) as "an irresistible urge to do something inadvisable." When I happened upon this term, the first question that came to mind was: how did I live so long with this condition and not know its name?

Cacoethes was in fairly wide use in English-speaking countries about 100 years ago, particularly in connection with the phrase *cacoethes scribendi,* to describe those afflicted with an insatiable thirst to write. Provincetown is said to have an overpowering pull for writers grappling with this particular affliction.

For well over a century, this outermost edge of the Cape has lured creatives from all over the world, not only to write poetry, prose and plays, but also to draw, paint, photograph, sing, dance, sculpt magnificent brick chimneys, weld extraordinary flowers and build splendid sailing vessels. Others have crafted award-winning wines, concocted delectable chocolates or dreamed up fusions of food from around the globe. Provincetown's allure is as expansive and eclectic as it is seductive.

Many who spend time here discover they've developed a *cacoethes* for one "inadvisable" penchant or another. If you notice yourself experiencing an onset of *cacoethes scribendi,* or perhaps *cacoethes chocolati* or *cacoethes vino,* you are likely to find ample opportunity to indulge in these irresistible pleasures—as well as most any *cacoethes* that overtakes you.

Whereas some might go so far as to call these pleasures "vices," I would not, for what is a vice, after all, but a pleasure with a bad reputation?

Indeed, some would consider Provincetown itself an irresistible pleasure with a bad reputation. If you stay here long enough you may find that, like many of us, you've acquired *cacoethes Provincetownum!*

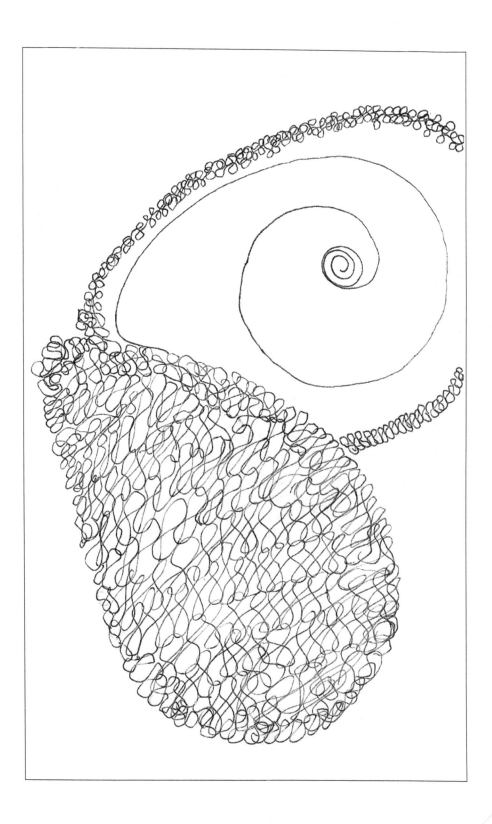

ACKNOWLEDGMENTS

I'd especially like to thank Caleb Johnson of MayflowerHistory.com, Librarian Nan Cinnater, Ana Ruiz, Julia Perry and Linda Fiorella at the Provincetown Town Hall, Peary-MacMillan Arctic Museum Director Genevieve LeMoine, Hauke Kite-Powell and Scott Lindell at the Woods Hole Oceanographic Institution, the helpful folks at The Sperm Whale Project, Harbormaster Don German, Skip Finley, Irish Railroad Workers Museum Managing Director Luke F. McCusker, volunteers with the Eastham Historical Society, David Wright and the Wellfleet Historical Society, Co-director Darias Coombs at Plimouth Patuxet Museums, the late George Bryant, Carole Pugliese, Daniel Gómez Llata, Char Priolo, Pat Medina, Robert Vetrick, Rosalyn Graham, Anne Vernon, Gwen & Scott Kazloukas-Noyes, Mick Rudd, Meg Garrity, Lisa King, Jim and Olivia Partridge, Tim Bryce, Josiah Mayo, Professor Karen Campbell, John Dowd, Boyko Terziyski and the Sunday Dock Crew.

I'm deeply appreciative for the help of Tim Burt, Stephen Kinzer, Lee Ann Cox, Priscilla Jackett, Barbara Grandel, Steve Barnes, Vivien Kirchner, Laurie Langelier, Bill Clark, Scott Penn, Tatiana Mikan, Suzanne Stringfield, Bill Fitts, and the ever-so amazing Sean Current, Virginia Simmon and Kitty Werner.

My heartfelt thanks to these folks for their assistance, contributions and/or permissions: David Dunlap, Mark Adams, Michael Cunningham, Zoë Lewis, Peter Donnelly, Nick Flynn, John Wiley Nelson, Daniel Trotter, Lenny Alberts, David Rodrigues/Matias, Steve Desroches and Tom Standage.

BIBLIOGRAPHY

Books

Amis, Kingsley. *Everyday Drinking: The Distilled Kingsley Amis*. New York: Bloomsbury, 2008.

Baxter, John. *Eating Eternity: Food, Arts and Literature in France*. New York: Museyon, 2017.

Berger, Josef. *Cape Cod Pilot: A WPA Guide*. Boston: Northeastern University Press, 1985.

Bourdain, Anthony. *Kitchen Confidential: Adventures in the Culinary Underbelly*. New York: Bloomsbury, 2000.

Civitello, Linda. *Cuisine & Culture: A History of Food and People*. Hoboken, NJ: John Wiley & Sons, Inc., 2011.

Coogan, Jim. *Sail Away Ladies: Stories of Cape Cod Women and the Age of Sail*. East Dennis, MA: Harvest Home Books, 2008.

Corbett, Scott. *The Sea Fox: The Adventures of Cape Cod's Most Colorful Rumrunner*. New York: Thomas Y. Crowell Company, 1956.

Cozzi, Ciro. *Ciro & Sal's Cookbook*. New York: Donald I Fine, Inc., 1987

Cunningham, Michael. *Land's End: A Walk Through Provincetown*. New York: Crown Publishers, 2002.

Drake, Gillian. *A Taste of Provincetown*. Provincetown, MA: Shankpainter Publishing Co., 1987.

Driver, Clive. *Looking Back*. Provincetown, MA: Cape Cod Pilgrim Memorial Association, 2004.

Dunlap, David. *Building Provincetown: A Guide to Its Social and Cultural History, The History, Told Through Its Architecture*. Provincetown, MA: Town of Provincetown, Provincetown Historical Commission, 2015.

Egan, Leona Rust. *Provincetown as a Stage: Provincetown, the Provincetown Players, and the Discovery of Eugene O'Neill*. Orleans, MA: Parnassus Imprints, 1994.

Finley, Skip. *Whaling Captains of Color: The World's First Meritocracy*. Annapolis, Maryland: U. S. Naval Institute Press, 2020.

Flynn, Nick. "Daughter." *I Will Destroy You*. Minneapolis, MN: Graywolf Press, 2019.

George, Jean Craighead. *The First Thanksgiving*. New York, NY: The Putnam & Grosset Group, 1993.

Hunt, Peter. *Peter Hunt's Cape Cod Cookbook*. New York: Gramercy Publishing Co., 1954.

Jurafsky, Dan. *The Language of Food: A Linguist Reads the Menu*. New York: W.W. Norton & Company, 2014.

Kemp, Harry. *Love Among the Cape Enders*. New York: The Macaulay Company, 1931.

Khayyam, Omar. "A jug of wine, a loaf of bread and thou." 1048-1131 AD. Translation: Edward Fitzgerald, *Rubáiyát of Omar Khayyám*, 1859.

Krahulik, Karen Christel. *Provincetown: From Pilgrim Landing to Gay Resort*. New York: New York University Press, 2005.

Kurlansky, Mark. *Cod: A Biography of the Fish that Changed the World*. New York: Penguin Books, 1997.

Kurlansky, Mark. *The Big Oyster: History on the Half Shell*. New York: Random House Trade Paperbacks, 2006.

Lawless, Debra. *Provincetown: A History of Artists and Renegades in a Fishing Village*. Charleston, SC: The History Press, 2011.

Lawless, Debra. *Provincetown: Since WWII: Carnival at Land's End*. Charleston, SC: The History Press, 2014.

Manso, Peter. *Ptown: Art, Sex and Money on the Outer Cape*. New York: Scribner, 2002.

Matias, David. *Fifth Season*. Provincetown, MA: Provincetown Arts Press, 1998.

McGee, Diane. *Writing the Meal: Dinner in the Fiction of Early Twentieth-Century Women Writers*. Toronto, Canada: University of Toronto Press, Inc., 2001.

Mitcham, Howard. *The Provincetown Seafood Cookbook*. Reading, MA: Addison–Wesley Publishing Company, 1980.

Museum of Art: Records, Files, and Publications, George J. Mitchell Department of Special Collections & Archives, Bowdoin College Library, Brunswick, Maine.

Paine, Nancy S. *The Provincetown Book*. Brockton, MA: Tolman Print, 1922.

Philbrick, Nathanial. *Mayflower: A Story of Courage, Community and War*. New York: Viking, 2006.

Porterfield, James D. *Dining By Rail: The History and Recipes of America's Golden Age of Railroad Cuisine*. New York: Saint Martin's Griffen, 1993.

Robinson, Ted. *The Beachcombers*. Provincetown, MA, 1947.

Skillings, R.D. *Where the Time Goes*. Hanover, NH: University Press of New England, 1999.

Standage, Tom. *A History of the World in 6 Glasses*. New York: Bloomsbury, 2005.

Standage, Tom. *An Edible History of Humanity*. New York: Bloomsbury, 2009.

Teller, Walter. *Cape Cod and the Offshore Islands*. Hoboken, NJ: Prentice-Hall, Inc., 1970.

Thoreau, Henry David. *Cape Cod*. New York: Bramhall House, 1951.

Vorse, Mary Heaton. *Time and the Town: A Provincetown Chronicle*. Provincetown, MA: Cape Cod Pilgrim Memorial Association, 1990.

Vowell, Sarah. *The Wordy Shipmates.* New York: Riverhead Books, 2008.

Wright, John Hardy. *Provincetown: Volume I.* Dover, NH: Arcadia Publishing, 1997.

Articles online

Alpem, Sara. "Helena Rubinstein." Jewish Women: A Comprehensive Historical Encyclopedia. February 27, 2009. Jewish Women's Archive. Accessed June 2020.

Atkinson, Greg. "Treasures of the Tide Flats: On a beach or at a bash, oysters are worthy of celebration." *Seattle Times*, March 14, 2003. Accessed June 2020.

Blakemore, Erin. "The Revolutionary War Hero Who Was Openly Gay." history.com, June 14, 2018.. Updated February 6, 2020. Accessed September 2021.

Clark, Edie. "Best Portuguese Kale Soup Recipe: Ruth O'Donnell." Newengland.com, *Yankee Magazine*, December 15, 2010. Accessed December 2019.

Desroches, Steve. "For the Roses." Provincetownmagazine.com. September 26, 2018. Accessed December 2019.

Rupp, Rebecca. "Rum: The Spirit that Fueled a Revolution." The Plate, nationalgeographic.com, April 10, 2015. Accessed September 2021.

Setterlund, Christopher. "The Story of Smallpox in Provincetown." capecod.com, February 15, 2018. Accessed January 2021.

Documentaries

George Bryant: A Personal Tour. Directed by Carol Pugliese. With George Bryant. Provincetown Community TV, 2011.

The Real McCoy. Written, Directed by Bailey Pryor. With Christopher Annuno, Kristina Joyce Utt. Telemark Films, 2012.

Songs and lyrics

Cole, Nat King,"Those Lazy, Crazy, Hazy Days of Summer." (Carst, Hans and Tobias, Charles), A side on *Those Lazy, Hazy, Crazy Days of Summer,* Capitol Records, 1963, vinyl record.

Donnelly, Peter, "Road With No End," track 6 on *Road With No End*, Tom Tracy Music Productions, 2007, compact disc.

Lewis, Zoë,"Bicycle," track 8 on *Rotary Phone*, CD Baby, 2011, compact disc.

Lewis, Zoë, "Squid Song," track 13 on Fishbone, Wishbone, Funnybone, CD Baby, 2001, compact disc.

Nelson, John Wiley, "Provincetown Rag," track 1 on *Another Day in Paradise*, JWN2022, 2022, compact disc.

Nelson, John Wiley, "Red Cranberries," track 5 on *Another Day in Paradise*, JWN2022, 2022, compact disc.

Porter, Cole, "Let's Do It (Let's Fall in Love)," 1928.

Redding, Otis and Cropper, Steve, "(Sitting on) The Dock of the Bay," track 1 on *Dock of the Bay*, Volt/Atco, 1968, vinyl record.

Writer unknown, "Wasn't That a Mighty Storm," American folk song, early 1900s.

Useful websites

Bowdoin.edu/arctic-museum [Peary-MacMillan Arctic Museum at Bowdoin College]

buildingprovincetown.wordpress.com [Dunlap, David. Building Provincetown: The History of Provincetown Told Through its Built Environment]

mayflowerhistory.com [Johnson, Caleb. Caleb Johnson's MayflowerHistory.com, 1994–present]

MassHist.org [Massachusetts Historical Society]

Newenglandhistoricalsociety.com [New England Historical Society]

Provincetownhistoryproject.com [town of Provincetown]

womenshistory.org [National Women's History Museum]

A BIT ABOUT THE AUTHOR

Portrait of the author by local artist Mark Adams.

This book grew out of Odale's many decades years working her way around the world, during which she learned to speak several languages—the most useful being the language of food and foodways. Her MA degree centered on Culinary Anthropology and Cultural Diplomacy. When she's in the US she can usually be found back in Provincetown where she found a homey welcome as a wash-ashore over 30 years ago.

Website: dialectpress.com

CPSIA information can be obtained
at www.ICGtesting.com
Printed in the USA
JSHW020637160623
43319JS00004B/15